The master spirit of the age

The Master Spirit of the Age

Canadian engineers and the politics of professionalism 1887–1922

J. RODNEY MILLARD

UNIVERSITY OF TORONTO PRESS

Toronto Buffalo London

University of Toronto Press 1988
Toronto   Buffalo   London
Printed in Canada

ISBN 0-8020-2652-4

∞

Printed on acid-free paper

Canadian Cataloguing in Publication Data

Millard, J. Rodney
  The master spirit of the age

  Includes bibliographical references and index.
  ISBN 0-8020-2652-4
  1. Engineering – Canada – History.
  2. Engineers – Legal status, laws, etc. – Canada – History.
  3. Canadian Society of Civil Engineers – History.
  4. Engineering Institute of Canada – History.
  I. Title.
  TA26.M54 1988   620'.00971   C88-093097-7

CREDITS FOR PHOTOS (following p. 78)
National Archives Canada: CSCE annual meeting 1894 (PA 148562), Keefer
(PA 33953), Gzowski (C 8620), EIC annual meeting 1919 (PA 121591); McGill
University Archives: McLeod; *Transactions*, Canadian Society of Civil
Engineers: Kennedy (6 [1892] frontispiece); University of Toronto Archives:
Galbraith, Haultain; Notman Photographic Archives, McCord Museum,
McGill University: Keith (326208-II)

This book has been published with the help of a grant from the
Social Science Federation of Canada, using funds provided by the
Social Sciences and Humanities Research Council of Canada.

Contents

To my mother

Bernice Millard

and to

the memory of my father

Ross Millard

Preface

Many people have helped to prepare this book. The Engineering Institute of Canada, Montreal, extended privileges and gave me unrestricted access to its papers and records; staff members were unfailingly helpful, friendly, and co-operative. The Canadian Institute of Mining and Metallurgy, Montreal, also accorded many courtesies and allowed me to read its council minutes. Archivists and librarians at the National Archives of Canada, the Archives of Ontario, McGill and University of Toronto archives and libraries, the D.B. Weldon Library at the University of Western Ontario, and the Metropolitan Toronto Library gave invaluable assistance.

Robert Craig Brown gave sound advice, time, and unflagging support over many years. Bruce Sinclair made many worthwhile suggestions and imparted much energy and enthusiasm. This book has benefited also by the recommendations of Michael Bliss, Edwin T. Layton jr, and readers at the University of Toronto Press and the Social Science Federation of Canada. Gerry Hallowell expertly guided the manuscript through its various stages, and John Parry improved it with his splendid editing.

A number of secretaries have typed drafts of this book, none more diligently than Sharon Sjalund. The Faculty of Social Science, University of Western Ontario, provided generous financial support for research and data processing. Special thanks are due to my colleagues at Western and especially to Marjorie Ratcliffe, Wilfrid Laurier University.

Associations

AAE American Association of Engineers (founded 1915)
AIEE American Institute of Electrical Engineers (1884)
APEO Association of Professional Engineers of Ontario (1922)
ASCE American Society of Civil Engineers (1852)
ASME American Society of Mechanical Engineers (1880)
BCTA British Columbia Technical Association (1919)
CAE Canadian Association of Engineers (1918)
CMI Canadian Mining Institute (1898)
CSA Canadian Standards Association (1917)
CSC Civil Service Commission (1908)
CSCE Canadian Society of Civil Engineers (1887)
DIAE Dominion Institute of Amalgamated Engineering (1898)
EIC Engineering Institute of Canada (1918)
ICE Institution of Civil Engineers (1818)
JCTO Joint Committee of Technical Organizations (1917)
OALS Ontario Association of Land Surveyors (1892)
RCI Royal Canadian Institute (1849)

The master spirit of the age

Introduction

Alan Macdougall was pleased. A year had passed since he had issued a circular calling for the establishment of a national, professional, engineering society. Now, on 24 February 1887, the first general meeting of the Canadian Society of Civil Engineers was about to begin in Montreal. Others had tried and failed to organize a Canadian engineering society; but Macdougall had succeeded – he was the ideal organizer and promoter. At forty-five, he was a successful and respected consulting engineer. Born in India, the son of a British army officer, and educated in Scotland, Macdougall arrived in Canada in 1868 and worked on various railway and public works projects, before entering private practice as a consulting sanitary engineer, in 1883.[1] Until his untimely death in 1897, he strove to place engineering on the same footing as law and medicine. The new engineering society was a major step towards that objective.

On the surface, conditions appeared favourable for the new engineering society, as well as the new Dominion. In 1887, Queen Victoria was about to celebrate the fiftieth year of her reign, and the Dominion, bound together by the recently completed Canadian Pacific Railway (CPR), was twenty years old. Although still a rural, small-town nation of church-going inhabitants, Canada was beginning to change. Everywhere, signs of progress were visible as Canada neared the dawn of the electrical age. In spite of these prospects, it was also apparent that the country had entered the most critical period of its existence.

Barely two years had passed since the North-West Rebellion and the hanging of Louis Riel had precipitated the first great crisis of Confederation. The following year, Honoré Mercier had gained power in Quebec on a rising tide of nationalist sentiment. Premier Oliver Mowat of Ontario campaigned to increase provincial power at the expense of the central government, and the Nova Scotia legislature had gone so far as to pass a resolution to repeal the province's membership in Confederation. Later, in October 1887, amid adverse economic conditions, dissident premiers would meet in Quebec City to vent their hostility at Ottawa.

Unfavourable economic conditions, together with regional and social unrest, however, posed a more serious threat to Confederation than the trend to provincialism. Although Sir John A. Macdonald miraculously had won the February 1887 general election, opponents, such as the new Liberal opposition leader, Wilfrid Laurier, charged that his National Policy had failed to make Canada prosperous like the United States. Many Canadians moved south, in search of prosperity, while others, particularly farmers and Maritimers, blamed bad times on the tariff. Some industrial workers owed their jobs to the tariff. During the 1880s, however, organized labour, although small in number, became increasingly more dissatisfied with working conditions and more critical of how Canada's new industrial wealth was distributed.

Despite the political rancour and economic gloom, there were grounds for optimism. The economy had grown continuously since Confederation.[2] Businessmen made money, and engineers were occupied designing and constructing new railway, municipal, and hydraulic works. Alan Macdougall and his colleagues were confident and enthusiastic. They were proud of their engineering achievements and inspired by the prospect of further technical progress. In 1887, less than two years after the completion of their most spectacular engineering triumph, the CPR, they had attained an impressive record of remarkable engineering accomplishments.

During the nineteenth century, transportation projects, usually canals and railways, were the principal works designed and built by engineers. Although the Great Lakes and the St Lawrence provided British North America with excellent natural transportation, much improvement was needed to enable Montreal to compete with New York for control of western trade, especially after the completion of the Erie Canal in 1825. Between 1824 and 1848, a series of canals – Welland, Lachine, Cornwall, Beauharnois, and Williamsburg – was built and improved, in order to lower transportation costs by circumventing Niagara Falls and the St Lawrence rapids. But, as the canals neared completion, construction of an American railway network to the south, like the canal system that preceded it, threatened Montreal's commercial hinterland. Eventually, this led to railway development in Canada.[3]

The railways were the foremost achievement of nineteenth-century

Canadian engineering. Able to operate year-round more efficiently than canals, they developed during the prosperous 1850s in response to the transportation needs of a rapidly expanding economy. Borne on a wave of popular enthusiasm generated, in part, by the widely circulated pamphlet of Canada's most celebrated engineer, T.C. Keefer's *Philosophy of Railroads*,[4] the railways were financed primarily with British capital and, like the canals, given generous government assistance. In the 1830s and 1840s, several railways were planned, but little construction took place, apart from short 'portage' roads. During the 1850s, however, at the height of Canada's first railway boom, four major railways were built: St. Lawrence and Atlantic, Great Western, Northern, and Grand Trunk. Spanning the St Lawrence at Montreal stood the Victoria Bridge, the world's longest tubular bridge, a mile-and-a-quarter-long masterpiece of Victorian engineering, connecting the eastern and western divisions of the Grand Trunk, the world's longest railway. By January 1860, there were nearly two thousand miles of track in the Province of Canada alone, compared with sixty-six in all of British North America in 1850.[5]

Canada's second railway boom developed after Confederation in response to political factors. The Intercolonial Railway was constructed because of Maritime insistence on a line from central Canada; the CPR was built as a condition of British Columbia's entry into Confederation. The CPR was Canada's most celebrated transcontinental line, an engineering triumph as well as a major tenet in Macdonald's plan to create a viable national, transcontinental economy. By 1888, T.C. Keefer could boast that Canada had more miles of railroad per capita than any other country in the world.[6]

Railway construction led inexorably to industrial development. Railways created demand for producer goods industries – foundries, rolling mills, car and locomotive works – that served the railways. In some cases, these industries were financed with capital accumulated from railway construction and investment. With a fortune made from building a section of the main line of the Grand Trunk Railway (GTR) from Toronto to Sarnia, for example, Casimir Gzowski, one of Canada's leading railway engineers and contractors, invested in the Toronto Locomotive Works and, later, the Toronto Rolling Mills.[7] These and other mechanical engineering industries provided the infrastructure for further industrial development.

Although railways were their principal achievement, by 1887 Canadian engineers were making other significant contributions. A growing number of mechanical engineers supplied the railways and industry with locomotives and stationary steam-engines. Municipal engineers provided Canada's rapidly growing cities with safe water and gas supplies, as well as sewers and paved, well-lighted streets. Electrical engineering, however, was still in its infancy in 1887; the invention of the transformer, which permitted long-distance transmission of electricity, was a decade away. And while substantial deposits of copper-nickel had been discovered in the Sudbury basin during construction of the CPR, the large-scale extraction of Canada's vast mineral wealth would await the twentieth century.

Comparatively few engineers worked on Canada's remarkable early engineering projects. In 1851, at the start of the first railway boom, only thirty-five men in the Province of Canada called themselves 'engineers.' Ten years later, there were 129; there were 451 in 1871 and 719 by 1881.[8] Many of these men, especially in the earlier years, came from Great Britain and the United States. The Rideau Canal (completed 1834) was built by Royal Engineers, whereas the Welland and Cornwall canals were the work of American engineers, such as James Geddes, John B. Mills, and Benjamin Wright. The Great Western Railway, designed as a short-cut across the southern Ontario peninsula, in order to connect with the Michigan and New York rail networks, was built almost entirely by American engineers and contractors. By contrast, the GTR was constructed to exacting British standards, sometimes with unfortunate engineering results, by the cele-brated British firm of Peto, Brassey, Jackson and Betts.[9]

Although these early projects were dominated by Britons and Ameri-cans, they nevertheless helped to develop a distinctive, national, technical style based on British traditions and American influences, reflecting Canada's more conservative outlook and culture.[10] At the same time, they also produced Canada's first generation of civil engineers. Keefer, for example, first president of the Canadian Society of Civil Engineers (CSCE) and the only Canadian to serve as president of both the CSCE and the American Society of Civil Engineers (ASCE), began his career on the Erie Canal, before serving as an assistant engineer on the Welland. His elder stepbrother, Samuel Keefer, also worked on the Welland and, later, the Cornwall Canal. By the end of the second railway boom, following completion of the CPR, Canada had developed a corps of capable and experienced native-born engineers.

Of the twenty members of the CSCE's first council, the society's governing body, half were Canadian born; half were born in Great Britain or the Empire – except for Casimir Gzowski, who was born in St Petersburg. These men were a cross-section of some of Canada's most successful and distinguished engineers. They were an extraordinarily gifted and accom-plished group. The 1887 council included a wealthy contractor and militia colonel, a noted essayist, an inventor, several chief engineers of railway companies and government engineering departments, as well as various city engineers, a dean of engineering, and a member of Parliament.[11]

Except for Louis Lesage, superintendent of the Montreal Waterworks, all the members of the 1887 council were English speaking. They were middle-aged (averaging about fifty-three years), largely self-made men. While Keefer had family influence to help him get started, all these men, including Keefer, had substantial, well-earned professional reputations. Best known for his views on railways – although he had never built one – Keefer's professional reputation stemmed from his work as a hydraulic engineer on the Montreal, as well as several other municipal waterworks.[12] Only one man, Herbert Wallis, was a mechanical engineer, employed by the GTR; the rest were civil engineers. Like Wallis, most of the 1887 council members, at one time or another, were associated with a major railway. Some had begun their careers on railways and then moved to other fields of engineering. Alan Macdougall, for example, took up municipal engineering following his employment with the CPR. Unlike Macdougall and a few other independent consultants, however, most council members were salaried employees of large public and private corporations.

Although some council members had attended university, only two – H.T. Bovey and, possibly, Casimir Gzowski[13] – had received any formal instruction in engineering. Until the mid-nineteenth century, Canadian engineers followed British practice and trained as apprentices. Keefer, for example, received his early training on the Erie Canal, and Macdougall was an articled pupil to consulting engineer Charles Jopp, North British Railway Company, Edinburgh. By 1887, however, with five Canadian universities – New Brunswick, McGill, Toronto, Royal Military College, and Ecole polytechnique – offering engineering courses,[14] an increasing number of students received formal university instruction in engineering, in spite of a lingering bias that engineers should be 'practical men.' By 1914, 78.6 per cent of CSCE council members were university engineering graduates; 87.5 per cent by 1921.[15]

In 1887, university engineering education in Canada was at a formative stage of development. Engineering schools were small, had few students, and usually taught only civil engineering. The School of Practical Science (later the Faculty of Applied Science and Engineering, University of Toronto, Canada's largest engineering school by the academic year 1920–21),[16] for instance, had but a single engineering professor and forty-seven regular students. Only twenty-eight students were graduated by the 1886–87 term.[17] With a curriculum heavily weighted towards traditional science courses taught by faculty members from university science departments, early engineering schools gave practical instruction in civil engineering, in order to supply engineers for resource development, public works, and, especially, railway projects. In 1887, the School of Practical Science offered courses only in civil and mining engineering; applications to study mechanical engineering were turned down until the following year, when the school was authorized to form a division of mechanical (including electrical) engineering. Until 1890, however, undergraduate enrolment in civil engineering was 75 per cent of the total.[18]

By 1887, the engineering schools were beginning to reflect broader changes in the profession, which led to a virtual scientific revolution in technology that transformed engineering from an empirical art to a scientific profession.[19] Prominent educators, such as John A. Galbraith, a prize-winning University of Toronto honours mathematics graduate who had ten years of practical engineering experience before his appointment to the School of Practical Science in 1878, believed strongly in giving students a solid grounding in scientific principles, before teaching how to apply them. As a consequence, curriculum, under this short and rather laconic, yet resolute and dedicated professor (later, the first dean of the Faculty of Applied Science and Engineering), became progressively more theoretical and scientific in content.

The trend to scientific engineering was evident in other ways. After long and bitter controversies in the early 1880s and, again, in 1903–4, the school acquired its own chemistry and physics instructors.[20] Electrical engineering was given the same status with mechanical engineering in 1891 (McGill established a division of electrical engineering the same year), and, in the 1891–92 term, the school received a large amount of laboratory equipment suitable for engineering experimentation. Later, in 1917, a School of Engineering Research would be established. By that time, mechanical and electrical engineering students at Toronto outnumbered the civils, who, as early as the 1892–93 term, had declined to 30 per cent of total enrolment.[21]

As the schools became more scientific in their approach to engineering education, they also acquired more of the outward trappings of 'professional' respectability: university affiliation and degrees. In 1871, from its institutional beginnings in the downtown School of Technology – a night school for artisans – the School of Practical Science had located on the University of Toronto campus; it had affiliated with the university in 1889 and had become a separate faculty in 1906. The professional degree of civil engineer (CE) was established in 1884, the bachelor of science in 1889, and the master of applied science in 1903.[22] Together, these developments gave engineers more prestige; but only to a point.

As one of the earliest expressions of professional institutional development, university engineering schools were only the most visible sign of the
growing 'professional' status of engineers. In spite of their increasing
respectability, however, Alan Macdougall and many of his colleagues were
extremely anxious about their status as professionals.

Macdougall had concluded that the profession was in a 'quagmire.'
Unethical competitive practices among engineers, he lamented, had made
engineering 'almost a trade.'[23] Years earlier, Keefer had called attention to
the problems arising from the engineer's dependent status as an employee
of large contracting firms. Only when engineers were financially secure and
accorded the same status as doctors and lawyers, he asserted, could they
maintain their professional integrity, without compromising professional
standards for commercial or political expediency.[24] Macdougall, Keefer,
and others were also keenly aware that engineers, despite their importance
to society, had not received much public recognition.

Canadian engineers constantly reminded themselves that they had
virtually created the modern industrial world: they had developed the
mineral and forest resources, constructed the vital transportation networks, presided over the rise of the cities, and laid the foundations of
Canada's modern industries. Yet while the public displayed genuine
interest in great engineering projects, the engineer was often overshadowed by the grandeur of his own work and soon forgotten after its
completion. The ordinary citizen, engineers complained, saw no romance
in such commonplace necessities as sewers and soon took them, and
engineers, for granted. Dealing indirectly with the public through large
corporations, without a legally protected title, engineers lacked a popular
identity. An 'engineer,' in the public mind, meant anything from a
locomotive driver to a plumber. Still closely identified with tradesmen,
engineers were stigmatized by negative nineteenth-century British aristo-
cratic attitudes to manual labour.[25] They were not quite gentlemen like
doctors and lawyers.

While engineers liked to think of themselves as independent professionals, most were salaried employees of large public and private corporations.
They possessed expertise essential to industry; but, as employees, they
could neither control their professional lives nor protect themselves from
competition. Unlike the practice of law and medicine, engineering had no
legal standing. Anyone could practise. In spite of a scientific revolution in
technology that gave birth to the modern engineering profession, most
employers, before the First World War, did not recognize engineers as
professionals. They continued to hire the cheapest professional, or
non-professional, talent. Forced to live on a fixed income, engineers were

vulnerable to inflation and unemployment. To this extent, they found themselves in relatively the same economic predicament as most other industrial wage and salary earners. This was profoundly demoralizing to men who had struggled for nearly half a century to rise above the level of tradesmen. They felt unrecognized and unrewarded.

Determined to raise their status, engineers adopted a strategy of professional development. They acquired vital esoteric, technical knowledge essential to their employers and, in 1887, institutionalized their expertise in an élite, professional engineering society, the Canadian Society of Civil Engineers. By 1918, however, as overcrowding intensified competition among engineers for scarce jobs, wartime inflation threatened to undermine their status. Moreover, various earlier initiatives to enhance their prestige had failed. Rejecting unionization, engineers campaigned instead for licensing to achieve the same ends as unionization. Posing as professionals protecting the public interest, they eventually obtained substantial monopoly powers through licensing, by 1922, without resorting to professionally undignified restrictive trade practices, such as strikes.

Professionalism was a uniquely middle-class solution to the uncertainty and insecurity accompanying rapid industrialization. It was distinct from and, in some respects, more effective than other contemporary collectivist initiatives, such as trade unions or business cartels. Organized to restrict competition and monopolize practice, licensing laws were a collectivist assault on the ideals of laissez-faire. Engineering licensing associations were the middle-class counterparts to trade unions, business associations, and combinations. They arose from a long struggle between two competing concepts of professionalism within the CSCE and represented the triumph of younger protectionist engineers over older free-market proponents. This victory heralded the rise of an aggressive, self-confident new breed of middle-class experts in Canada and the Western world.

This book examines the engineers' struggle to acquire power and prestige. It covers the relatively short, yet crucial period between the founding of the CSCE in 1887 and the granting of registration laws to Ontario's engineers in 1922. Rather than a comprehensive analysis of engineers as a profession, or even of professionalization, it is primarily a social and institutional history of a small but important group of organized civil engineers. Its focus is on engineers, not engineering. This book is the story not so much of how engineers changed society but of how they survived that change through collective action.

While engineers often compared themselves to doctors and lawyers, they differed substantially from the older, pre-industrial consultative professionals. Engineers were employees, not independent consultants; they sometimes viewed engineering as a business rather than a profession and, before the First World War, rarely discussed the idea of professionalism. Instead, engineering 'professionalism' was a pragmatic political device. Engineers deliberately adopted the outward professional trappings of doctors and lawyers to raise their status and legitimize the acquisition of restrictive licensing laws. As such, the process of obtaining power and prestige constituted the essence of the engineers' peculiar kind of 'professionalism.'

In background, status, and outlook, engineers were part of an emerging group of urban middle-class experts – administrators, foresters, town-planners, public health advocates, educators, social workers, and others – that rose to prominence during Canada's transformation from a rural agrarian country to an urban industrial nation. Engineers formed the vanguard of this 'new middle class.' They personified its spirit and aspirations. They saw themselves in the van of history as the foremost participants in a dramatic national adventure and believed that they had a special destiny to fullfil. They had a vision of a new social order and assumed that they were uniquely qualified to lead society and solve its problems with engineering methods. Preaching the secular gospel of social engineering, they helped to supplant the authority of traditional professionals. As unabashed apologists for an acquisitive, materialistic society, engineers were, perhaps, more influential in shaping the values of the developing industrial state than were many contemporary social reformers, such as the Social Gospellers. An examination of the development of their ideas, institutions, and politics leads to a better understanding of how Canadians, especially middle-class Canadians, adjusted to rapid industrialization.

1

'The master spirit of the age'

The engineer and his world

Canadian engineers did not regard themselves as philosophers. They believed that they were practical men of action, not thinkers. According to Sandford Fleming, engineers 'are not as a rule gifted with many words ... [They] must plod on in a distinct sphere of their own, dealing less with words than with deeds, less with men than with matter.'[1] Engineers were distrustful of doctrine and contemptuous – sometimes envious – of the more articulate members of society. Few seemed to have either the time or the inclination for much non-technical writing. There were a few notable exceptions, of course, the most celebrated being T.C. Keefer and the engineer-historian William Kingsford.[2] Occasionally, some abstract subjects were attempted, such as C.E.W. Dodwell's extraordinary treatise, *Righteousness versus Religion*, but without much popular success or critical acclaim.

Nevertheless, in their speeches, articles, and letters, Canadian engineers periodically made philosophical statements that revealed a unique Weltanschauung. When arranged logically, these statements roughly outlined the engineer's vision of the world. This vision, however, reflected the view of a small minority of articulate engineers, mostly engineering leaders, journalists, and educators. They functioned as the profession's thinkers and spokesmen and generally formulated the ideas that were accepted by most rank-and-file engineers.

Canadian engineers were not very accomplished ideologists. Their ideas were largely derivative of British and, especially, American engineers.[3] Their analyses were often superficial and unsystematic. Their arguments tended to be ill conceived and naive, more polemical than analytical, and were sometimes confused, even contradictory. Yet, in spite of their shortcomings as philosophers, engineers developed a distinct and remarkable philosophy that stressed the pre-eminence of technicians in an industrial society.

Engineers viewed Canada as a vast engineering frontier. 'No matter to which section of Canada you turn,' observed the *Canadian Engineer* in 1908, 'crude forces and huge stores of natural wealth lie ready to lend themselves to processes that create wealth and concern themselves with the larger movements of human progress.'[4] Canada's destiny lay in the scientific development of this immense natural wealth. In turn, this would place Canada in the forefront of modern civilized nations. 'It only remains,' declared one enthusiast, 'for these resources to be ascertained and properly developed to place this country in a foremost position as a great producing nation.'[5] Canada's potential was virtually unlimited, and it was confidently assumed that Canada would soon rival the United States as an economic power.[6] In his retiring presidential address to the Toronto Engineers' Club, in 1911, C.M. Canniff asserted that for years Canada had been 'a poor relation to England,' overshadowed by the United States. But with the return of prosperity after 1896, Canada had come to the attention of the whole world; 'at last,' Canniff declared, 'the Dominion is coming into its own.'[7] It was Canada's turn to assume its rightful position among the great industrial nations.

No other group of Canadians was in such direct and constant contact with the physical evidence of substantial material improvements as engineers. They saw history as a splendid record of growth and improvement. 'In Canada,' announced Sandford Fleming, 'we are in a constant state of general and continuing development. Year by year we advance forward as our fathers did before us.'[8] Science and technology were the keys to achieving progress. Years earlier, in his *Philosophy of Railroads*, T.C. Keefer waxed eloquent about the great civilizing tendency of the railway. Keefer and his engineering colleagues had boundless faith in the capacity of technology[9] to substantially improve the material and moral condition of Canadians. They were the consummate apostles of progress.[10] The practical application of science to Canada's natural resources, they believed, would not only transform the country into a modern industrial utopia but would also provide a series of blessings, from increased population to cheap consumer goods, and ameliorate social evils associated with industrialism.[11]

Canada's immense unexploited natural resources and tremendous industrial potential excited engineers' imagination and provided them with a great mission: to transform Canada from a backward wilderness into a powerful industrial nation. They accepted this noble calling with evangelical fervour and boldly appointed themselves, as one engineer observed, 'the guardian of the whole industrial development of the country.'[12] Canada's resources, moreover, provided engineers with an opportunity, as well as a mission. According to an engineering journalist: 'Canada is pre-eminently the engineer's country ... The vast extent of the country, its magnificent lakes and rivers, its agricultural and mineral riches, its forests, its unrivalled water-power, and many other potential sources of future wealth and progress furnish exceptional incentives and opportunities to the engineer.'[13] Canniff remembered that the twentieth century belonged to Canada and, going beyond Laurier, proclaimed that the 'Twentieth Century belongs also to the engineer.'[14]

The engineer's sense of mission was not confined to narrow nationalist objectives. As Canadian nationalists, they also had a broader imperial vision. Before the First World War, many engineers expressed the belief that Canada's future lay within the British Empire. By building a strong industrial economy, they felt that they were strengthening the empire. As engineers, they had a special mission to unite the empire physically with transportation and communication works.[15] Unlike some other Canadian imperialists, however, engineers had no reservations about industrialism, no arcane longing for a more virtuous agrarian past, or even fear of social disorder arising from industrial evils. Industrialism, like the empire, was *a priori* good.

Thus, Canadian engineers had a profound sense that they were major participants in a dramatic national adventure. Armed with the conviction that they were the guardians of Canada's industrial development, they marched forth with crusading zeal as the shock troops of British civilization to battle all the stubborn adversity of nature, in the name of progress and empire. At the same time, however, they also realized that not all Canadians shared their vision and appreciated the advantages of technology. They were convinced that unprogressive and reactionary forces were impeding Canada's industrial progress and thwarting their mission.

Many engineering leaders and thinkers were deeply alarmed about the lack of industrial and political leadership in Canada. Everywhere they turned they saw inefficiency and mismanagement. They believed that these undermined Canadian society and stifled national industrial progress. They felt that many of society's fundamental values had been eroded. In his presidential address to the Engineering Institute of Canada, in January 1920, Col. R.W. Leonard, a wealthy and prominent civil engineer and mining promoter, observed:

A few years ago it would have been unnecessary to deal with the fundamentals of our civilization; they were so imbued in our being that it was almost silly to formulate them into words. We rested securely in the belief that 'Truth is might and will prevail'. Of late, however, so much false teaching and distortion of fundamental truths has been disseminated, and accepted by so many, that downtrodden Truth would appear to need the assistance of some Minister of propaganda if she is to hold her place and prevail before the structure of our civilization is badly shaken.[16]

Much of this 'false teaching,' according to Leonard, was spread by sensationalist newspapers that gave 'undue prominence ... to any radical or extreme utterance of even the most ignorant' and printed exaggerated reports of profits and corrupt business practices of a few large companies.[17] Engineers also believed, like many businessmen, that the labour movement had been radicalized and was controlled by revolutionaries. Youthful and inexperienced union leaders made unrealistic and irresponsible wage demands, which they did not deserve, and business could not afford, because of the iron law of wages.[18] Strikes and labour violence resulted.

The dramatic rise in industrial conflict, climaxing in the Winnipeg General Strike of 1919, frightened engineers. They believed that industrial strife had far-reaching consequences. Not only did it harm employers and workers, it also constituted a direct assault on society. 'On our own Continent,' Leonard declared, 'we have to day attempts by the ignorant and misguided to destroy both the foundation and arch stones of our industry and civilization.'[19] Some engineers suspected that even their colleagues, not just the working class, were vulnerable to pernicious ideas. Amid the post-war hysteria, generated by the Bolshevik revolution and the Winnipeg General Strike, one engineer feared that 'minor and inferior elements in the profession, if not dominated by its intellectual leaders, may stray into the wilderness of chaotic thinking.'[20]

In their approach to labour unrest and other problems, engineers' social thought was influenced deeply by their belief in a Newtonian universe ruled by immutable natural laws that governed man and the physical world. Universal social principles, like physical laws, could be ascertained scientifically by the same objective and rational methods that engineers applied to engineering. Education, especially of the technical sort, enabled man to perceive correctly universal social principles through rational thinking. Engineers divided society broadly between the educated, progressive forces and the unenlightened, unprogressive elements. They assumed that they themselves were the foremost members of an élite community of right-thinking progressives. They were singular in this conviction and untroubled by doubt. According to E.T. Clark, engineers were 'accustomed to dealing with facts and with immutable natural laws. They feel instinctively that there is about everything a definite position which must be right; what differs from it is wrong.'[21]

Engineers viewed the economy almost as if it were a complex machine that functioned properly when operated in conformity with correct design specifications. Malfunctions, they believed, arose from minor disorders and were amenable to objective analysis and rational solutions. Labour conflict, they thought, was caused not by faulty design, since the economy, in spite of shortcomings, was fundamentally sound. Capitalism, like progress, was accepted by engineers on faith as an accurate reflection of the natural order. Industrial conflict arose from ignorance of a fundamental principle: capital and labour were mutually interdependent, integral parts of Canada's developing industrial economy. Peaceful coexistence and industrial progress hinged upon mutual recognition of this principle.[22]

The ordinary worker, if properly guided with sound principles, for example, was content and loyal to his employer.[23] Lack of education, however, made him susceptible to the pernicious propaganda of 'irresponsible, self-seeking agitators,' who easily led him astray, often on the pretext of 'alleged grievances.'[24] Only by countering the agitators' insidious propaganda with reason and sound principles could society avert labour unrest.[25] Col. Leonard warned that 'until the wise heads in the Unions get together, take control and educate the others along lines of duty and honest service to their fellow men, there can be no industrial peace.'[26] Unfortunately, even at this critical juncture in Canada's development, when various 'reactionary' forces threatened to undermine society, engineers had little confidence in political leaders to restore order and to foster progress.

Engineers were repelled by government corruption and scandals. They believed that public affairs at all levels were being mismanaged. The *Electrical News* observed: 'Every live Canadian has a growing feeling of unrest and dissatisfaction at the methods adopted in the management of our various public affairs. Charges of graft are becoming every day matters; evidences of incompetence in our administrators are available on all sides; proof, unmistakable in its directness, that the public good is being placed in a secondary position to the demands of party politics or personal gain daily confront us.'[27] In a society so heavily dominated by partisanship, engineers had developed an aversion to politics. T.C. Keefer considered himself a casualty of politics,[28] and, in the continuing tradition of hostility to party politics of the Canada First movement, Sandford Fleming bitterly attacked 'partyism' and became a staunch advocate of electoral and parliamentary reform. He cautioned his colleagues not to become involved with politics in its debased condition.[29]

Most engineers sensed that there was something fundamentally wrong with Canadian democracy. As one engineer asserted: 'The manifest tendency of the times [is] to put more and more power into the hands of the ignorant and uneducated.'[30] Although most engineers tacitly accepted democracy as an ideal, provided the electorate were well educated and informed, they had little confidence in the intelligence of the ordinary voter. Suspicious of the American ideal of majority rule and inclined towards conservative and monarchical principles of order and authority, they feared that, with the aid of the sensationalist press, personable and articulate demagogues could be elected by arousing the baser instincts of the 'ignorant and uneducated.' Once elected, such people put political interest before the public interest.[31]

Much of the engineers' hostility to democracy was directed at municipal government. As rapid urban growth drew an increasing number of them into municipal engineering, city engineers soon came into conflict with elected civic officials.[32] In an 'age of efficiency,' these engineers were highly critical of the fact that cities were controlled by popularly elected amateurs – ward aldermen. Judging by the professional standard of the city manager concept, they commonly portrayed aldermen in a crude, one-dimensional stereotype: lower class, self-seeking, unprogressive, and unproductive. Engineers maintained that, as failed businessmen or ambitious tradesmen seeking personal fame through politics, most aldermen were incompetent civic administrators, because their main qualification for office was political, rather than technical or administrative, ability. Ignorant of the technical aspects of municipal administration, aldermen decided vital public issues on political, not technical grounds.[33] This adversely affected and eventually retarded Canadian urban progress.

Rejecting parliamentary methods of government as inefficient, before the First World War, engineers were inspired by the management techniques of an efficiently run modern business corporation, with its clearly defined hierarchical lines of authority, long-term planning, continuity of management, and, above all, decision making by experts, based on objective and rational considerations. Parliamentary government was the antithesis of this ideal, and engineers developed a contemptuous disdain for it, reinforced by the inefficiency, patronage, and corruption rampant in all levels of government. Ideally, engineers preferred government by experts. They endorsed the city manager, or commission government concept,[34] a panacea that promised to take politics out of municipal administration and stressed expertise, rationality, efficiency, and security of tenure. According to R.A. Ross, president of the Engineering Institute of Canada and Montreal's city commissioner, the city manager had 'no election pledges to keep, and no dependence upon the fickle and foolish decisions of the voter, but [was] free to carry out as a real manager the necessary work of the community in the same way as the manager of a company.'[35]

Engineers' advocacy of commission government and their earlier critique of municipal government were inspired in many respects by the urban reform movement that swept Canada between 1890 and 1920.[36] Engineers sided with the commercial élite of many cities in an effort to have civic affairs run in a more efficient, business-like manner.[37] Motivated by a high degree of self-interest and employing popular democratic reform rhetoric, engineers and prominent businessmen attempted to lessen popular participation in municipal government by minimizing the power of local ward politicians.[38]

At the same time, however, engineers differed from the mainstream of contemporary urban reform thought. Whereas business reformers viewed the city as a corporate enterprise and justified reform in the name of the people, engineers saw the city, especially its government, almost exclusively in engineering terms. 'City government,' the *Canadian Engineer* explained, 'is largely an aggregation of engineering problems.'[39] If a city were properly designed and maintained by knowledgeable experts, it would function smoothly, with orderly precision. Engineers were less interested in the human aspect of urban reform and did not rationalize their actions in terms of the commonweal. Their sole concern was to eradicate inefficiency from municipal government. They justified efficiency for its own sake and reasoned that if city governments were well run, the public, in turn, would be well served.

While most articulate engineers had little faith in Canadian political leaders, they also believed that other groups – particularly business and professional men – were unfit to lead a modern industrial society. They set themselves up as the standard against which leadership was measured and tended to judge other callings by their own rigid materialistic values, assuming that engineering had greater practical value for humanity. In their view, the older learned professions – theology, medicine, and law, for example – were anachronistic, doing little to advance society's material progress.

Although engineers acknowledged the clergy's authority in earlier times and probably accepted their spiritual guidance, they nevertheless regarded this profession with respectful condescension. This attitude was not prompted by anti-clericalism but arose from an assessment of the clergy's relative social importance. While the church was considered a legitimate, though declining institution, its other-worldliness probably appeared irrelevant amid the materialism of modern industrial society.

Medicine was considered more progressive, since it was more practical;[40] but its social importance was proscribed by the scope of its responsibility. 'The physician,' argued consulting engineer Walter J. Francis, 'heals the sick and deals with individuals while the engineer holds in his hand the health of towns, cities and nations.'[41] A doctor's responsibility was individual; an engineer's, collective. Moreover, doctors could easily elude blame for professional incompetence. An engineer, however, had no escape; his structures were material and stood openly on their own merits. If a train crashed through a badly designed and constructed bridge, he alone was responsible.[42] As Francis put it: 'The doctor buries his mistakes. The engineer erects monuments to his ability or lack of it.'[43]

Law was regarded as the least productive of the learned professions. Lawyers did not create wealth. They lived off surplus wealth and profited from the misfortune of others. They were unprogressive, since they looked to past precedent rather than future potential. The *Canadian Engineer* maintained: 'The average lawyer's mind is dilatory, bound with redtape, tied by precedent. It does not create, it takes advantage of minute divisions and side issues. It is bound by the shackles of the past in an extraordinary manner. It cannot organize, and its achievements are verbal triumphs, not executive deeds.'[44] By contrast, the engineer possessed a 'creative mind': 'He walks warily among the teeming possibilities which surround him. He is a cautious selector, never prone to haste, but progressive in general trend. Sufficiently conservative not to adopt unproven remedies or devices, he is willing to consider any new possibility in the light of past experience and technical judgment. He looks to the future more than to the past, while he does not despise precedent – more often than not he creates precedent by further advance. No other modern mind has quite the same cast.'[45] Not only were lawyers regressive, they were confined to man-made provincial boundaries, while engineering was practised universally, like science. While lawyers became tangled in a web of man-made laws, engineers were in touch with a more perfect order – natural law.[46]

Engineers also dismissed businessmen. Like lawyers, businessmen did not create wealth. Merchants and bankers, the *Canadian Engineer* argued, were only mediums of exchange, not true producers.[47] While business accumulated wealth, engineers, according to the *Contract Record*, were 'engaged in building larger, better, and more lasting structures than "fortunes".'[48] The engineer designed and built the means of production, provided power and raw materials, and organized production and distribution.[49] Francis believed that there were two classes in society: producers and non-producers. Real estate brokers and speculators were the lowest of the non-producers, while engineers headed the producers. Other callings fell somewhere in between. Farmers were occasionally included among the select group of producers, because of the need for food and clothing;[50] but labour's classic claim to be the true producers of wealth was ignored. Engineers perhaps assumed that, without their machines and management, labour could not produce anything.

Undoubtedly the most fundamental tenet in the engineers' creed was the belief that they had created the modern industrialized world and fostered its material development. Francis asserted:

It is the engineer who harnesses the Niagaras of the world to transform the night of our cities into noonday, and to turn the wheels of commerce. It is the engineer who develops the mining and furnishes the metal with which he builds machines that by their ingenuity compel us to stand in awe and admiration. It is the engineer who produces the steel to form a network of highways over our continents and that makes possible the myriads of floating palaces on our oceans. It is the engineer who has abolished famine and pestilence. It is the engineer who has annihilated distance with his telegraph and his telephone. It is the engineer who has made possible the conquest of the air.[51]

Engineers had raised humanity from the darkness of semi-barbarism to the enlightened civility of the industrial age. 'The human race,' declared E.H. Keating, general manager of the Toronto Street Railway, in his president's address of 1902 to the CSCE, 'would still be clothing itself with the skins of animals, using stone implements and dwelling in caves or wigwams' but for engineers.[52] The civilized world, many engineers believed, was dependent on engineers; without them, government could not function and the modern world would be, according to Walter J. Francis, 'immediately plunged into the darkness of the middle ages.'[53]

Finding others wanting, engineers simply concluded that they were society's natural leaders. By the First World War, they were confidently asserting that engineers were uniquely qualified to manage public affairs. This conviction was predicated on the notion that the major issues affecting Canada were essentially engineering problems. By implication, only the engineer, who possessed technical knowledge, training, and experience, was capable of leading society and solving its problems.[54] Assuming that problems in society, like those in engineering, were amenable to scientific solutions, engineers proposed to apply science to society. In short, they intended simply to engineer society. As one engineer proclaimed: 'Statecraft is merely national engineering.'[55]

Engineers would bring to public life the combined advantages of training in applied science and extensive managerial experience. The engineer's mind, they argued, was schooled to solve practical problems scientifically.[56] As senior corporation executives and managers of various industrial and engineering concerns, they were experienced organizers, skilled in co-ordinating large numbers of people into, as one engineer put it, 'effective human machines.'[57] While lawyers and politicians had failed to resolve industrial conflict, engineers, occupying a neutral position, intermediate between capital and labour, were accustomed to dealing effectively with labour. After all, industrial relations were merely a problem in 'human engineering.'[58]

Engineers would also bring morality to public life. Amid the corruption and duplicity of party politics and the unrestrained exploitation of the country's natural resources, engineers, like farmers, had a moral vision of themselves as producers and guardians of the nation's natural wealth. They were honest and honourable,[59] uncorrupted and incorruptible – 'The engineer's clean, wholesome mind,' wrote a Toronto civil engineer, 'the sterling character derived from his close association with nature, would in a great measure tend to elevate the trend of politics in this country.'[60] By training and disposition, the engineer was non-political and non-partisan.[61] All judgments involving the public interest would be made objectively, consistent with the principles of efficiency and public utility.

That engineers, not elected representatives, should lead society was not regarded as a particularly revolutionary, or even radical doctrine. The notion stemmed from conservative precepts of order and authority and was considered by many a progressive ideal, uniquely suited to a modern industrial society. In an 'engineering age,'[62] engineers reasoned that government's problems were essentially technical. While politicians were elected, they were not experts; they were forced to rely on engineers for advice. Good government – economy and efficiency – depended on sound technical advice. 'Thus in the end,' the *Contract Record* concluded, 'the responsibility rests upon the shoulders of the expert.'[63] The engineer, not the politician, was ultimately responsible to the people. To this extent, engineers were already *de facto* leaders.

While Canadian engineers expected ultimately to rule society, they had no manifesto, no doctrine of radical social engineering, no master plan to transfer production and distribution from businessmen to engineers and organize society on a technical basis. They were hardly a 'Soviet of Technicians' or the indispensable 'General Staff' of the industrial system envisaged by Thorstein Veblen.[64] They lacked strong messianic leaders like the American engineer-technocrat Howard Scott, and they were unassertive and highly conservative – almost apolitical. They neither expected nor condoned revolution.

Although engineers had no plans to assume power, their philosophy did reflect their aspirations. The city manager panacea, for example, was never seriously promoted by any organized engineering group. It remained essentially an abstract concept in the engineer's mind rather than a practical objective. Its real significance was its symbolic appeal. Rejecting the traditional entrepreneurial and professional ideals, engineers identified instead with the city manager. The city manager represented a unique ideal that defined their role and embodied their aspirations. This non-elected, non-partisan expert, who managed the city rationally and objectively, with business-like efficiency, was ultimately the personification of the engineering ideal – the quintessential technocrat.

The main thrust of engineers' thought was technocratic,[65] not professional. They believed that technology would transform Canada into an industrial utopia, that social problems were essentially technical ones, requiring technical solutions. Although engineers had begun to develop a concept of professionalism, their close association with business arrested the growth of professional consciousness. For years they had argued about whether engineering was a profession or a business. In 1923, C.R. Young, later dean of applied science and engineering, University of Toronto, concluded that engineering was 'part profession and part business.'[66] This concept, in effect a dichotomy in the engineer's mind between idealism and pragmatism, overshadowed the engineer's thinking on professionalism.

Engineers thought like businessmen and regarded engineering as a business. They recognized that engineering depended on business and was ultimately justified by the profit motive: 'Will it pay?'[67] An engineer's professional success, moreover, depended on business success. 'A successful engineer,' asserted M.J. Butler, 'is a good business man.'[68] An engineer could not rely exclusively on technical knowledge, and a common complaint was his lack of business sense.[69] 'Engineering is business,' the *Canadian Engineer* declared, 'and there should be better business methods in engineering.'[70]

Like businessmen, engineers were fiercely competitive in their drive to attain financial success and social recognition and often used engineering as a stepping-stone to more lucrative business careers in contracting. Engineers were the embodiment of the Victorian creed of the entrepreneurial ideal, or the success ethic – the individualistic counterpart of the idea of progress.[71] They upheld the required virtues of industry, hard work, and perseverance and subscribed to the 'self-help' philosophy of Samuel Smiles.[72] Their ideal was the self-made man who was not only professionally accomplished but also wealthy and socially prominent. Engineers respected Fleming and Keefer, but Sir Casimir Gzowski (and later C.D. Howe) were their real heroes.[73]

Although they were entrepreneurial by instinct, engineers differed in some fundamental ways from businessmen. Their basic objectives were not necessarily compatible, and many engineers found it difficult to reconcile science with the profit motive. Moreover, engineers believed that they belonged to a much higher and more dignified calling. The engineer was not merely a businessman engaged in technical work or an integral part of business, but a learned professional – a repository of esoteric scientific knowledge. For moral and practical professional reasons, engineers believed that they were not governed exclusively by business values and maintained that they had a special concern for the public interest.

Engineers were not willing to justify either profit or success by any means. They denounced dishonest and corrupt businessmen who, in their view, were preoccupied with the pursuit of profit. 'The small cunning needed in some businesses,' the *Canadian Engineer* observed with gentlemanly indignation, 'has no place in the broader transactions of the engineer who is often disgusted with the methods of so-called purely business men.'[74] The pursuit of financial success, engineers believed, often became an end in itself, justifying all acquisition no matter how sordid or corrupt. They were repelled by the competitive and deceptive aspects of business, thinking them, as one engineer put it, 'undignified and unmanly.'[75] It was important how wealth was accumulated; real success could not be measured without moral consideration.[76]

Engineers also argued that they must have integrity. They were often placed in positions of trust, charged with spending public funds, or privy to secret trade information of value to a client's competitor. As such, they were subject to insidious temptations, by 'shifty contractors and capitalists,'[77] to compromise themselves for short-term gain. Under these circumstances, young engineers were advised to maintain a scrupulous distance from contractors with whom they were dealing, always refusing any gifts.[78] 'The ideal Engineer,' according to Charles T. Harvey, 'must use the plumb line of integrity, and the square of equity'[79] in professional work and place the public interest ahead of personal gain. Otherwise, his usefulness would cease and his income would decline with his reputation.

The developing strains of professionalism – expertise, public service, and professional trust – never coalesced and matured, in the engineer's mind, to form a coherent system intellectually on a level with other philosophies of professionalism. Engineers had remarkably little to say on the subject. They produced no thinkers or literature on engineering professionalism, and their ideas were largely borrowed from other professions. As an abstract concept, professionalism was intellectually at variance with the engineer's quasi-business mentality and incompatible with being an employee of large corporations. The engineer was too preoccupied with bureaucracy and the vicious competition of the market-place, too divided in his thinking by business and science, to develop an original philosophy suited to his condition.

As a partially formed, abstract, and dimly perceived concept, suspended precariously between the opposing and sometimes contradictory notions of engineering as both 'part profession and part business,' professionalism had an artificial, almost shadow-like existence in the engineer's consciousness. Ultimately his professionalism was still-born. Rather than develop into a viable philosophy, it merged half formed, half digested, into the mainstream of the engineer's technocratic thought. Later, it was arbitrarily conscripted as a publicity device to legitimize the engineer's political initiative in obtaining restrictive licensing laws. To this extent, professionalism was a practical device, lacking any intrinsic quality. As technocrats, engineers would masquerade in professional clothing in order to achieve political objectives.

The engineer's technocratic philosophy was at once naive and paradoxical: naive, because engineers had little political influence in society; paradoxical, because, as Canada's foremost pragmatists, they developed an impractical and delusive philosophy. To this extent, it was also tragic. When the 'pioneers of civilization and progress'[80] were confronted with the harsh reality of having little power or status in society, they became bewildered and, later, embittered. The disparity between expectation and reality soon generated a fierce determination – almost an obsession – among engineers to raise their status and assume their 'rightful' place in society.

Engineering leaders, nevertheless, were confident that, one day, they would realize their destiny. They believed that engineering would soon be recognized as the leading profession. At various times in history, they argued, different professions had occupied positions of leadership, but centuries before the advent of law, medicine, or even the priesthood, the engineer (although using a different name perhaps) practised his profession and uplifted humanity.[81] From its remarkable beginning with the 'great engineer of the universe,'[82] engineering, unlike other professions, had evolved and adapted to modern conditions and become, according to C.E.W. Dodwell, district engineer, Department of Public Works, Halifax, 'the most important Profession.'[83] In future, as mankind increasingly looked to engineers, the profession would assume leadership. The

Canadian Engineer concluded: 'The evolution of the modern world, of civilization itself, largely rests upon the engineer's shoulders. As his numbers increase and his talents are more and more exercised, the future must inevitably look to him in an increasing manner for the solution of its difficulties. To-day the engineer is a servant to many other interests; tomorrow – since only the fit survive – he may dominate and control those interests. The future largely belongs by right of conquest to the engineer.'[84]

Engineers fully expected to inherit the earth. Through an almost divine process of natural selection, engineering had evolved far beyond other callings to meet the challenges of the modern industrial age. Engineers had emerged as a new élite, the high priesthood of progress, that alone possessed the esoteric knowledge essential for civilization's advancement. Full of restless, youthful vigour and aggressive self-confidence, engineers were determined to overcome reactionary and unprogressive forces, in order to build a new social order, a new steel-and-concrete utopia, founded on rationality and efficiency after their own image. By the dawn of the twentieth century, the engineer believed he had become 'the master spirit of the age.'[85]

2

'The Montreal clique'

Formation of the CSCE

Traditionally, Canadian engineers had advanced their careers by building individual reputations for technical achievement. But, by the late nineteenth and early twentieth centuries, as business, labour, and professional groups were organizing collectively to protect and further their interests, engineers also began to organize themselves into a number of societies. These organizations served a variety of technical, business, and social needs. They reflected the engineers' values and aspirations and were the primary means through which engineers sought to fulfil their collective ideals and to realize their ambitions.

The world's first national engineering society was the Institution of Civil Engineers (ICE) of Great Britain. Founded in 1818, it flourished under the influence of one of Britain's foremost engineers, Thomas Telford. As a result of continuing occupational specialization in engineering, accompanying the industrial revolution, new societies emerged to address the particular needs of engineers. In 1847, the Institution of Mechanical Engineers was organized in Birmingham, with George Stephenson, founder of the world's first locomotive works, as its president. The Society of Telegraph Engineers, established 1871, became the Institution of Electrical Engineers in 1880. The earliest permanent American organization, the Boston Society of Civil Engineers, was organized in 1848. The American Society of Civil Engineers (ASCE), founded in 1852 and revived in 1867, was the first national society in the United States. Although it claimed to represent all civil, that is, non-military engineers, rival groups – the American Institute of Mining Engineers (1871), the American Society of Mechanical Engineers (1880), and the American Institute of Electrical Engineers (1884) – soon appeared. These four national bodies (known collectively as the 'founder societies'), like their British counterparts, could not prevent the creation of numerous other engineering societies.

Prior to 1887, there were no professional engineering societies in Canada, and Canadian engineers sometimes belonged to British or American societies, as corresponding members. Foreign societies were generally unsuccessful at organizing Canadian branches. After 1887, two major Canadian engineering societies emerged: the Canadian Mining Institute (CMI) and the Canadian Society of Civil Engineers (CSCE).

Organized, in 1898, from a loose federation of provincial mining societies,[1] originally created to monitor and to fight legislation harming the mining industry,[2] the Canadian Mining Institute[3] claimed to represent an industry, not a profession. Its chief aim was to develop Canada's mineral resources, rather than to educate engineers.[4] Unlike the British Institution of Mining and Metallurgy, which confined itself to the advancement of mining and metallurgical science, the CMI organized on broader lines similar to the American Institute of Mining Engineers, in order to represent the various professional and business interests comprising the mining industry.[5] It formed a pragmatic and organic alliance of science and business, dedicated to a common industrial objective. Mining engineers valued their association with business and regarded it as an essential precondition to developing Canada's mineral resources.[6]

The CMI's membership was organized along industrial, rather than professional lines. It reflected a cross-section of the mining industry and included non-professionals – mine owners and managers – along with various professional groups, including mining engineers, geologists, metallurgists, and chemists. These people, in turn, were divided into two classes, members and associate members, which, in practice, served to distinguish professional from commercial interest in mining. This classification, however, was only nominal, since non-professionals, though barred from holding office, enjoyed all privileges and could be admitted to full membership at the discretion of the CMI's governing body.[7]

Although four-fifths of the membership were professional,[8] the CMI resisted attempts to form a purely professional society. Mining engineers were more entrepreneurial than civil engineers in outlook; they regarded themselves primarily as employees and engineering as an integral part of business. Professional advancement was pursued within the context of the mining industry. By facilitating the application of science to industry, while safeguarding the interests of the mining industry, particularly against 'ill-advised clauses in provincial legislation,'[9] mining engineers believed that they advanced their own interests and served the public.[10] The CMI was content to leave professional development to the CSCE.

Founded in 1887, the CSCE[11] was organized as a professional society. Unlike the CMI, the CSCE did not represent an industry or admit non-professionals to full membership. It was national in scope and claimed to represent all 'civil,'[12] or non-military engineers in Canada. Before 1918, much of the professional development of Canadian engineers was promoted by the CSCE.

When the CSCE was organized, Canadian engineers had already laid the foundation of the nation's new transcontinental, urban-industrial economy. By 1887, the first phase of the great transportation works, culminating in the completion of the CPR, had been built and Canadian engineers were on the verge of constructing a new generation of works, ranging through municipal, electrical, chemical, and other industrial projects. Although the idea of forming an engineering society was discussed years before 1887,[13] it was not until the construction of the CPR that engineers began to consider the idea seriously. The ranks of engineers swelled as the CPR neared completion in 1885, and engineers thought that there were sufficient numbers of qualified professionals in Canada to form a viable national organization.

One of the major factors behind the formation of an engineering society was dissatisfaction arising from the legal advantage that land surveyors enjoyed over civil engineers. Engineers could conduct canal and railway surveys, but they were prohibited from practising as surveyors, unless they fulfilled certain statutory requirements and passed an examination. By contrast, land surveyors, whether competent or not, could practise as civil engineers.[14] Some engineers believed that engineering should also be governed by statute and that they should enjoy the same privileges as land surveyors.[15] After consultation with C.E.W. Dodwell and other engineers in Toronto, during 1884 and 1885,[16] Alan Macdougall issued a circular, in January 1886, calling for legal recognition of engineering and formation of a national society.[17] This initiative represented the organizational beginning of the CSCE.[18]

In February 1886, Macdougall issued a second circular that led to a number of meetings, the most important held in Montreal on 4 March 1886. This meeting unanimously resolved to form a national engineering society to include all branches of engineering and to draft a preliminary constitution. Local committees in Toronto, Ottawa, and Montreal amended the draft constitution and elected representatives to a provincial committee, which was then given authority to complete preliminary organizational work.[19]

Macdougall's plan for a national society was highly controversial, since it advocated the comparatively radical measure, for that time, of securing legal recognition for engineers and closing the profession to unqualified practitioners. The new organization was perceived to be more than an educational body dedicated to advancing professional knowledge; it would have considerable legal power. Macdougall and his supporters wanted not only the recognition already obtained by surveyors but also much broader powers, remarkably similar to those delineated in a bill respecting civil engineers, presented to the Ontario legislature in 1881.[20] This bill, which had failed to become law, called for a full measure of professional self-government, with complete statutory authority to control and regulate all aspects of professional practice. Thus the new society, as Macdougall saw it, would become the means to acquire legal powers, with which to establish engineering on the same footing as law and medicine.

Macdougall and his supporters, however, were opposed by a group of conservative engineers – mostly older and more successful consultants, corporation managers, and senior government engineers, such as T.C. Keefer and John Kennedy – who were generally sympathetic to raising the status of engineers but disagreed with the means. Convinced that higher status could not be legislated, the conservatives believed that the standing of the profession could be improved only through the efforts of individual engineers raising the standard of practice by acquiring professional knowledge. In their view, the primary function of an engineering society was to educate individual members. They saw the new organization primarily as a learned or educational society. To the conservatives, Macdougall and his supporters were proposing an unacceptable, collectivist remedy, bordering on trade unionism. The conservatives placed their faith in the success of the mother of all engineering societies, Britain's ICE, which had rejected legal protection.[21] According to Keefer, the first president of the CSCE, the founders of the profession in Great Britain and the United States were born engineers and 'sought only a free field and asked no favors.'.[22]

Although Macdougall was elected to the influential post of provisional secretary of the provisional committee, his plan had already lost considerable ground, as the nascent organization grew and drew in more conservative engineers, especially from the Montreal area. General sentiment opposed any plan to establish a closed corporation at that time, and Macdougall's dream was submerged in a wash of conservative reaction. At the first general meeting, 24 February 1887, called to ratify the work of the provisional committee, John Kennedy, a vice-president, announced that any plans to acquire powers similar to the law society had been abandoned. 'The profession,' he declared, 'was left an open one and the ranks of the profession were accessible to those in whom the public had confidence.'[23] The Macdougall plan was overturned, and Kennedy announced that the new society existed for the 'interchange of ideas among members of the profession.'[24]

The conservatives believed that the primary function of an engineering society was educational. They viewed the CSCE as a learned society, similar to the ICE,[25] and held that the CSCE's principal object was, in the words of the new constitution, 'to facilitate the acquirement and interchange of professional knowledge among its members, and ... to encourage original investigation.'[26] Until the First World War, the conservatives stubbornly adhered to this objective and steadfastly refused to allow the new society to serve business or to promote the careers of individual members.

The conservatives argued that the CSCE, unlike the CMI, represented a profession, not an industry. The diversity of engineering specialties – civil, mechanical, electrical, and mining – precluded any organizational attachment to a particular industry. Although engineers appreciated business support,[27] in order to preserve their professional integrity they jealously guarded their independence. Whereas mining engineers valued their association with business, civils often viewed business with suspicion, even as a potential threat to their autonomy. In the late 1880s the greatest danger to an engineer's professional independence came from business, not from government. Emerging corporations, such as the great railway, bridge, and ironwork companies, exerted enormous bureaucratic pressure on engineers to subordinate science to business. Since the conservatives regarded engineering societies as the guardians of professionalism, it followed that such a society must be autonomous, free of interference by non-professionals, to ensure full collegial control over professional development. The use of an engineering society by unscrupulous business-men for selfish commercial purposes, the conservatives asserted, might easily subvert a society's professional priorities and lower the status of individual members. 'It is absolutely necessary to have it understood,' stated one engineer in 1887, 'that we do not intend to sacrifice our independence and are determined to keep our society a professional one.'[28]

The conservatives maintained also that the CSCE was constituted not to further members' careers or to serve their business and social needs; that was the purpose of the private engineers' clubs.[29] It was inappropriate that the society should intervene on behalf of individual members to protect reputation or livelihood. The conservatives regarded interference between an engineer and his employer as simply a form of trade unionism. Moreover, the conservatives held that it was contrary to the society's aim to comment on, or attempt to influence, public opinion. They felt that the

CSCE, as an educational society, would serve the public indirectly by improving Canadian engineering. To this end, the conservatives planned to raise the standard of professional practice through the interchange of professional knowledge and by accepting only highly qualified engineers as CSCE members. This approach was explained later by Phelps Johnson in his 1914 president's address: '[The] basic purpose of the Society can best be achieved by having enrolled in its membership a large proportion of the able and active engineers of the country, by the interchange of thought and of experience at its meetings and particularly by the reading, discussion and circulation of papers on important and interesting works or investigation.'[30] Papers would be presented and published. Special research committees, chaired by prominent engineers, would study important practical engineering problems, and high admission standards would be imposed. The conservatives assumed that these measures would raise not only the standard of professional practice but also, as a consequence, the engineer's status.

High admission standards were central to the conservatives' plan to raise the standard of professional practice. They were the principal means of creating an élite organization of highly qualified professionals, ranking with and accepted by the older and more prestigious engineering societies, such as the ICE and the ASCE. Prior to a time when civil engineering qualifications were determined by statute, the conservatives hoped that CSCE membership would distinguish professionals from non-professionals (particularly tradesmen and practical men), as well as certify an engineer's professional competence without government regulation.

Both the CMI and the CSCE admitted businessmen, or 'associates,'[31] to membership, but there was a fundamental difference. Whereas the CMI permitted associates to vote and actively encouraged their participation in institute affairs, the CSCE maintained a rigidly graded hierarchy that excluded associates, as well as students and honorary members, from full membership.[32] They could neither vote nor hold office. The CSCE was entirely dominated by professionals and offered little of interest to businessmen. The financier and engineer H.S. Holt, for example, vigorously protested being classified as an associate and insisted on, and later qualified for, full member status.[33] Significantly, by 1921, the CSCE had only a dozen associates – about one-third of 1 per cent of the total membership.[34]

The CSCE restricted full membership to professionally qualified engineers, that is, men[35] who could design and direct engineering works and had at least ten years of experience, five in responsible charge of work. According to the 1905 by-laws:

Every candidate for election as Member must be at least thirty years of age, and must have been engaged in some branch of Engineering for at least ten years, which period may include apprenticeship, or pupilage in a qualified Engineer's Office, or a term of instruction in some school of Engineering recognized by the Council. The term of ten years will be reduced to eight years in the case of any candidate who has graduated with honours in his engineering course. In every case the candidate must have had responsible charge of work for at least five years, and this not merely as a skilled workman, but as an Engineer qualified to design and direct Engineering works.[36]

These requirements constituted the CSCE's definition of a 'professional' engineer and effectively barred tradesmen and other non-professionals from membership.

At the heart of the CSCE's admission requirements was the provision that an engineer must have been in 'responsible charge in engineering work.'[37] The requirement that a member be 'qualified to design and direct Engineering works' merely distinguished the engineer from the skilled workman; it did not make him a professional. Professional engineering went beyond design and construction to include managerial functions. The engineer thus had to combine executive ability with technical knowledge; but he was more than just a technically knowledgeable business manager. He had to be responsible for the design and construction of engineering works. Responsibility implied an element of trust which, in some respects, was comparable to the fiduciary relationship between a client and a member of the older consultative professions, particularly law. Engineers were frequently placed in positions of trust and charged with the expenditure of large amounts of public or private funds.[38] Employers had to be assured that an engineer was not only technically competent but also responsible enough to assume charge of a complex project. Thus the CSCE insisted that its members be mature and experienced.

From the beginning, the CSCE had very high educational requirements, which also served as a convenient method of excluding non-professionals. It demanded a university-level engineering education, or its equivalent. After 1912, a board of examiners was established to consider candidates who were not graduates of a recognized school of engineering, in order to determine who was qualified to design and direct engineering work.[39]

Of equal and, in some respects, greater importance, were unwritten provisions regarding the character and non-technical requirements for student members. Such people first had to be high school graduates pursuing a recognized course of study in engineering. Students were also expected to have a good general education, in order to think and to express themselves clearly and to interact with educated and intelligent people.[40] Voicing a commonly held view that the educational-cultural attainment of individual members would reflect the society's social and professional standing, some engineers warned that 'the admission of students who [did] not possess a proper degree of culture would lower the tone of the Society.'[41]

Thus, the conservatives saw the engineer not just as a skilled workman possessing esoteric technical knowledge, but also as a well-rounded and cultivated individual, a gentleman, competent to assume responsibility and to win the acceptance of colleagues and associates, as well as the respect of subordinates. The engineer, stated John Gallbraith, 'must be a many-sided man thoroughly acquainted with his own side of the work, and able to co-operate with all sorts and conditions of men.'[42]

The CSCE's exclusiveness was further enhanced by a strict admission procedure, which placed enormous discretionary power in the hands of its council.[43] Prior to 1918, all candidates for admission were elected by letter ballot submitted to the general membership. When the society grew larger, the council elected all members. Following practice established by the ICE and the ASCE, it first issued a 'preliminary list' containing a concise summary of the applicant's qualifications for members' careful scrutiny, before making its decision.[44] Any three councillors could reject a candidate,[45] and council could effectively veto any 'unacceptable' applications by not approving or classifying them.[46] As a further safeguard, all applications had to be accompanied by the personal recommendation of no less than five members.

The CSCE's high admission standards, however, did not restrict the practice of engineering to qualified professionals. As the society was a self-constituted, private, and voluntary organization, it could not force non-members to conform to its admission standards, which, after all, had no standing in law. The standards were arbitrary and subjective and were ultimately predicated on the assumption, perhaps the expectation, that CSCE membership, like ICE membership in Great Britain, would be recognized by all employers as the only reliable guarantee of professional competence. Unlike ICE membership, however, CSCE membership was not recognized by most corporate employers. Anyone in Canada could call himself an engineer and practise engineering; it was not necessary to belong to the CSCE.

High admission standards could not protect members from competition. Apart from tightening admission requirements and redoubling efforts to bring the majority of qualified professionals voluntarily into the CSCE, the only effective and logical alternative to restricting practice further was to make the CSCE's admission requirements mandatory. This, in turn, would require legislation to compel engineers to belong to the CSCE in order to practise. While the CSCE never became a licensing authority (except in Quebec), engineering was eventually restricted by law to qualified professionals. The admission requirements, adopted by provincial licensing associations, were originally defined by the CSCE, acting independently as a private body.

Although the conservatives had originally rejected Macdougall's plan for a closed profession, by imposing high admission standards they had, nevertheless, created the conditions that would lead to licensing. Thus, in many respects, their attempt to exclude non-professionals from membership, by high admission standards, represented the first major step towards restricting competition and monopolizing engineering practice in Canada.

To preserve the CSCE as a learned society and to maintain high admission standards, the conservatives instituted a form of society government that enabled them effectively to control the CSCE until the First World War. Although the society's new constitution prescribed a democratic system of government similar to other major engineering societies in Great Britain and, especially, the United States, in practice, the CSCE was an oligarchy run by a coterie of prominent conservative Montreal engineers. In style and substance, the CSCE's organization resembled corporate and bureaucratic structures and reflected conservative notions of order, hierarchy, and deference to authority.

The CSCE's governing body was the council. It was elected at the annual meeting and consisted of president, three vice-presidents, secretary, treasurer, the last three surviving past presidents or honorary councillors (non-elected), and twenty councillors. According to the society's constitution, the council had 'general supervision of the affairs of the Society,'[47] including approval and classification of applications for membership and appointment of the secretary and treasurer and the standing and special committees. CSCE presidents were essentially figureheads. They were men of great prestige, and their election to the society's highest office was usually regarded as the ultimate tribute to an outstanding professional career; but, while presidents could exercise short-term influence, they had no prescribed powers beyond chairing meetings.[48] Their duties were largely ceremonial. Ironically, they appeared to have exercised more power collectively with their fellow past presidents and as members of the powerful nominating committee after their tenure as presidents.

The secretary was the CSCE's most powerful officer.[49] Charged with the general management of the society, the secretary, rather than the president, was the real executive head. As a non-elected yet full voting council member, the secretary combined all the covert authority and executive initiative of a deputy minister and corporate general manager. Enjoying an extended tenure of office, while possessing the most comprehensive knowledge of the CSCE's internal operation, he provided continuity of management and wielded power and influence over the CSCE quite out of proportion to his single vote on council. Moreover, as the general editor of the society's publications and the head of a network of contacts and loyalties built up over years of service, the secretary also enjoyed special influence with the general membership, independent of council.

The CSCE was blessed in having as its secretaries remarkably able and dedicated men whose personalities influenced the development of the society. The first secretary, Dr H.T. Bovey, dean of the Faculty of Applied Science, McGill University, together with Alan Macdougall, helped to organize the CSCE and, throughout his five years in office, this cultivated and articulate Englishman imparted a sense of integrity and dignified professionalism to the new society.

In 1891, Bovey was succeeded by Professor C.H. 'Bunty' McLeod, vice-dean of the Faculty of Applied Science at McGill, undoubtedly the CSCE's most important and powerful secretary. In his twenty-five years in office, until his retirement and death in 1917, McLeod presided over the most critical phase of the CSCE's development and played a leading part in the society's management. McLeod was a truly remarkable man of wide interests and accomplishments. Born in 1851, the son of a Cape Breton merchant, he worked under Sandford Fleming on the Intercolonial Railway, before his graduation from McGill's new engineering department in 1873. McLeod had a keen interest in university athletics and, like most engineering professors, did independent consulting work and gave expert evidence in court. For forty-three years, McLeod was superintendent of the McGill Observatory, and he achieved some distinction in determining the exact longitude of Montreal.[50] McLeod was strong-minded and did not hesitate to resort to unorthodox means to attain what he regarded as worthy ends.[51] To an admirer, McLeod possessed great executive ability and had a keen understanding of men.[52]

The secretary's position was part-time and paid a modest honorarium.[53] For years, as the CSCE expanded, McLeod laboured unselfishly under an increasingly heavy and crippling burden of work. Then, in 1917, death overtook him in his office at McGill, in his sixty-sixth year. The same year, McLeod's long-standing annual recommendation for a full-time secretary was realized with the appointment of the energetic and efficient Fraser S. Keith. Keith established the *Engineering Journal* and presided over the critical period, immediately following the First World War, when engineers lobbied for restrictive provincial licensing laws. But, while he became the CSCE's first well-paid, full-time secretary,[54] unlike his powerful predecessor he was not accorded full voting rights in council.

Originally, the CSCE elected its officers by a simple majority vote at its annual meeting; but, as the society grew, it was forced to abandon this system and to create a nominating committee, an innovation borrowed from the ASCE.[55] Officially, the new procedure was intended to secure more equitable provincial representation on council.[56] In practice, however, the nominating committee effectively transferred the control of the society's electoral machinery from the general membership to a small group of prominent Montreal engineers.

It was extremely difficult for committee members to recommend a slate of thirty-one suitable candidates from a large and diverse membership scattered across the Dominion.[57] This was especially true of younger engineers, resident outside Montreal, who were less familiar with available candidates. For those in Montreal, however, the task was simpler. Since the city was the headquarters of Canada's largest railway and engineering companies, it had the largest pool of engineers, with proven administrative and executive experience, from which to nominate worthy and 'acceptable' candidates.

At the same time, Montreal had other important advantages. Since it had the largest number of members – 367 in 1916, for example, as opposed to 168 in Ottawa, the next largest centre[58] – it had disproportionate representation in the election of the nominating committee and councillors. The eight elected members of the nominating committee (six from Ontario and Quebec) nominated twenty-five councillor candidates, ten of whom, according to the by-laws, were to be Montreal residents and the remainder from anywhere in Canada, including, presumably, Montreal.[59] Moreover, the Montreal members of the nominating committee, combined with non-elected committee members – the three past presidents, who usually supported the Montreal establishment – easily constituted the simple majority necessary to nominate the society's officers. As the nominating committee sometimes nominated only the exact number of candidates,[60] it could virtually elect the council, because the general membership was given no alternative to the official slate.

As a result, the nominating committee annually selected what appeared, at least to outsiders, as a disproportionate number of Montrealers,[61] who seemed to monopolize office. Analysing council membership (excluding vice-presidents and presidents) in the ten years preceding 1913, one critic observed: 'Eight members have served four years on the Council and one for six years. Ten have served three years and several have been on for two years.'[62] Moreover, because the duties of councillors demanded a substantial personal outlay of time and money,[63] in an era of uncertain and irregular employment even for experienced engineers, only older and more established engineers could stand for nomination, thus effectively excluding the younger ones.

The selection of the society's senior officers was even less democratic. In practice, the presidential and vice-presidential candidates were chosen by the honorary councillors on the nominating committee. As conservative apologists argued, the past presidents were more familiar with the character and ability of other members of council and therefore could best judge who was competent to occupy the society's highest responsible positions.[64] Moreover, because it was customary each year for the past presidents to nominate only one presidential candidate from among the three vice-presidents, a kind of self-perpetuating presidential oligarchy was established, which, in effect, deprived the general membership of democratically choosing its senior officers. Attempts to change the by-laws, in order to permit the nomination of more than one presidential candidate, failed because conservatives argued successfully that it was, in John Kennedy's words, 'a most indelicate thing' to ask two presidential candidates – or even two vice-presidential candidates – to run against one another.[65]

Although the CSCE's constitution provided for a separate opposition ballot, signed by any ten, or, later, twelve, voting members,[66] attempts to upset the official slate were rare and unsuccessful. Opposition ballots never challenged the authority of the nominating committee. They appeared to carry a stigma of illegitimacy,[67] as a result of being conspicuously labelled and presented to the membership separately.[68] In 1892, when E.P. Hannaford contested John Kennedy's presidential nomination, for example, Kennedy's supporters argued that he had 'a prescriptive right' to the presidency, because he was the senior vice-president and the unanimous choice of the nominating committee. Since a contest for the presidency was unknown in the ICE and infrequent in the ASCE, Kennedy's supporters successfully characterized the whole affair as being undignified and injurious to the society. Hannaford was easily defeated.[69]

To outsiders, the concentration of power among a few prominent members in Montreal appeared to be cliquish, and, according to one report, the belief arose that the CSCE was 'run for the glorification of a few prominent engineers'[70] by a 'McGill Clique,' or, as it later became known, a 'Montreal Clique.'[71] This belief stemmed not only from the fact that many of the society's officers were prominent Montrealers who appeared to dominate council affairs, but also from the major organizational and administrative role that McGill engineers played during the early history of the CSCE. For example, the important office of secretary was occupied by McGill engineers. With the exception of Fraser S. Keith, a McGill graduate in electrical engineering, three out of four secretaries between 1887 and 1925 held teaching positions in the Faculty of Applied Science.[72]

The 'Montreal Clique' was not an organized or structured group, nor composed exclusively of Montrealers. It took form mainly in the minds of critics and outsiders as a kind of informal grouping of prominent Montreal-oriented engineers who controlled society affairs and shared similar conservative beliefs about the nature of professionalism. To this extent, the Montreal clique was the successor to the conservatives headed by Keefer and Kennedy.

To its severest critics, however, the Montreal clique was associated with the society's undemocratic nature. 'The Society [was] founded on demo-cratic principles,' lamented one of the oldest members of the CSCE, 'but practically it is governed by a handful of men in Montreal.'[73] The power and influence of non-elected councillors were particularly resented. For instance, the honorary councillors, combined with the secretary and treasurer – two other non-elected yet voting members – constituted a quorum in council which, potentially, could manage the society's day-to-day affairs if several elected councillors did not live in Montreal. In 1897, one group of members charged: 'The Council contains six past Presidents five of whom are practically resident at headquarters and accordingly owing to the small number of elected councillors who are also resident at headquarters, it is quite possible for this large non-elective vote to control the action of Council.'[74] While these critics had, perhaps, overstated their case, by the First World War there was a growing and widespread feeling that the Montreal clique had lost touch with the membership and was serving its own interests.

The Montreal clique's control over the CSCE affairs was also reinforced by council's tendency towards secrecy. Council decided what information about its proceedings was disclosed to members. Although council concerned itself mostly with routine administrative matters, it also discussed private and confidential matters such as the admission and classification of members. As a rule, council kept all of its proceedings secret and released only a brief synopsis of its affairs in the annual report.[75] While some members complained that council was not taking the member-ship sufficiently into its confidence by disclosing more information,[76] most members were apathetic and generally accepted the situation, believing that nothing untoward happened in council.

Although the Montreal clique was often called 'arrogant' and sometimes 'autocratic,' it was able to control the CSCE, because it had the tacit, albeit grudging support of the membership. Most members accepted authority and deferred to their professional betters. They viewed the Montreal clique essentially as honourable men and believed that the early success of the society was due to their hard work and dedication. The Montrealers formed the backbone of the society, laid strong foundations, and kept the society going in times of trouble. Moreover, the prestige of the clique's more prominent members gave the CSCE professional standing.[77] Even the harshest critics reluctantly conceded that the clique managed the society's affairs competently. To H.E.T. Haultain, a professor of mining, University of Toronto, the Montreal clique was 'an autocracy of leadership rather than of domination.'[78] However, neither these sentiments, nor the clique, were to last beyond the First World War. As the demand for reform grew, the clique's authority was eclipsed and its power diffused more equitably throughout the CSCE.

The CSCE was the institutional expression of the Montreal clique's pre-industrial professional values.[79] Modelled after the ICE, it combined the advantages of a learned society and of a gentleman's club. Engineers such as Keefer and Kennedy were essentially gentlemen professionals. They were professionally and financially secure, and the CSCE's principal value was prestige enhancement.

Unfortunately, the CSCE offered little for the mass of ordinary members led by Alan Macdougall. These young, university-educated, middle-class members were bureaucratically oriented and did not entirely share the Montreal clique's professional values. As junior salaried employees of large public and private corporations, their immediate concerns were employment and salaries. The CSCE, as an educational body, was institutionally at variance with their needs. Moreover, although the CSCE, like the ASCE, was not controlled by business,[80] it nevertheless indirectly served business. Dominated by the Montreal clique (the majority of whom were corporate managers and high-ranking civil servants), the CSCE discouraged members from collectively pursuing their natural interest as employees. For example, on the pretext of being a learned society, the CSCE could remain strictly neutral in all labour disputes involving engineers, as well as stand aloof from public-works controversies that could embarrass governments.

While the CSCE would continue to serve the interests of the Montreal clique, it would have progressively less appeal for most other members. As a learned society, it would not promote their economic interests.

Confronted by fierce competition for jobs, these engineers would be less concerned with the interchange of professional knowledge and more preoccupied with immediate economic survival. Although the Montreal clique had firmly established the CSCE as a learned society, it had not suppressed protectionist sentiments. In the 1890s, younger engineers, led by Macdougall, would mount an insurrection against the clique and demand licensing laws to close the profession.

3

'A sort of outcast people'

Engineers and bureaucracy

Engineers were not independent professionals. Most of them were employees of large corporations and governments. This was the most important factor affecting their professional life. Emerging from the canal- and railway-building enterprises of the nineteenth century, the engineer was a creature of large bureaucratic organizations – the original 'organization man.'[1]

The majority of Canadian engineers were salaried employees, not self-employed consultants. Independent consulting engineers comprised a small portion of the profession in Canada; some observers estimated 10 to 15 per cent.[2] Exact figures are difficult to obtain because neither government nor the CSCE kept yearly totals. One indication of their relative numbers, however, can be calculated from CSCE applications for membership or reclassification. Between 1887 and 1922, only 7.2 per cent of applicants (excluding student and junior members) were consultants,[3] in contrast with 66.3 per cent who worked for private corporations – including 4.9 per cent who were senior management engineers – and 20.7 per cent employed by governments (see Figure 1).

In this respect, engineers differed substantially from the older consultative professions. Lawyers and doctors functioned independently in the market-place; many were self-employed, owned and managed their own consulting businesses, and, more important, were paid by fees. They maintained their independence, partly by providing an essential consulting service directly to the public; engineers, by contrast, dealt only indirectly with the public as employees of corporations. Even the élite private consulting engineers did not enjoy the same degree of independence as lawyers and doctors. Consultants' remuneration was measured by business profit,

Figure 1
Employment status of CSCE applicants 1887–1922
Source: National Archives of Canada, Engineering Institute of Canada Papers,
MG 28, 1–277, Membership Files, 1887–1922

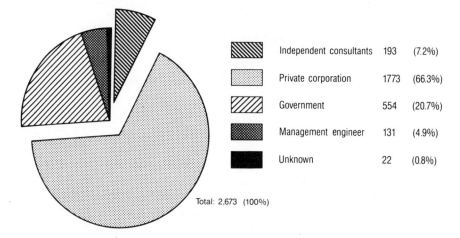

Independent consultants	193	(7.2%)
Private corporation	1773	(66.3%)
Government	554	(20.7%)
Management engineer	131	(4.9%)
Unknown	22	(0.8%)

Total: 2,673 (100%)

not professional fees. They depended for work mainly on large corporations – especially municipal governments – and moved in and out of
consulting, depending on prevailing economic conditions. Some consultants eventually became either salaried employees, or even contractors,
like Sir Casimir Gzowski.[4]

As employees within a large bureaucracy, engineers had little control
over their professional lives. Except for a few well-paid management
engineers, most were as vulnerable and insecure as any corporate
employee. Even the short hierarchical distance separating engineers from
skilled workmen did not give them greater security. Although engineers had
exclusive access to technical knowledge essential to business, they were
unable to achieve greater independence because, unlike lawyers and
doctors, they could not control competition. Employers could hire anyone
claiming to be an engineer and force him to compete against another.[5]
Moreover, while engineers were an essential part of a corporation and
enjoyed more prestige than skilled workmen because of their status as
experts, in some respects engineers had less power than the workmen
they supervised. Whereas workmen were willing to use their power collectively through trade unions in order to bargain for higher wages and job
security, before the First World War engineers, essentially for ideological

reasons, refused to combine and use their collective power for similar ends.

As well, the engineer's employment was determined by market forces over which he had no control.[6] During periods of economic growth, such as the building of Canada's transcontinental railways, the demand for engineers was high and employment available; but during harsher times demand slackened and engineers faced hardship.[7] The mysterious forces of economics and finance placed them in a precarious position. More than any other professional, engineers were directly affected by business slumps.[8] When capital was scarce, corporations could not finance capital expansion. Chronic unemployment became the scourge of the profession, and even eminent engineers, such as T.C. Keefer, could not escape it.[9] Although one engineer believed that many of his colleagues survived by marrying their employers' daughters,[10] most remained barely solvent. 'The result, in a great number of cases,' observed Arthur Surveyer, a highly respected and prominent French-Canadian engineer, 'is a bare living wage in boom times, and a hand-to-mouth existence in times of depression.'[11] This uncertainty of income, noted Surveyer, recalling the findings of Britain's Lunacy Commission, was the primary reason why engineers had the highest rate of insanity in Britain, compared with other liberal professions.[12]

Although engineers preferred to think of themselves as independent professionals, they were, nevertheless, acutely aware of their dependent status and their subordination to business. They deeply resented their dependence on financial interests[13] and tended to regard themselves, as one engineer bitterly lamented, as 'simply tools of men who know less than they do but are good at business and draw bigger salaries.'[14] 'To-day,' protested a Montreal consulting engineer in 1920, 'we are too frequently but the creatures of "politicians" and "profiteers", doing their bidding; or, at any rate, practising our professions very largely by their leave.'[15]

Although corporations collectively employed more engineers than governments, after the First World War, with nationalization of two transcontinental railways, the Dominion government became the largest single employer of engineers in Canada.[16] While government engineers were not subject to the same uncertainty and unemployment as their colleagues in private companies, their lack of standing as independent professionals created some unique problems.

When the Civil Service Act was passed in 1868, the Dominion government employed comparatively few engineers.[17] According to C.E.W. Dodwell, engineers were regarded as 'necessary evils temporarily employed, to carry out specific works, and to be discarded at the earliest possible moment.'[18] The government had no professional standards for engineers. They were not required to pass an examination or produce testimonials, diplomas, or credentials, or even questioned about their educational background, before assuming positions of responsibility which, in some cases, required the judicious expenditure of large sums of public money.[19] Non-professionals were hired along with eminently qualified engineers. Political appointments in such patronage-ridden departments as Public Works cut across professional standards and often resulted in the appointment of incompetents.

As government engineering work became more specialized, however, a permanently employed corps of highly qualified engineers evolved; but, while government engineers had assumed responsibility for important and costly public works, they were not officially part of the civil service. The Civil Service Act, 1868, divided public servants into two classes: departmental staff, or the inside service (generally civil servants employed in Ottawa), and the outside service – postal clerks, customs agents, etc.[20] No provision was made in the Civil Servant Act, 1878, or in any subsequent amendment prior to 1918–19, for inclusion of a corps of engineers in any government department. The government did not officially recognize its engineers. The handful employed with the inside service (3 out of over 100 in the Public Works Department in 1918, according to C.E.W. Dodwell) were simply classified as clerks and, as a rule, were not promoted unless the clerk immediately senior died or resigned.[21] With the exception of these fortunate ones, most engineers were employed with the outside service and were excluded from the civil service.[22] Thus, government engineers were, as A.B. Warburton, a member of Parliament, explained to the House of Commons in 1910, 'a sort of outcast people'[23] who lacked the rights, privileges, responsibility, status, and security of tenure enjoyed by ordinary civil servants.

Government engineers enjoyed the relative security of steady employment and were, as William Pugsley, minister of public works in the Laurier government, pointed out, no worse off than other employees in the outside service.[24] They nevertheless felt dissatisfied because of poor employment opportunities and low status. The government was an important source of employment – in some cases the only one – for many engineers who had given years of service and who professed unselfish devotion to the public interest. Alternative employment was not always available, or desirable. More important, these engineers believed that their professional education, responsibility, and accomplishments entitled them to special consideration. In their view, their lack of status was unjustified and demeaning.

The government's failure to recognize its engineers was reflected also in low salaries.[25] Although government engineers constructed important public works, their remuneration was not commensurate with their responsibility. In some cases, salaries were so low that Fraser S. Keith considered them 'an affront to the profession.'[26] Relatively unskilled clerks, with modest educational qualifications, often earned more than university-educated engineers. Since labour had become well organized and relatively well paid by the end of the First World War, supervising engineers were sometimes placed in the humiliating position of earning less than foremen and mechanics under their charge.[27]

While many engineers spent their entire professional lives in government service, because they were excluded from the civil service they were not entitled to any benefits, such as pensions or superannuation. Low salaries prevented many from saving, or investing sufficiently large portions of their earnings in annuities and life insurance. Government engineers had no real security against accident, sickness, or death; if they died, or were incapacitated while in government service, neither they nor their families could receive any compensation.[28] These and other disadvantages contributed to their growing sense of discrimination and alienation. While the government eventually brought them under the regulation of the Civil Service Commission after 1918, they still faced a long struggle to win recognition as professionals.

No other government engineers had as much trouble with their employers as municipal engineers. As cities grew in size and number, under the impact of industrialization and immigration, there was a corresponding growth in conflict between city engineers and city councils. Although much of this trouble had its roots in the byzantine intrigue of municipal politics, its real cause was lack of professional autonomy. Like their counterparts in the Dominion government, city engineers could not function with the power and authority of independent professionals.

As cities become more technically complex, elected officials were forced to hire experts, especially engineers, to help run the new metropolises. A leading consulting engineer, R.O. Wynne-Roberts, who specialized in municipal work, estimated that 300 to 500 engineers in Canada were engaged in city work by 1913.[29] Although the city engineers' responsibilities grew as urban technology became more sophisticated,[30] they did not experience a corresponding growth in authority; executive power rested with non-technically trained ward aldermen, who governed with a different set of values and priorities. As the heads of major municipal departments, city engineers complained that their executive powers were not clearly defined and that they could not exercise the necessary authority to carry out their responsibilities.[31] As ordinary municipal employees, they were entirely subject to the will of elected officials and their political appointees. They had no authority to initiate work or set policy and resented the fact that, while municipal administration was the prerogative of a political appointee – usually an ex-ward politician – it was the engineer who ran the department and kept the political head out of trouble.[32] The city engineers' influence varied directly with their ability to persuade politicans to adopt their recommendations – a talent few possessed.

In contrast with other professionals, city engineers did not command authority and respect from municipal politicians. These officials viewed them with indifference and suspicion. Civil engineering, unlike electrical or industrial, did not have an aura of esoteric mystique in the public mind. Civic politicians, raised in rural nineteenth-century Canada, were accustomed to the rule-of-thumb methods of the practical man. They regarded themselves as pragmatic men fully equal to understanding most practical problems. A municipal engineer, in their view, was nothing more than a glorified and slightly pretentious mechanic who failed to comprehend the more important political imperatives of city government.

This attitude adversely affected city engineers. They frequently complained that elected officials interfered in all phases of their work, offered gratuitous professional advice, and made important engineering decisions without understanding the technical implications. More important, city engineers bitterly protested that their expert advice was often ignored – even distorted – for partisan reasons.[33] As civic officials appeared to respect the professional opinions of medical and legal advisers, city engineers could not understand why a municipality would engage them and then proceed to ignore their advice.[34] This behaviour was entirely inconsistent with their experience in private corporations.

City engineers also deeply resented their lack of independence and authority. They disliked not having full charge of city engineering and being subject to politicians whom they disdainfully regarded as their intellectual, social, and moral inferiors. 'Could anything be more humiliating to a member of the engineering profession,' lamented one engineer, 'than to have a board of men [city council], selected from the ranks of the trades and industrial classes, preside over his deliberations?'[35]

As well, city engineers were torn by conflicting loyalties to science and to their employers. They recognized that professional judgments had to be made objectively, without regard to political considerations, even at the risk of dismissal;[36] yet they also realized that they were bound to serve their employers' interests. This situation presented a cruel dilemma: if an engineer were influenced politically, he compromised himself professionally; if he were strictly professional, he risked alienating his employer and destroying his livelihood.

This predicament was further complicated by the fact that, unlike a business corporation with clearly defined lines of authority, in which an engineer was ultimately responsible to one employer, the city engineer, in effect, had several employers – the city council – which, in turn, was divided by many factions, each anxious to enlist the engineer in its partisan schemes. If an engineer's professional report unintentionally supported one faction, for example, he was invariably attacked by the opposition.[37] As well, in the normal course of their duties, city engineers constantly risked offending individual citizens, or interest groups, who had influence with city government.[38]

At the same time, the political priorities of politicians often conflicted with the technical capabilities of city engineers. Ambitious politicians, with grandiose engineering projects, for example, or newly elected councils with election promises to keep, frequently made unrealistic and technically unsound demands.[39] When ill-conceived policy resulted in engineering trouble, city engineers, who were responsible for implementing policy, were usually held accountable. Moreover, they were expected to master a wide range of specialties, which cut across many branches of engineering – electrical, mechanical, sanitary, waterworks, transportation – in addition to possessing considerable administrative and legal knowledge.[40] In towns and smaller cities, they often had to work in both design and construction and, unlike doctors and lawyers, could not seek specialized advice from outside consultants. As urban technology became complex and their duties expanded, it was inevitable that something would go wrong.[41]

As public works was the municipality's largest spending department,[42] and more than any other department directly affected the health and comfort of ratepayers, any engineering problem often resulted in serious political trouble. City engineers maintained that unscrupulous politicians, ever mindful of their political survival, used them as scapegoats for their own administrative incompetence.[43] Indeed, many were subject to frequent violent attacks on their professional and personal characters, in the press and in city councils. This usually resulted in arbitrary dismissal without impartial hearing, ruining professional reputations and civic standings. It often undermined the confidence of respected, eminent engineers and lowered the status of the profession in the eyes of the public.[44]

To a certain extent, the city engineer's lot was not appreciably different from that of most employees in large corporate bureaucracies.[45] Lack of recognition, interference, internal power struggles, and arbitrary dismissals were not confined to municipal corporations. It could be argued, with some justification, that city engineers were partly the architects of their own misfortune. They failed to assert themselves adequately and to impress politicians with the esoteric nature of their technical problems, in order to reinforce their own positions as experts.[46]

City engineers never fully accepted their dependent status and continued to think of themselves – perhaps somewhat unconsciously or through wishful thinking – as noble, independent professionals,[47] unjustly caught up in a tangled web of bureaucracy and political intrigue. In part, this was a reflection of their technocratic outlook, which placed them at the centre of an ideal municipal administration with executive, almost authoritarian power. From this perspective, they failed to appreciate, or even admit to, non-technical or political factors affecting municipal government. They seemed almost blinded by the conviction that all municipal problems were amenable to scientific solutions. This was the reason for their reluctance to perceive realistically their own shortcomings and for their readiness to blame other factors. Most city engineers, however, probably would have been content with more professional autonomy within the existing municipal structure. As one of them, who did not want to be identified, put it: 'A city council should direct on general lines the policy they wish their engineer to follow, leaving technicalities and details of construction to the engineer.'[48]

While engineering leaders and thinkers realized that their predicament ultimately stemmed from lack of professional autonomy, they also recognized that ordinary market forces made their existence even more tenuous. City engineers, for example, were forced to compete for work with non-professionals, especially in smaller urban centres. As a rule, small towns, like small businesses, could not afford engineers[49] and rarely appreciated their value. While local practical men fulfilled minor engineering requirements by using traditional rule-of-thumb methods, larger projects, such as waterworks or sewers, were given to contractors who sometimes attempted to avoid hiring engineers in order to minimize expenses.[50]

City engineers, moreover, were not well paid; they generally earned less than their counterparts in private business, doing comparable work. With a large supply of civil engineers on hand, municipal employers could easily offer lower salaries. Toronto, for example, paid its assistant department heads in the Public Works Department, engineers in actual charge of construction work, less than foremen under their charge. The city had such a high turnover of engineers that it became known as a training ground for engineers who moved on to other cities for higher salaries. In other centres, professionals, such as city solicitors, sometimes earned twice as much as they did.[51]

City engineers did not have security of tenure. Their employment was directly dependent on market forces, which allowed councils to retain them during prosperous times and dismiss them or reduce their salaries during difficult times. An extraordinary example of this process occurred in Kitchener in 1917.

Pursuing a policy of retrenchment, council voted to fire its engineer, Herbert Johnson, and hire another at a much lower salary. Johnson, a CSCE member, with fourteen years in Kitchener's engineering department (seven as city engineer), was not charged with incompetence or asked to take a lower salary. He had not had any serious dispute with council. The whole affair arose from an attempt to lower the municipal tax rate by reducing the budget of a number of civic institutions. As a further economy measure, one alderman proposed to reduce the city engineer's salary by 50 per cent. With the support of a local citizens' group (as well as a shabby attempt to bribe two aldermen to vote for Johnson's dismissal), Johnson was fired and another engineer was hired at half his former salary.[52]

Council's high-handed treatment of Johnson upset many engineers. The *Canadian Engineer* described the incident as 'cold-blooded commercialism,'[53] and the CSCE was criticized for its inaction and failure to protect city engineers. The city engineer of Moose Jaw, for example, bitterly described the society's attitude as 'Each Man for Himself.'[54] Remembering similar incidents in other municipalities, city engineers lamented their powerlessness to protect themselves.

One manifestation of this mounting discontent was an attempt to form a separate society, dedicated exclusively to municipal engineers. This idea, however, did not have much support. Promoters, as well as the technical press, were divided as to forming a branch of an existing British or American society in Canada or organizing a distinct Canadian society.[55] More important, the proposed society, like the CSCE, could not protect its members, since it was conceived primarily as a learned society.[56]

Nevertheless, a growing number of engineers wanted other, more direct and effective measures to protect their municipal colleagues. These men saw the CSCE as the most effective instrument to achieve this end. They argued that the society should intervene on behalf of city engineers, particularly in cases of unjust dismissal without a fair hearing, especially for frivolous reasons.[57] The *Contract Record*, for example, called upon the CSCE to be more active in protecting its members:

In a lower plane the unions protect the interests of the humblest worker ... Why then, in the highest sphere, should not a professional body such as the C.S.C.E. concern itself with the interests of its members? The main object in view in the organization of the Society, – the promotion of engineering knowledge, is a somewhat different matter from the arbitration of private disputes, but times are changing and the Society must also change – the scope of its usefulness must be widened – if the profession is to maintain its place above the sordidness of competion, graft, and the influence of city councils.[58]

But, while the *Contract Record* and other critics of the CSCE wanted the society to intervene on behalf of city engineers, they stopped short of advocating interference between an engineer and his employer. Instead, they suggested a different form of intervention whereby a committee of the CSCE would act as an impartial expert commission, in order to investigate charges of professional incompetence. This idea was predicated on the belief, popular with all professions, that only an expert is qualified to judge other experts, because professional work involves esoteric knowledge. Like the disciplinary committees of the legal and medical professions, a commission of engineers would be advantageous because it would tend to shelter city engineers from the arbitrary control and scrutiny of the despised ward aldermen and other laymen, particularly judges.[59] This, in turn, would enhance the status and independence of city engineers, even though they remained essentially employees.

Nevertheless, the idea of an expert commission was never systematically developed by opinion makers, such as the *Contract Record*, or seriously entertained by the CSCE. The idea stemmed from the naive assumption that ward politicians would relinquish partial control over such an important public servant as the city engineer or even desired objective, non-partisan investigation of his work.

The question whether the CSCE should protect individual members in their disputes with employers had been debated at the CSCE's annual meeting in 1911. At this meeting, a controversy arose over what action the society should take in regard to the treatment of W.A. Clement, city engineer of Vancouver. Prior to the 1910 municipal elections, he was harshly criticized for the construction of certain streets. Immediately following the election, Clement requested an impartial investigation of the allegations by a board of engineers. The mayor, an opponent of the engineer and publisher of a newspaper hostile to Clement, appointed an investigation committee composed of newly elected aldermen. This committee hastily reported within twenty-four hours and arbitrarily recommended the appointment of a new supervising engineer.[60] Vancouver members of the CSCE appealed in vain to city council for a fair hearing for Clement. They felt that the CSCE was obliged to defend an unjustly treated brother engineer, especially when his reputation was at stake. Accordingly, at the 1911 annual meeting, they read a motion censuring Vancouver city council.[61]

The Montreal clique's response was immediate and predictable. G.H. Duggan, second vice-president and chief engineer of the Dominion Bridge Company,[62] thought that while it was proper for the Vancouver members as individuals to try and influence city council, the CSCE, as a society, should take no action. Although the CSCE's primary object was to further professional knowledge, Duggan maintained that while the society had advised Dominion and provincial governments on legislation affecting the welfare of the profession, it had 'kept strictly out of politics and out of all controversies with the public.'[63] CSCE interference was unprecedented and unconstitutional. For John Kennedy, the issue was more clear-cut. The CSCE, he declared, was 'a scientific body and not a trade union.' Although he regretted that Clement did not receive a fair hearing, he argued that the CSCE did not have the right to interfere between engineer and employer.[64] In a committee report to the annual meeting, some of the leading members of the Montreal clique – John Kennedy, C.H. Rust, and G.A. Mountain – strongly recommended that the CSCE take no action. The annual meeting concurred, and the Montreal clique won another major victory – its last.[65]

The Vancouver members never contemplated interfering in what was essentially a labour dispute. They recognized the employer's prerogative of dismissal and never entertained any thought of coercion through collective action. Their main concern was to clear Clement's name by a proper investigation – especially urgent since no charge had ever been brought against him. Their abortive attempt to censure Vancouver council was an act of exasperation,[66] since the CSCE had neither the power nor the prestige to influence city councils. It was a dramatic demonstration of the city engineers' growing frustration with their tenuous position within municipal governments.

Even if the CSCE possessed the will and the constitutional authority, it could not have interfered in a labour dispute. Unlike a trade union, the CSCE had no coercive power; it could neither organize a strike nor boycott a bad employer.[67] Employers could easily hire any engineer, including CSCE members and non-professionals, because, unlike other professionals, engineers did not control or regulate practice. Above all, engineers did not command authority and respect from employers, like independent professionals. Before the First World War, employers regarded engineers merely as ordinary skilled workmen with essential practical knowledge.

The CSCE's refusal to intervene in labour disputes was consistent with its earlier decisions involving the Grand Trunk Railway in 1896[68] and the Grand Trunk Pacific Railway in 1904. The controversy over Vancouver's city engineer, in 1911, dramatically revealed the CSCE's deficiencies as a learned society. These shortcomings would fuel a more heated debate after the First World War, which could erupt into unyielding demands for substantial radical change. In the mean time, as ordinary employees, engineers had no control over their professional lives. They were at the mercy of their employers, and the CSCE had neither the will nor the means to protect them.

4

'The foreign invasion'

Engineers and competition

During its early stages of development, Canada needed foreign engineers; but, by the end of the nineteenth century, it had produced a corps of capable and experienced engineers that was already building spectacular new works that were attracting world-wide attention. By this time, Americans had displaced British as the dominant outside engineering group in Canada, and, as their ranks expanded, Canadian engineers increasingly found themselves in competition with Americans.

Unlike lawyers and doctors, Canadian engineers were not protected from foreign competition. Even after the enactment of Canada's weak and ineffectual Alien Labour Law in 1897,[1] a free North American engineering labour market existed, and Canadians were forced to compete with Americans on an equal basis in their own country. But, as Canadian engineers acquired confidence, drive, and ambition, they began to resent being passed over in favour of Americans of equal or lesser ability, especially for government contracts. Moreover, American competition threatened the livelihood of many engineers, particularly during hard times, when large numbers of Americans travelled north in search of work.[2] Ultimately, the problem of foreign competition raised serious questions about whether the CSCE, as a learned society, could or even should attempt to restrict foreign competition, in order to protect the interests of its members.

One of the most celebrated cases involving alien engineers in Canada occurred during the survey and location of the Grand Trunk Pacific Railway (GTP), a subsidiary of the Grand Trunk Railway. Although this case was highly controversial, in many respects it was typical of several that occurred before the First World War.

In May 1902, Charles H. Hays, an American who was general manager of the Grand Trunk Railway, offered H.D. Lumsden an assistant chief engineership, at $4,000 per year, for what Lumsden understood was maintenance work on the Grand Trunk. The GTP was not mentioned, according to Lumsden, who declined the offer. Without attempting to recruit another Canadian, Hays wrote a confidential letter to J.W. Kendrick, third vice-president of the Atchison, Topeka & Santa Fe Railway, asking him to recommend an engineer to take charge of the GTP surveys. Kendrick replied and suggested a young American engineer, J.R. Stephens, who was subsequently retained by Hays at the substantially higher annual salary of $7,500.[3]

About thirty years of age, Stephens was considerably younger than most engineers in charge of comparable work. Except for a few years spent in South Africa, engaged in mining – until he was compelled to leave under mysterious circumstances in 1896[4] – Stephens had spent his entire career in the United States. He had no experience in Canada and did not know any Canadian engineers.[5] As he was not a member of the CSCE or even of the ASCE, he lacked the essential contacts with which to locate suitable Canadian engineers.[6] Following Van Horne's hiring practices on the CPR, Stephens employed American engineers he knew. All the division engineers (his immediate subordinates), the chief clerk, and the office engineer, for example, were Americans and former associates of Stephens in South Africa or on the Santa Fe or Northern Pacific railroads.[7]

Stephens also used a network of US railway company executives to help him recruit other American engineers. He personally intervened to persuade some American employers to release engineers for service on the GTP and even obtained a harbour engineer who took temporary leave from his position with the US Hydrographic Service. Stephens and his associates offered the American engineers – as an inducement to come north – higher salaries than they were receiving in the United States.[8]

Although the GTP head office in Montreal received at least one hundred applications from qualified Canadian engineers, in addition to a large number of applications for subordinate positions, such as levellers, topographers, transitmen, and draughtsmen,[9] none of these applicants was employed, in spite of company policy to give Canadians preference where qualifications were equal. Stephens and his associates made virtually no attempt to employ Canadians. They did not advertise and made no serious inquiry of the CSCE or even of the School of Practical Science. Stephens's total effort to employ Canadians, he later admitted, was confined to 'occasional talks' with engineers whom he 'happened to meet.'[10]

Recruiting of the survey parties was delegated to the division engineers. In many cases, they also hired engineers directly from the United States, at higher salaries, through their own recruiting networks. Not only did G.A. Kyle, division engineer at Winnipeg, hire his brother and nephew, but he also forced the resignation of a Canadian engineer, Cecil Goddard, as a result of hiring an American, at a higher salary, to a position originally promised to Goddard.[11]

Kyle's preference for American talent stemmed perhaps from his unfavourable opinion of Canadian engineers. 'We are in the unpleasant situation,' Kyle wrote to a US applicant, 'where it is advisable to fill the minor positions with natives, and are therefore rather handicapped.' To an engineer in Idaho, Kyle said he regretted that company policy was to use Canadians but added that he thought that 'later on we will have to import some American brains in order to carry the thing out successfully.'[12]

Although the CSCE had anticipated trouble as early as 1903 and advised the government that Canadian engineers should be employed,[13] the Liberal government did not take notice of the problem until the Conservative Leader of the Opposition, Robert L. Borden, raised the matter in the House of Commons on 13 May 1904, during debate on the GTP bill.[14] Realizing that the government was facing an election later that year, Sir William Mulock, the postmaster general, on 25 May 1904 tactfully shelved the matter by appointing a royal commission chaired by a prominent Toronto Liberal and county court judge, John Winchester, who had served on a number of royal commissions and inquiries.[15]

In his report, submitted in January 1905, Winchester found that, of 101 employees (as of 25 May 1904), upwards of 30 per cent were Americans. This contrasted sharply with Hays's claim that (on the basis of data supplied by Stephens)[16] 97 per cent of the employees in GTP survey parties were Canadians or British subjects, while only 3 per cent were Americans.[17] More important, Winchester found that only one of the nine senior management engineers was a Canadian.[18] While GTP officials pleaded that they were forced to hire Americans because no qualified Canadians were available, Winchester's investigations revealed that this was incorrect. In his concluding remarks, Winchester stated:

There was no earnest endeavor made to obtain Canadian engineers for the location of the Grand Trunk Pacific Railway by those having authority to employ such, that had such an effort been made there would have been no difficulty in obtaining a sufficient number capable not only of locating but of constructing the whole work. There was, however, a very earnest desire to obtain American engineers for the work, and in some cases applications were made to the heads of other railway companies to relieve men for the purpose of having them brought to Canada to be employed on this road.

In his final assessment, Winchester concluded 'that discrimination has been made, against them in my opinion, there is no doubt.'[19] In accordance with his terms of reference, Winchester reported on several American citizens, employed on the GTP, who violated the Alien Labour Law. Later several engineers resigned voluntarily, and warrants for deportation were issued for others.[20]

During the inquiry Winchester became impatient with Stephens. On one occasion in Montreal, he was forced to adjourn proceedings because the chief engineer was, in Winchester's words, 'not in a position to be examined.' A Winnipeg police constable later testified that he had helped Stephens to his feet after he had fallen in an intoxicated condition in front of a hotel. And on several other occasions, Stephens had been observed by some of his subordinates to have been unable to attend to business, because of his intemperance. Winchester believed that one of the reasons why Stephens hired his American friends was to shield his personal misconduct.[21]

Officially, the CSCE's response to the GTP case was similar to other incidents: aliens should not be discriminated against. In theory, an engineer's professional qualification, not his nationality, should determine his employment in Canada, although, as a matter of principle, Canadians should be given preference when qualifications were equal. Because they were professionally competent and could compete successfully with Americans, the CSCE believed, Canadian engineers did not require protection. Even among the more articulate and outspoken CSCE members, there was little support for the principle of excluding alien engineers from Canada. Engineering, like science, it was assumed, was universal and transcended national boundaries.[22] 'In the truest sense,' declared Secretary McLeod, 'the engineer is a citizen of the world.'[23] Engineering professionalism was based on scientific knowledge. Restrictions founded on national distinctions were antithetical to this concept; they placed political expedience ahead of science. The paramount consideration was professional qualification, not nationality[24] – 'the man ... best fitted for the position, irrespective of nationality,'[25] as one Canadian engineer, practising in the United States, put it.

The engineering labour market, many of these engineers believed, was governed by the natural law of supply and demand. Competition among equals, unfettered by artificial bonds of nationality, invariably produced the best man and the best work, to the mutual benefit of employer and country.[26] National distinctions inhibited the pursuit of professional excellence and encouraged second-class work. Moreover, excluding alien engineers from Canada was considered unprofessional. It was often compared to trade unionism and was perceived as an arbitrary intrusion into a free market that infringed upon an employer's right to obtain the best advice available. If the CSCE used its influence to restrict aliens, it would, according to one engineer, 'no longer be regarded as a technical organization for the promotion of scientific knowledge but as a mere trades union.'[27] More important, it would bring the profession and the CSCE into public disrepute. 'I can conceive of no course,' asserted Phelps Johnson, president of the CSCE and president of the Dominion Bridge Company, 'so sure to discredit and disrupt the Society as to adopt Labor Union methods, and interfere in the disputes of engineers with their employers.'[28] While engineers, as individuals, could claim preference on Canadian work, it would be improper for the CSCE to interfere between employer and employee. As a learned society, the CSCE would only advise, not interfere with corporate bodies.[29]

Practical considerations also militated against restrictions. As a young developing country, Canada needed outside help, especially advanced engineering methods.[30] Americans did not discriminate against Canadians practising in the United States; the ASCE admitted all nationalities and even elected a Canadian, T.C. Keefer, as president.[31] Canada and the United States were too closely tied to erect artificial barriers. Restrictions would be unfriendly and ungentlemanly and would destroy the mutually advantageous, unofficial reciprocity between the two countries in engineering talent. They would certainly invite retaliation. Moreover, many aliens were CSCE members; by 1922, 241 members resided in the United States.[32] The society could not discriminate against its own members. If an alien engineer met the CSCE's admission requirements, he should be free to practise in Canada.[33]

For the CSCE, the problem was not so much legal as psychological. The society never disputed the fact that Canadian engineers were sometimes discriminated against. Rather than blame Americans, however, it first blamed those employers who hired Americans because they thought that they were superior. Ultimately, the CSCE censured Canadian engineers who, it thought, lacked confidence and self-assertion. As American engineers confidently promoted themselves, Canadians had not made their qualities known sufficiently to employers. According to consulting engineer and CSCE past president W.F. Tye, Canadians had been duped by American pretensions to superiority: 'If the Americans insist that they are the greatest engineers in the world, and we don't insist that we are equally good, when the government want engineers it is natural for them to go there – to go to the people who say they are the greatest engineers.'[34] Thus, rather than agitate for restrictions, Canadian engineers merely should aggressively inform and re-educate employers. 'If we are given fair play,' C.B. Smith maintained, 'we don't need protection; our qualifications are sufficient.'[35]

Although the CSCE was genuinely committed to an 'open-door' policy, it made one important, almost contradictory, exception: it was unalterably opposed to the employment of aliens on government projects or works that were being publicly subsidized (such as the GTP),[36] when qualified Canadians were available. Alien engineers working for private companies were not a source of complaint, because Canadian engineers never questioned the private-property prerogatives of employers.

Of all the cases involving alien engineers, none angered the CSCE as much as the employment of Professor George F. Swain, in 1916. Although Swain's appointment was not the most objectionable case of discrimination against Canadian engineers, it occurred at an awkward time and appeared to threaten some vital interests.

During the First World War, the ambitious Liberal railway building program of the previous decade foundered under Robert Borden's Conservative government, and the two new transcontinental lines, the GTP and the Canadian Northern, collapsed. In view of the political difficulties attached to continued public subsidization of the lines, in July 1916 the government appointed a royal commission to study the whole vexatious railway problem. The commission, chaired by A.H. Smith, general manager of the New York Central Railroad,[37] immediately appointed an American engineer, Professor Swain, then of Harvard University,[38] to assist the inquiry in the valuation of railway property.[39]

Swain's appointment enraged the CSCE. On behalf of the council, Secretary McLeod issued a circular to all CSCE members, condemning the appointment on the grounds that alien engineers should not be appointed to a government inquiry.[40] According to McLeod, the 'inferences to be drawn' from the incident were: '1st. That the Canadian engineers who built the railways are not competent to report upon them. 2nd. That the Canadian universities, in many cases enjoying Government subsidies, are not producing competent engineers; and 3rd. That the Canadian Society of Civil Engineers, although embracing a membership of about three thousand, is not considered worthy of consultation on an important engineering question.'[41] In a deliberate attempt to influence government policy, the CSCE launched a vigorous campaign to protest Swain's appointment and to pressure the government into appointing Canadian engineers to all public bodies.[42] At the same time, the CSCE co-ordinated its protest with other interest groups.

During the First World War, Canadian architects, manufacturers, and contractors resented the fact that some government contracts were awarded to foreigners. They felt discriminated against and warned that the employment of aliens had undesirable consequences. Since foreigners naturally preferred men and materials with which they were familiar, they usually specified foreign assistants and machinery.[43] The *Contract Record* argued that 'the employment of a United States architect or engineer is generally followed by the letting of the contract to a United States contractor, who, in turn, employs a United States staff and purchases, in large measure, United States materials.'[44] Ultimately, Canadian money flowed out of the country. Recognizing that Canadian architects, engineers, and contractors had a common interest,[45] the Toronto branch of the Canadian Manufacturers' Association called a meeting of interested businessmen and professionals late in 1916. This group later formed a committee and drafted a memorial to Borden[46] protesting the awarding of the Lindsay Arsenal contract to foreigners but also expressing the CSCE's concerns about the employment of aliens on government works. After some delays and misgivings, the document was endorsed by council.[47]

This action represents a significant departure from previous CSCE policy. The CSCE had been reluctant to criticize the government's employment policy, for fear of compromising its learned society status. Instead of demanding that Canadians be given preference on the GTP surveys, for example, the CSCE merely advised the government that, for professional and technical reasons, it was in the interest of the country to hire Canadian engineers.[48]. Thus, whether commenting on the GTP surveys, or even on Swain's appointment, the CSCE's representation never varied: it was unnecessary to employ aliens, since qualified Canadians were available. But after 1916, although the message remained the same, the method changed.

For the first time, the CSCE attempted to press its case by a co-ordinated approach to members of Parliament, the press, and boards of trade, in addition to marshalling its political influence with the government through its prominent members.[49] In short, it employed all the classic methods of interest group lobbying. 'It would be difficult to imagine,' Sir Henry Drayton, the only Canadian commissioner on the railway inquiry, stated in a report to Borden, 'a more complete ... attempt to achieve a result by political influence.'[50]

Although the CSCE's campaign was neither effective nor particularly successful, it was remarkable because the CSCE chose to make a major issue out of an essentially weak case. The *Canadian Engineer* pointed out that compared to other more numerous and more serious cases on the municipal level, Swain's appointment was not a particularly flagrant case of discrimination.[51] The appointment of A.H. Smith, it argued, was more serious, since Smith was the head of a rival American railroad that controlled important railway interests in Canada.[52] Further, it was doubtful that any Canadian engineer could have taken over Swain's job. Sir Henry Drayton offered the compelling argument that 'all Canadian railway engineers of standing have been some time or other, or are now, in the employment of railway companies.' Examining the CSCE's council, Drayton observed that there were 'two Canadian Pacific engineers, two Grand Trunk engineers, two Canadian Northern engineers, as well as engineers on the Intercolonial or National Transcontinental systems.' Even McLeod was employed by the GTR as timekeeper, in his capacity as superintendent of the McGill Observatory.[53] A Canadian could not be reasonably expected to make impartial valuations of his own or rival railways.

As well, the CSCE was attacking one of its own principles: that, under exceptional circumstances, the service of an outside expert may be required for certain specialized work. In the absence of a truly impartial Canadian engineer, it was not unreasonable to appoint a highly qualified expert of international standing – such as Swain, a former president of the ASCE and member of the CSCE – to study such a highly charged subject as Canada's railways.

Under these circumstances, in the face of much worthier cases of discrimination, why did the CSCE attack the government? Nationalist fervour and professional pride played a role, but other factors that threatened the engineers' livelihood also combined to produce the CSCE's shrill response.

Like many other Canadians, engineers were caught up in wartime hysteria and patriotism. With nearly one-third of the CSCE's members at the Front, Canadian engineers may have been less tolerant, perhaps a little resentful of Americans entering Canada and taking Canadian jobs, particularly when the United States had not entered the war. As incidents of Canadians being passed over in favour of Americans grew more numerous and flagrant, Canadian engineers became more sensitive. They began to lose a certain measure of balance and perspective and easily over-reacted to real or imagined discrimination. Swain's appointment became the focus of much anger and frustration. It had enormous symbolic importance and was interpreted as an affront to Canadian engineers – especially the Montreal clique – and a blow to the prestige of the CSCE.

Most Canadian engineers did not object to aliens moving north and making Canada their home; but they resented American consulting engineers working in Canada on short-term government contracts.[54] They argued, somewhat self-righteously, that, while Canadian engineers in the United States had become American citizens and participated fully in the civil and professional life of their adopted country,[55] American consultants did not settle in Canada and, therefore, had no commitment to Canada. The main concern of these men was monetary gain, and this was not in the national interest. Protesting British Columbia's appointment in 1912 of alien engineers under R.H. Thompson, an American engineer, to survey Strathcona Park, R.W. MacIntyre had observed that, while Canadians paid taxes, supported families, and spent their earnings in the province, 'Mr. Thompson and his alien assistants owe no allegiance to Canada and the Empire and ... having no stake in the country, are simply here for financial gain.'[56]

Although most Canadian engineers conceded that a highly qualified American might be employed temporarily in an advisory capacity under a Canadian for certain specialized work, there was no need to go outside the country to hire Americans, especially for routine work, since Canada had enough qualified engineers.[57] By virtue of their knowledge and experience with Canadian conditions and materials, Canadian engineers believed that they were equal, perhaps superior to American engineers.[58] Engineering triumphs of international standing, as well as the success of Canadian engineers abroad, attested to their professional stature. Whether coping with sink-holes north of Superior on the CPR,[59] or installing generators at Niagara,[60] Canadian engineers believed that they possessed special native expertise. Aliens lacked this crucial advantage, and this deficiency sometimes had calamitous results. 'The outstanding blunders in Canadian engineering work,' the *Canadian Engineer* maintained, 'can be laid at the door of the man brought into Canada to report and then depart, to be followed by his fee.'[61]

Many engineering thinkers also assumed that an engineer required something more than technical competence to achieve professional excellence. He must have national commitment. Writing to Judge Winchester in connection with the GTP survey investigation, Sir Sandford Fleming cautioned that, since Canada was embarking on a great national enterprise, it required 'able upright engineers in full sympathy with our national aims and aspirations.'[62] Perhaps remembering the Northern Pacific Railway's attempt to gain control of the CPR, Fleming warned that it was dangerous to hire aliens who might, as he stated, 'come under the influence of those who would profit most by the non-success of the Canadian line.'[63]

Beneath this concern for the national interest, however, lay deeper anxiety about the ability of Canadians to compete in the North American labour market. Canadians complained, for example, that there was no reciprocity between Canada and the United States in engineering talent. Although US immigration officials interpreted the Alien Labor Law in such a way as to admit members of recognized professions – including CSCE members[64] – many Canadian engineers believed that they did not have free access to American contracts and jobs. They argued that the US Army Corps of Engineers was responsible for federal government works and that most state and municipal governments preferred American citizens. Even a growing number of private employers demanded US citizenship. Far more American engineers were employed in Canada than vice versa.[65] As an increasing number of Americans filled Canadian city engineerships and other government posts before the First World War, Canadian engineers realized that they were at a decided competitive disadvantage. Moreover, when governments passed over Canadians and hired Americans, Canadian engineers felt humiliated and stigmatized by an 'inference of Canadian inferiority.'[66] They contended that this damaged their professional reputation and set a bad precedent for private employers. Ultimately, it resulted in lost contracts and lost jobs.

More important, the main thrust of the agitation came from consulting engineers. They relied on government – especially municipal – contracts for a large portion of their practice. When funds for public works dried up, as during the war, and many Canadian engineers were hard pressed for work,[67] American consultants cut sharply into the profits of Canadian consulting firms.

Although protest was heated – especially in provinces furthest from Montreal, like British Columbia – Canadian engineers did not blame Americans or manifest any anti-Americanism. They simply believed that their governments should favour Canadians. This, they reasoned, was consistent with practice in other countries, particularly in the United States. Noting that all protests regarding alien engineers in British Columbia were confined to government-funded works, C.E. Cartwright, a Vancouver consulting engineer, stated that there 'is nothing to which American engineers can take exception in this, as it is simply asking that our governments follow the example of the United States and all other nations.'[68] Going to the heart of the matter, Cartwright continued: 'The protest is not against American engineers, but against the lack of knowledge of our own governments of the fact that qualified engineers can be obtained without sending abroad.'[69]

On the surface, restricting alien engineers from employment on government-funded works ran counter to the CSCE's professed free-labour-market policy. Restrictions, no matter how necessary and justified, were still founded on non-scientific grounds. This contradiction further undermined the CSCE's status as a learned society and generated more controversy over the society's role and purpose.

For the most part, the 'open-door' policy was supported by older, more established engineers, associated with the Montreal clique. Some engineers, such as Phelps Johnson, were American born and educated. As a management engineer, Johnson usually favoured large-scale engineering immigration, to keep salaries down, and reacted negatively to any real or imagined infringement on management prerogatives, particularly in labour relations. Still others, perhaps many, had worked in the United States and were reluctant to jeopardize future employment or to alienate American colleagues and friends.

By 1914, however, these engineers realized that the climate of opinion had changed. It had become apparent that foreign competition hurt many CSCE members. Younger engineers, for example, were particularly affected; many were forced to leave Canada in search of work.[70] As well, prior to the war, editorial opinion in the technical press began to turn against the employment of aliens. In a long and carefully prepared editorial, 'The Foreign Invasion,' published in May 1910, the *Canadian Engineer* opposed alien employment on the grounds that Canada no longer required outside help.[71] Later, in February 1913, the *Contract Record* ignited a heated controversy by claiming that the 'isolated few' 'open-door' supporters had international vested interests to protect.[72]

In spite of their opposition to labour restrictions, by 1916 the 'open-door' advocates were actively protesting the employment of alien engineers on government-funded works. While perhaps influenced by the mounting opposition to aliens, they undoubtedly realized that some restrictions could serve their business and professional interests, for example, by lessening demands for legislation to exclude all alien engineers from Canada. Such legislation could hurt Montreal's major private employers of engineers, such as the Dominion Bridge Company, or the CPR. Moreover, by simply urging governments to recognize the advantages of Canadian expertise and voluntarily employ Canadians, instead of enacting restrictions against aliens, the 'open-door' advocates technically avoided compromising their free-labour-market principles. In effect, they protected their interests by pursuing the apparently contradictory policy of advocating both restrictions and a free market.

This ambiguous policy was counter-productive. Virtually all the complaints about alien engineers originated from public works, especially on the municipal level. Restricting aliens from government-funded works would effectively preclude most alien engineers from practising in Canada. This discredited the CSCE's 'open-door' policy and further eroded its façade as a learned society. At the same time, younger engineers and some consultants were angered by the CSCE's failure to protect them from foreign competition. They rejected the idea of requesting governments voluntarily to restrict aliens from public works and demanded mandatory restrictions to repel 'The Foreign Invasion.'

5

'Iniquitous and impertinent' legislation

The CSCE and the politics of professionalism

Towards the end of the nineteenth century, CSCE members tried to solve their professional problems by legislation. In 1896, the CSCE began seeking restrictive licensing laws to close the profession to 'unqualified' practitioners. This tactic had been attempted before. An engineering licensing law was introduced in 1881, but never passed, in the Ontario legislature,[1] and, in 1887, Alan Macdougall endeavoured to have the CSCE incorporated as the licensing and regulatory body for Canadian engineers.[2] Although the legal profession had been self-governing for over a century[3] and the world's first dental act was passed in Ontario in 1868,[4] licensing was a comparatively novel and extraordinary measure for an era that still extolled the virtues of laissez-faire. Moreover, as a predominantly 'civil' engineering society, the CSCE found that its licensing program soon encountered fierce opposition which persisted until well past the First World War.

While Canadian engineers deeply resented competition from alien engineers, they also regarded land surveyors as a threat. Surveyors often practised civil engineering and usually called themselves 'civil engineer.'[5] Although engineers were confident that they could compete with surveyors on an equal basis, they believed that surveyors' licensing laws gave them an unfair competitive advantage.

Land surveyors had always enjoyed special privileges. Originally, boundary lines were set by government officials, usually military engineers and surveyors, but this responsibility was gradually delegated to private surveyors, who functioned as public officials. Surveyors were expected to uphold the public interest by protecting third parties, such as landowners whose property adjoined lands surveyed, and to be familiar with complex land laws and systems of measurement.[6] In the interest of accuracy and impartiality, governments reserved the right to examine, license, and regulate surveyors.[7] By the late nineteenth and early twentieth centuries, these powers were conferred on provincial land surveyors' societies.[8] This gave surveyors extraordinary power to control all aspects of professional practice – in effect, a monopoly similar to that enjoyed by lawyers and doctors.

Engineers were excluded from surveying, but surveyors, whether competent or not, could practise engineering.[9] Engineers were also excluded from some aspects of traditional engineering practice by other laws favouring surveyors. Under the Northwest Irrigation Act, 1894, for example, only Dominion land surveyors (who had exclusive rights to survey Dominion lands) could sign maps and plans.[10] Employers, unable to afford both surveyors and engineers, were forced to engage surveyors. Gradually, government and CPR work, in the Northwest, was taken over by Dominion land surveyors. This caused friction between engineers and surveyors. Engineers not only felt at a severe competitive disadvantage but also believed themselves discriminated against. 'We are,' protested one irate engineer, 'actually being crowded out by legal enactments from a fair chance to secure employment except as assistants to Dominion Land Surveyors on purely Engineering works.'[11] During the depression of the 1890s, as migration to the Northwest declined, engineers believed that unemployed surveyors were drifting into civil engineering, in competition with engineers who were already hard pressed for work. Some engineers suggested that the only solution was to imitate the surveyors: restrict competition by closing the profession to 'unqualified' practitioners.[12]

By 1892, many CSCE members favoured restricting competition by licensing. Following completion of the CPR, the demand for engineers declined and younger ones believed that licensing would eliminate competition from aliens, surveyors, and non-professionals. This would increase demand, create employment, and help to stem the flow of recent engineering school graduates to the United States. Government engineers recognized that licensing might help to eliminate patronage and give them professional standing.

While the Montreal clique rejected licensing, it did not vigorously oppose it at this point. It undoubtedly recognized, during the 1890s, that the weight of opinion, particularly among a growing number of prominent engineers, had dramatically shifted in favour of political action. Voicing perfunctory objections, the Montreal clique was forced to yield, temporarily, to majority opinion.[13] It was not until the First World War that it raised strong philosophical objections.

The CSCE's independent consulting engineers had the most to gain from licensing. Unlike most CSCE members – salaried employees shielded by employers from outside competition – consulting engineers were directly affected by competition from aliens and surveyors, especially during hard times. However, while hurt by competition, consultants rarely complained of real hardship. Had they seriously wanted access to surveying, they could easily have passed the surveyors' licensing examinations. Many, especially city engineers, were licensed provincial land surveyors by necessity.[14] The surveyors' monopoly appeared to have injured their professional pride, not their pocket-books. Consultants did not consider surveyors their equals. It was demeaning, not financially ruinous, to be compelled to join the surveyors' guild, in order to practise some traditional aspects of engineering. Other more compelling reasons inspired licensing.

As Canada moved deeper into the depression of the 1890s, a growing number of consultants competed for a decreasing number of contracts. In the 'scramble for work,'[15] as the *Canadian Engineer* described it, consulting engineers engaged in competitive practices considered unethical by contemporary legal and medical standards. Underbidding, advertising, lobbying, and giving gratuitous professional advice were prevalent and sometimes the subjects of controversies in engineering newspapers. Respected consulting engineer Willis Chipman, for example, believed that these practices, especially what he described as 'American methods' of lobbying small municipalities for work, were corrupting and degrading the profession.[16] As well, consultants were forced to compete with salaried engineers. It was a common practice for engineering professors (and even some government engineers) to accept outside consulting work. At a time when contracts were scarce, consultants charged that government engineers and, especially, professors had an unfair competitive advantage, with secure incomes and free use of publicly endowed facilities, such as university laboratories. Consultants complained bitterly that they had to provide their own facilities.[17] Although the CSCE had had a code of ethics since 1896, unethical practices continued.[18] The code was ineffective and unenforceable. It applied only to CSCE members, ignored the engineer's quasi-business mentality, and, most significantly, did not specifically prohibit unseemly competitive practices. Predicated on the ethical imperatives of the 'Golden Rule,'[19] it merely set forth broad guide-lines for professional conduct. CSCE members, asserted President John Kennedy in 1893, were men of honour, 'who merely stand in need of guidance and not of restraint.'[20] Thus, instead of regulating competition, the code served as a kind of gentleman's code of honour, which enhanced the CSCE's prestige but did little to improve its ethics.

The consultants recognized that the CSCE must acquire licensing powers to enforce a code of ethics and regulate competition. To this end, they first appealed directly to members' sense of professional pride. Unseemly competition, they argued, harmed the profession by lowering its status. 'As the profession stands to-day,' Macdougall stated, 'it is almost a trade.'[21] A more successful tactic, however, was to arouse members' anger over land surveyors encroaching on engineers' prerogatives. Macdougall and other consultants used this issue as a pretext to agitate for licensing laws. They were responsible for subtly promoting the idea that laws favouring surveyors discriminated against engineers. This enabled them to portray licensing as a pragmatic defensive measure, which, in turn, temporarily neutralized the Montreal clique's opposition.

Although Macdougall failed in 1887 to have the CSCE incorporated as a self-governing licensing and regulatory body, he did not abandon the idea, in spite of strong opposition from the Montreal clique. Encouraged by growing demand within the CSCE for legal recognition, he rallied his forces and organized a powerful crusade to place engineering on the same legal footing as law and medicine.

In April 1892, Macdougall launched his campaign at a regular Montreal CSCE meeting. In his paper, 'The Professional Status: A Plea for a Close Corporation,' he argued that a close corporation (the popular term for an incorporated professional society closed to non-professionals) was a natural and necessary development in establishing engineering as a profession. Engineers had only to take the next step. 'The profession,' he declared, 'is like a man standing on the brink of a river, afraid to take a header into the stream in which his companions are sporting.'[22]

Macdougall's views were soon endorsed by engineers outside Montreal, but a request that council take action to secure licensing legislation was turned down, on the grounds that it was not then feasible.[23] Undaunted, Macdougall circumvented the Montreal clique and appealed directly to the membership. At the 1893 annual meeting, a committee on professional status was appointed, with Macdougall as chairman.[24] For the next two years, however, Macdougall's initiative faltered and lost momentum. With committee members scattered across Canada, committee business was conducted awkwardly by correspondence; Macdougall assumed most of the work-load. The committee made little progress until 1895, when, in response to its circular, committee members approved of creating a close corporation. In October, council authorized the committee to retain legal counsel to draft bills of incorporation.[25]

Macdougall knew exactly what he wanted: licensing privileges, not government regulation or certification, similar to those enjoyed by the Ontario Association of Stationary Engineers or the Institute of Chartered Accountants of Ontario. The 1891 legislation creating the Ontario Association of Stationary Engineers only empowered that body to hold examinations and grant certificates of qualification and efficiency; an employer was not obliged to hire association members. The Institute of Chartered Accountants of Ontario functioned as an educational and certification body. It offered classes, lectures, and examinations, tested candidates for admission, and granted diplomas of fellowship, enabling members to use the letters FCA after their name.[26] In 1892 in Ontario, only lawyers, doctors, dentists, and provincial land surveyors had the exclusive statutory authority to control and regulate their respective professions. Pharmacists enjoyed similar powers under the pharmacy act. The architectural profession, however, was not a close corporation. The Architects Act, 1890, incorporated the Ontario Association of Architects (OAA) and gave it power to certify, not license members. Only the title 'Registered Architect' was protected; no penalties were prescribed for non-members who practised architecture.[27] For Macdougall, nothing less than the full powers possessed by the Law Society of Upper Canada would be acceptable. But, while this organization was an ideal example of a close corporation, the recently incorporated Ontario Association of Land Surveyors (OALS) appeared to be Macdougall's practical model. He believed that the CSCE, like the OALS, should have full self-governing powers to regulate all aspects of professional practice – administration, admission, discipline.[28]

Macdougall also thought that the CSCE, although a private organization, should be federally incorporated as the national licensing and regulatory authority.[29] CSCE leaders had always assumed that their society was, as one memorandum stated, 'the representative body for Canadian Engineers of all branches,'[30] which comprised practically all the professionally qualified engineers in the country. Like the ASCE, the CSCE claimed to represent all 'civil' engineers, including mining engineers, whom it considered, at least theoretically, a 'sub-department of civil engineering.'[31] This claim, however, was not based on actual membership; while it was Canada's only federally incorporated engineering society before 1898, the CSCE was still essentially a 'civil' engineering society, with its membership concentrated in Quebec and Ontario. Rather, the CSCE claimed to represent 'professionally qualified' engineers, or all scientifically trained men who could design and construct and had ten years of experience, five in responsible charge. These standards, the CSCE contended, were internationally recognized by the world's leading national engineering societies – the ICE, the ASCE.[32] Measured against these standards, other Canadian engineering societies were not considered professional, and those unable to qualify for CSCE membership were believed to be unfit to practise. Thus, Macdougall assumed that it was only reasonable that the CSCE, like the OALS, should be given licensing and regulatory powers.

Unfortunately, Macdougall's licensing scheme had two major problems. First, under the CSCE's Dominion charter, it was empowered only to 'facilitate the acquirement and interchange of professional knowledge among its members.' It could acquire property, elect officers, and pass by-laws; but, like the ICE, it had no authority to reconstitute itself as a close corporation. Second, and related, although engineering was practised nationally and the CSCE had a Dominion charter, only the provinces could confer licensing powers. Under the British North America Act, 1867, professional societies were regarded as educational bodies. While Macdougall preferred Dominion incorporation,[33] he understood the legal problems and accepted a solution proposed by the society's lawyers: the society should obtain an amendment to its Dominion charter, while applying for incorporation in each province with a standarized act.[34] With some difficulty, the lawyers drafted the legislation, and council sent confidential copies to senior CSCE members.

Of the two draft bills, the Dominion one was simpler but potentially more important. Framed along lines suggested by Walter Shanly,[35] it proposed to restrict all Dominion and publicly subsidized engineering works to CSCE members.[36] On the surface, this bill appears to have been inspired by the Dominion Lands Act, which granted Dominion land surveyors exclusive surveying privileges on Dominion lands. However, while the Dominion land surveyors' statutory powers were strictly proscribed, a simple amendment to the CSCE charter would give engineers wide-ranging monopolistic powers over all aspects of government engineering and publicly subsidized works, including, presumably, many railways. This would restrict competition from aliens, surveyors, and non-professionals and expand employment opportunities, especially for consultants. It would also deprive the government of an important source of patronage.

The draft provincial bill attracted more attention. Modelled after other Canadian licensing laws, it proposed to incorporate a separate, self-governing licensing and regulatory society, with power to restrict the use of the title 'Civil Engineer,' as well as access to any provincial or provincially subsidized works.[37] Although Macdougall wanted greater powers, he rationalized that it was a good beginning; amendments could follow. Other engineers, however, were more critical. Unlike lawyers and doctors, they argued, engineers were, of necessity, constantly moving. The proposed bill, they claimed, would restrict mobility by forcing engineers to belong to seven separate provincial societies.[38] In defence, Macdougall explained that provincial barriers could be overcome by passing a standardized act in each province, and, since the bill was framed in very general terms, provincial councils would have wide powers to make adjustments to ensure national uniformity.

In spite of these misgivings, a large majority of the members attending the CSCE's 1896 annual meeting approved the provincial bill. Council was authorized to apply to Parliament for an amendment to the charter; Macdougall's committee was dissolved and replaced by a central committee of five and several provincial committees of three.[39] Although some members, such as C.E.W. Dodwell, thought that it would be 'practically impossible'[40] to get the proposed bill passed, especially before the Dominion charter was amended, the Manitoba committee acted with such dispatch that the legislature passed the bill almost without changes. It became law 1 July 1896. According to the *Engineering News* of New York, Manitoba's became the first government in the world to make engineering a close profession. Eleven years later, the first US engineering licensing law would be passed, in Wyoming.[41]

Meanwhile, acting on instructions from the membership, council appointed a subcommittee to study the feasibility of amending the Dominion charter. But, after two trips to Ottawa, the committee concluded that it was unadvisable, at that time, to seek amendment.[42] The bill was set aside and never introduced. The CSCE then turned its attention to the provincial legislatures.

In Quebec, the government accepted and introduced a revised CSCE bill as a government measure. Unlike the Manitoba bill, the Quebec legislation did not propose incorporation of a separate provincial governing body. Acting on the advice of the society's Quebec lawyer, the CSCE accepted the idea that the provincial government should merely recognize the Dominion charter and grant the society special regulatory powers in Quebec. It was believed that this would help to preserve the CSCE's unity by avoiding the creation of autonomous provincial societies.[43] As well, to prevent discrimination, the revised bill stipulated that new members should be admitted by examination, not election. Unfortunately, the bill was introduced late in the session and died when the legislative assembly was prorogued.

It is ironic that the bill's only real opposition came from within the CSCE. At the 1897 annual meeting, some members charged that the bill was killed because an unnamed CSCE member complained to the attorney general.[44] W.J. Sproule, an energetic supporter of the bill, stated later that some councillors were passively resisting the bill by needlessly delaying its reintroduction.[45] It was at this point, when Sproule despaired of the bill's passage that session, that Professor McLeod took charge and saw the bill through the legislature. Anticipating trouble from the Quebec Mining Society, McLeod moved quickly to forestall opposition by simply exempting mining engineers from the legislation.[46]

As well, recognizing that Quebec provincial land surveyors were, as he put it, 'very strong politically,'[47] McLeod neutralized potential opposition by including them in the bill, while excluding some engineering works, such as government colonization roads, ordinary roads in rural municipalities, and bridges not exceeding $600, from the definition of 'civil engineering' activities in the bill, at the surveyors' request. Engineers did not usually work on colonization roads, and surveyors could not build expensive bridges. Most Quebec surveyors, McLeod reasoned, were engaged in some form of civil engineering, and nearly a third of their ranks were already CSCE members. They could not be excluded. At the same time, however, suspecting that some surveyors were attempting to delay and, ultimately, defeat the bill, McLeod took the precaution of requesting CSCE members, who were also provincial land surveyors in Quebec, to attend a surveyors' meeting, in order to explain the CSCE's position.[48]

McLeod was confident, nevertheless, that there would be no conflict of interest between engineers and surveyors. Engineering licensing laws would not interfere with the rights and privileges of provincial land surveyors, because there was a commonly recognized distinction between land and engineering surveyors. The principal function of a land surveyor, according to a CSCE memorandum, was to determine 'the boundaries, dimensions and areas of properties,' whereas engineers surveyed the 'location of various works of construction.'[49] In the end, the surveyors were accommodated.

The Quebec bill finally became law on 15 January 1898. Securing its passage had been difficult, time-consuming, and expensive, yet its enactment represented a major achievement for the CSCE. Twenty years would pass before a provincial legislature would pass another licensing law.

Encouraged by its success in Quebec, the CSCE quickly proposed similar bills in Nova Scotia and Ontario. But, unlike the Manitoba and Quebec legislation, these bills immediately encountered fierce and well-organized opposition from mining and other non-civil engineers, who saw them as a direct threat to their interests. In spite of the CSCE's willingness to compromise and overcome objections, opposition persisted, grew stronger, and eventually destroyed the CSCE's legislative campaign in other provinces.

Mining engineers resented the prospect of being forced to join the CSCE to practise. 'We don't want to be forced into any kind of societies in order to make a living,'[50] protested one irate mining engineer. The CSCE neither represented mining engineers nor was competent to judge their qualifications. B.T.A. Bell, the energetic and forceful young editor of the *Canadian Mining Review* who became the CMI's secretary, called the Nova Scotia bill 'the most iniquitous and impertinent piece of legislation'[51] he had ever seen. It did not, he believed, represent the true sentiments of most CSCE members. It was the work of an arrogant and egotistical coterie in Montreal. Moreover, the CSCE's high compulsory membership fee (described by John Hardman, the CMI's first president, as a 'tax')[52] was a desperate attempt to increase the revenues of a dying society.[53]

The Dominion Institute of Amalgamated Engineering (DIAE), founded 1898, a large engineering society that admitted non-professionals to membership and claimed to represent civil, as well as other engineers,[54] argued that the Ontario legislation would grant monopoly powers to a small private-interest group.[55] This view was supported by newspapers in Halifax, Kingston, and Toronto. The authority to regulate all aspects of professional practice, the DIAE contended, would lead to abuse and threaten the legitimate interests of students, tradesmen, and non-civil engineers. Engineering in Great Britain and the United States, it noted, was an 'open' profession. Restrictive licensing laws to protect the public from unqualified engineers were unnecessary, because, unlike doctors and lawyers, engineers did not deal directly with an unsuspecting public. Their employers – railways and governments – were sophisticated organizations and could protect themselves from imposters and incompetents.[56]

At the heart of this criticism was the conviction that the CSCE bills would constitute unfair competition. While the DIAE and CMI approved of protecting the public from unqualified practitioners, they were enraged by the prospect of a monopoly being conferred on their rivals. In their view, the CSCE legislation was simply a brazen and cynical attempt to eliminate competition. Professor R. Carr-Harris, Queen's University, the CSCE's fiercest critic, warned the CMI that the bills were 'simply nothing more nor less but an attempt to sweep out of existence any competition with [CSCE] members.'[57] Other critics denounced the bills as 'class legislation' and accused the CSCE of forming an engineering 'trust,' on the pretext of protecting the public.[58] This, in their judgment, was undemocratic and an affront to liberal values. Carr-Harris advised the CMI not to make any compromise with the CSCE. He warned that the bills were merely the 'thin edge of the wedge,'[59] part of a larger movement to obtain restrictive legislation throughout the Dominion. Adopting a common DIAE polemic, one Halifax newspaper saw grander and more sinister designs. The CSCE's legislative scheme was 'a well planned and persistent movement to control the whole of the vast and intricate series of engineering operations in Canada from a little office in Montreal.'[60] The CSCE must be stopped.

In 1899 and 1902, Bell and Carr-Harris argued forcefully against the CSCE's bills before the Private Bills Committee of the Ontario legislature. In 1902, Sandford Fleming, then chancellor of Queen's University and a DIAE member, publicly condemned the 1902 bill as being 'repugnant to the spirit of Canada.'[61] Principal Grant of Queen's and Dr W.L. Goodwin, director of the School of Mines, Kingston, as well as faculty and student representatives from Queen's, also lobbied against the Ontario bill, with the result that it did not survive for second reading.[62]

Dismayed at first by this opposition, the CSCE responded pragmatically and moved quickly to accommodate critics. Adopting the same tactics employed a year earlier in Quebec, the CSCE approached the OALS, regarding its co-operation as essential. Rationalizing that many Ontario surveyors were also CSCE members, the CSCE offered to admit OALS members to associate (not full) membership. After some further concessions concerning membership fees, the OALS approved the 1899 Ontario bill; only a few surveyors, acting as private individuals, opposed the measure. Apart from some misgivings about the 1902 bill, the CSCE experienced no further opposition from surveyors.[63]

Accommodating the CMI, however, proved more difficult. Beginning in 1899, McLeod wrote conciliatory letters to Bell and Carr-Harris, conveying the society's good intentions and reassuring them that the CSCE had no desire to interfere with their rights and privileges. McLeod and other councillors met CMI officers and offered to exempt all mining engineers and managers from the bill. Although McLeod believed that he had made some progress in modifying the CMI's attitude, he was genuinely bewildered by its continued opposition. The blanket exemption, he thought, was a major concession. It had been acceptable to Quebec mining engineers in 1897.[64]

After years of hard work, frustration, and bitter disappointment over the Ontario bill, McLeod gradually began to suspect that other factors were involved. Finding no rational explanation for the CMI's opposition, he and other councillors concluded that it was the result of a 'misunderstanding'; mining engineers and, especially, the public had been badly misinformed about the bill.[65] McLeod also tended to reduce the problem to personalities and privately hurled some ill-tempered invective at CMI leaders. In 1900, for example, he declared that mining engineers were being 'manipulated' by men such as Bell, and, in 1902, he charged that Queen's University (or, more precisely, Carr-Harris) was behind the CMI's continued opposition.

McLeod questioned Carr-Harris's competence as an engineering professor and accused him of misleading Queen's engineering students about the CSCE's bill.[66] Blinded by his contempt for Carr-Harris, McLeod believed that his opposition to the CSCE was, as he revealed confidentially to a colleague, 'founded upon personal animosity.'[67]

There is some evidence to suggest that Carr-Harris was inaccurate, if not deliberately misleading, in some aspects of his critique of the CSCE's bill. There was also considerable public misunderstanding. The bill was a novel and extraordinary expedient for its time, and even some CSCE members were confused. However, much of the misinformation was of a minor nature. Preoccupied with the superficial aspects of their opponents' criticism, the CSCE failed to probe and to comprehend its significance. The CSCE seemed insensitive to, and largely ignorant of, the bill's wide-ranging implications. For example, it never fully appreciated that, in spite of its own attempt to protect the rights of mining engineers, the bill still threatened some important vested interests. Although mining engineers were exempted from the proposed legislation, their rights were still not fully protected.[68] Traditionally, mining engineers encompassed many branches of engineering: mechanical, electrical, as well as civil. Under the Ontario bill, for instance, only CSCE members could legally design and construct mine roads and railways.[69] Similarly, some 'practical' engineers and tradesmen were also threatened. Small municipalities, unable to afford a township or county engineer, contracted local 'practical' men for public works. Enactment of the CSCE's bill would immediately deprive these men of their livelihood because, lacking scientific training, they could not become CSCE members and qualify as licensed engineers.[70]

At the same time, other important interests felt threatened. Although the University of Toronto approved of the CSCE's 1902 bill, it seems clear that Queen's University and, probably, the School of Mines feared that, if the bill became law, the CSCE could control university engineering education by virtue of its power to recognize degrees and set admission standards. As well, if CSCE membership were compulsory, membership in the voluntary societies – CMI, DIAE – would decline, because most engineers would not pay double dues. This prospect frightened the CMI. It confirmed an old suspicion that the CSCE had been scheming to take over the society.[71] The CMI was also deeply concerned that foreigners might not invest in the Canadian mining industry if their trusted technical advisers were barred from practising in Canada because of licensing restrictions.[72] This might deprive the industry of investment and, thus, deny Canadian mining engineers work. After 1918, this point would become central to the CMI's case against engineering licensing laws.

Another major indication of the CSCE's insensitivity was its approach to admissions in the 1902 bill. Unlike the 1899 bill, this one had no statutory provision for an examination board to admit engineers to membership. The legislation simply validated the CSCE's by-laws which, in turn, governed qualifications and admissions. Under these regulations, a candidate could be rejected if 10 per cent of the votes cast by letter ballot were negative. To outsiders, however, this provision appeared arbitrary. Dr W.L. Goodwin, for example, characterized it as medieval,[73] while the Toronto *Globe* called attention to the potential for abuse arising from granting undisclosed powers to a private interest group.

Both Goodwin and the *Globe* clearly understood that the CSCE, essentially, was asking the government to delegate part of its legislative and judicial functions. In their view, this was not only an abrogation of government responsibility but a manifest injustice; it would confer extraordinary powers on a private organization that did not represent the whole profession. Moreover, the validation of the CSCE's by-laws, they argued, would give it undisclosed powers that would be used arbitrarily against the interests of non-civil engineers. It could determine, for example, who was qualified to practise, since, as Goodwin observed, the CSCE by-laws would give the society power to define what was a 'civil' engineer and, therefore, who could earn a living practising engineering.[74]

It is not clear why the examination board was dropped from the 1902 bill. CSCE members, at least in Quebec, recognized the serious implications of admission by election. As early as 1896, members of the Quebec provincial committee on legislation argued that exclusion from membership by a 10 per cent negative vote, through professional jealousy or, perhaps, personal dislike, would be a 'manifest injustice'[75] because it would deprive a man of his livelihood. They warned that it would also constitute a major impediment to a bill's enactment. Secretary McLeod doubted that a cabal would form against a candidate when his livelihood was at stake. But, he admitted, a few men had been excluded from membership in the past and only ten negative votes could exclude a candidate, since approximately one hundred election ballots usually were returned.[76]

Perhaps organizers felt that an examination board was unnecessary. Admission by election was an accepted and well-established procedure employed by leading national engineering societies. The members of Canada's only representative national society of professionally qualified engineers may have felt quite capable of judging a colleague's professional qualifications without formal examination. Moreover, older, more conservative engineers, who were hostile to university engineering education, undoubtedly believed that experience was the only true measure of ability;

anyone could master theory and pass an examination. Nevertheless, the deletion of the examination board, combined with the threat to important vested interests, had serious consequences; it discredited the CSCE and made it appear élitist and self-serving. This virtually guaranteed the unflagging opposition of non-civil engineers and created such a legacy of bitterness and suspicion that civil engineers in Ontario were not granted full licensing powers until 1937.[77]

The CSCE's handling of its licensing bills was awkward, high-handed, and politically inept. Never again would it attempt to establish itself as the governing licensing body. This was the main lesson the society learned during this period. In the mean time, since council viewed legislative success in Ontario as an essential preliminary to obtaining similar laws in the west and the Maritimes,[78] defeat of the 1902 Ontario bill effectively terminated the first phase of the CSCE's legislative program, a later (1907) attempt to secure legislation notwithstanding.

By 1914, the CSCE had obtained legislation only in Manitoba and Quebec. Unfortunately, these acts had serious limitations. The Manitoba act did not have a penalty clause. According to McLeod, the bill was passed 'in a very great hurry,'[79] before council realized the absence of such a clause. The society's lawyer earlier had advised that its omission would be 'politic' and suggested that a penalty clause could be obtained later through an amendment.[80] Although H.N. Rutan, city engineer, Winnipeg, defended the act on the grounds that it at least had the moral force of law, nevertheless, without a penalty clause it amounted to little more than a mild registration law, and the American engineering press charged correctly that the act was unworkable. Attempts to amend it were postponed pending passage of licensing laws in other provinces.[81] By contrast, the Quebec act had a penalty clause; but the council was reluctant to have the law enforced, for fear of jeopardizing licensing legislation in other provinces.[82] Although McLeod characterized the Quebec act as 'very stringent,' unenforced it was worthless, and McLeod concluded that its main effect was to inform the public about the engineer's high educational qualifications.[83]

By 1902, the campaign to close the profession was already in sharp decline. Macdougall's death in April 1897 deprived the movement of momentum and enthusiasm. McLeod was able and persistent, but Macdougall had had the talent and determination to unite and to inspire engineers with his vision of greater power and prestige. After his death, consulting engineers, like Willis Chipman, could not mobilize the full support of the mass of ordinary salaried engineers.[84] By 1904, as employment opportunities increased and competition among consultants eased with the building of the transcontinental railways, the demand for protective legislation declined.[85]

During this period, rather than vainly pursuing legislation, the CSCE became more concerned with protecting its existing privileges. Unable to monopolize engineering practice by licensing, it then attempted to monopolize the title 'engineer' by opposing the incorporation of 'non-professional' engineering societies. In 1903, for example, the CSCE lobbied the Dominion government and blocked the incorporation of its old nemesis, the DIAE.[86] But, in 1911, it could not prevent the Ontario government from incorporating the Society of Domestic Heating and Sanitary Engineers. The CSCE deeply resented the usurpation of a legitimate engineering title – sanitary engineer – by plumbers and steamfitters.[87] It feared that the prestige of tradesmen would be enhanced at the expense of engineers; 'Bill Dobbs, the plumber, will become Mr. William Dobbs, the Sanitary Engineer.'[88]

At the same time, the CSCE also carefully monitored Parliament and provincial legislatures for bills that might encroach on traditional engineering prerogatives. It was particularly vigilant with respect to legislation concerning land surveyors. By 1910, amid growing demands from angry Quebec members to enforce the Quebec act against aliens practising illegally in the province,[89] the council began systematically to notify offenders and their employers of violations. It also explored the possibility of a test case and retained lawyers to scrutinize private bills admitting unqualified engineers to practice.[90]

Although these initiatives appear inconsequential, in contrast to earlier attempts to close the profession, they kept the CSCE politically active and served as a necessary prelude to the next attempt to obtain restrictive licensing laws, after 1918. In the mean time, with the completion of the transcontinental railways and the onset of the 1913 depression, younger salaried engineers grew progressively more dissatisfied with the CSCE's failure to solve their economic problems. During the war, they began to raise serious questions about the CSCE's structure and purpose.

CSCE members, annual meeting, Montreal, 1894

T.C. Keefer, first president, CSCE, 1887

Sir Casimir Gzowski, president, CSCE, 1889–91

C.H. McLeod, secretary, CSCE, 1891–1917

John Kennedy, president, CSCE, 1892

H.E.T. Haultain, chairman, Committee on Society Affairs, CSCE, 1916

John Galbraith, president, CSCE, 1908

EIC members, annual meeting, Ottawa, 1919

Fraser S. Keith, secretary, CSCE / EIC, 1917–25

6

In search of a 'tribal soul'

The birth of the EIC

The CSCE's detractors became more vocal and critical. By the First World War, not only was the society attacked for its failure to protect its members, but its role as an educational society was also questioned. This criticism peaked in 1916 and resulted in major changes that marked the most important turning-point in the CSCE's institutional development.

There was a widespread feeling among engineers that the CSCE had not benefited individual members or significantly raised their status. The society was neither recognized by the public nor even accepted by all qualified engineers. 'It must be confessed,' admitted John Galbraith in his 1909 president's address, 'after an existence of 21 years, that the Canadian Society has not succeeded in gaining recognition by the various classes of engineers in the country as the representative and authoritative engineering society.'[1] To a certain extent, this was a consequence of the CSCE's failure to fulfil its primary function, the interchange of professional knowledge.

The reading and discussion of professional papers were the principal means by which the CSCE functioned as a learned society. However, if a learned society is judged by the quality of its publications, the CSCE lacked professional stature. It was originally incorporated as a general engineering society, but while many of its early papers examined subjects from all fields of engineering, most papers concerned civil engineering, particularly construction and hydraulic engineering. They were descriptive rather than theoretical, too general or too narrowly defined to compare favourably with papers published by the ICE or ASCE.[2] They had little practical value for practising engineers and were, according to one cynic, 'essentially for the benefit, or amusement, of those few men in Montreal who have the honor of running the society.'[3]

CSCE presidents rarely missed an opportunity to point out that reading papers was not only good for the society but also an excellent way to bring members, especially younger ones, into professional prominence.[4] Even so, the CSCE always experienced difficulty in obtaining good papers.[5] While members were obliged to give presentations as a condition of membership, the number of papers presented, compared with the CSCE's increasing membership, steadily declined.[6] Moreover, because of lengthy publication delays, many interesting and valuable articles were published in the technical press instead of the society's *Transactions*.[7] There was also some doubt about whether the CSCE was advancing engineering research. Dissatisfaction periodically erupted over the quality of CSCE engineering standards and specifications, prepared by various standing committees.[8]

Dissatisfaction soon resulted in widespread apathy. Meetings were poorly attended – even some councillors were delinquent[9] – and discussions following the presentation of papers were, in John Galbraith's words, 'meagre and incomplete.'[10] The CSCE fell into a lethargy from which it was only temporarily aroused at the annual meeting, which was, prior to the inauguration of the professional meetings in 1918, the society's premier event. This somnolence reminded C.S. Leach of a bear named Barney, chained to a pole in White River. During the summer, he explained, Barney would walk around the pole all day, and then he would retire to his den for the winter. 'Now, I think the Canadian Society of Civil Engineers is very much like that bear,' the engineer mused. 'We come out of our dens once a year, hold our Annual Meeting, walk around and around the same propositions ... and then – go back to our dens and sleep for the balance of the year.'[11]

Judged by its own standards as a learned society, the CSCE was inadequate. 'The general feeling among the majority of engineers,' claimed A.N. Worthington in 1917, 'is that the Canadian Society of Civil Engineers has neither significance nor status and as such there is no advantage in belonging to it.'[12] Three groups were particularly ill served: non-civils, westerners and Maritimers, and young engineers.

By 1921, although less than half the engineers in Canada were 'civil' engineers (43.0 per cent),[13] the CSCE was predominantly made up of that category.[14] Between 1887 and 1922, 84.9 per cent of all initial CSCE applicants (excluding student and junior members) were engaged in some form of 'civil' engineering, usually railway, municipal, or hydraulic work (see Table 1). Mechanical and electrical engineers preferred to join American societies, while mining engineers, after 1898, generally belonged to the Canadian Mining Institute.

As well, the CSCE was mainly a central Canadian engineering society.

TABLE 1
Field of specialization of CSCE applicants
1887–1922

Specialization	Number*	Percentage
Civil	2,269	84.9
Electrical	178	6.7
Mechanical	154	5.8
Mining	38	1.4
Chemical	12	0.4
Unknown	22	0.8
Total	2,673	100.0

SOURCE: Calculated from: National Archives
of Canada, Engineering Institute of Canada
Papers, MG 28, 1–277, Membership Files,
1887–1922
*Excludes student and junior members

TABLE 2
Regional distribution of CSCE applicants
1887–1922

Region	Number	Percentage
East	345	8.7
Central Canada	2,825	71.1
West	437	11.0
British Columbia	255	6.4
Other	111	2.8
Total	3,973	100.0

SOURCE: As in Table 1

Between 1887 and 1922, 71.1 per cent of all initial applicants lived in
Ontario and Quebec (see Table 2). And with society affairs concentrated in
Montreal, non-resident members enjoyed few benefits. Discontent was
strongest in regions furthest from Montreal. Vancouver engineer G.R.G.
Conway, for example, declared that BC members felt that headquarters was
'somewhat out of touch, both geographically and in spirit, with western
ambitions' and noted that western members did not want to form 'a purely

local society for members in the neighborhood of Montreal and Ottawa, living under the influence and fostering care of McGill University.'[15] Maritime engineers were also indifferent to the CSCE. In 1921, for example, less than half of the civil engineers in New Brunswick and Nova Scotia were members.[16] Antipathy towards the CSCE among some Nova Scotia members developed to such an extent that a separate group, the Nova Scotia Society of Engineers, was organized in 1907.[17]

With the possible exception of McGill engineering graduates, young engineers did not join the CSCE until they were well established.[18] Membership conferred few professional advantages, and older members neither encouraged nor aided the professional development of younger members.[19] 'Nobody is ever asked for references from the Canadian Society,' declared a New Brunswick engineer, 'nor is the question raised as to his standing in the Society; indeed, his membership in the body is never considered except in such places as Montreal or Toronto, where the Society is well known.'[20] In view of the intention to make CSCE membership, like ICE membership in Great Britain, the mark of professional distinction, his statement is a strong indictment.

Criticism focused on the Montreal clique. It appeared first in 1908 and later in 1913. These attacks eventually forced concessions, during the Great War, which substantially altered the CSCE's constitutional structure and undermined the Montreal clique's power. Yet it is remarkable that, in spite of these changes, the Montreal clique maintained its power and forestalled change for so long. In large measure, this was a consequence of clever management and pragmatic reforms.

Although the Montreal clique's power ultimately stemmed from inequities in the CSCE's electoral system,[21] the group had other advantages. There was no organized and articulate opposition.[22] In the face of widespread apathy, the clique's benevolent rule was tolerated because it was the only faction capable of governing the organization. Few critics possessed the time or the means to attend the annual meetings, and the Montreal clique adroitly deferred opportunities for criticism to the dying hours of the meetings.[23] As well, younger members were intimidated by the professional stature and corporate rank of clique members, many of whom were either employers or potential employers.[24] The clique, in turn, took advantage of this to deflect criticism.

In its analysis, tactics, and rhetoric, the Montreal clique reflected its corporate background. When criticized, it adopted an uncompromising paternalistic attitude and treated opponents as if they were ill-behaved employees. It diminished criticism by denying the existence of serious trouble and discredited outspoken members by calling them vindictive malcontents.[25] More significant, it turned criticism back on the critics by blaming the membership for the society's shortcomings. With some justification, it argued that some members held unrealistic expectations, that others were ignorant of the society's limited purpose, and that most were apathetic.[26] Taking a narrow view of its constitutional responsibilities, the Montreal clique asserted that its role was strictly administrative; initiative for change must originate from individual members.[27] As Ernest Marceau, the CSCE's first French-Canadian president, explained: 'The Society's usefulness to its members depends upon the usefulness of each individual member to the Society, and that free and liberal interchange of ideas should be encouraged and practised by every member. In this way the Society will be improved, and by keeping this in mind and acting together the standard of the Society will be raised and it will be more able to impress its influence on the larger questions of the times, and compel the respect which such a national body of engineers should command.'[28]

At the same time, other, more constructive measures were taken which helped pacify discontent. The annual meetings were held periodically in major centres outside Montreal in order to encourage greater participation. Prizes for outstanding papers, such as the Gzowski Medal, were awarded for professional excellence. To broaden the professional scope of the society and increase its attractiveness to non-civil engineers, the CSCE, in 1903, formed four sections: electrical, mechanical, mining, and general (i.e. civil). Each section was headed by an appointed officer who presided at meetings held in Montreal. Papers read and discussed at these meetings were published by the society, if approved by a committee on papers. Believing that Canada was not large enough for more than one engineering society, CSCE leaders thought that it was difficult to separate the various branches of engineering and that overlapping and cross-fertilization were the norm among all specialties.[29] The formation of these sections was significant, because it helped prevent the fragmentation of the CSCE into separate specialized societies, as had already occurred in Britain and the United States.

The establishment of branch societies was perhaps the most important pre-war initiative. As CSCE activities were centred in Montreal, non-resident members, unable to attend the annual meetings, had virtually no contact with the society, except through its publications and notices.[30] Although the founding members had foreseen the need for branches and made provision for them in the constitution,[31] none existed prior to 1906. As hostility to Montreal mounted, branches were encouraged in order to counter centralist tendencies and to accommodate regional interests. Also, branches may have been promoted as a means to forestall the growth of separate organizations, such as the Regina Engineering Society and the Nova Scotia Society of Engineers.[32]

A branch was a microcosm of the parent society. An elected executive managed its affairs,[33] and, with a few minor variations, by-laws were the same. Provision for sections was made, and a system of fee rebates from Montreal financed the branches. All CSCE members automatically belonged if they resided within a specified distance of a branch. Normally, any ten corporate members could petition to form a branch, but occasionally branches were organized from a few existing, independent engineering societies. For example, the branches in Halifax (founded 1918) and Peterborough (1919) were outgrowths of the Nova Scotia Society of Engineers and the Peterborough Engineers' Club respectively. CSCE by-laws forbade the society from taking over existing organizations. Thus, existing societies had to disband before a branch could be formed.[34] Although enthusiasts claimed that branches were 'practically independent,'[35] they were, nevertheless, effectively controlled by the CSCE and made to conform to specific objectives.[36] They were constituted strictly as learned societies,[37] and membership did not release engineers from their obligations to the parent society. By 1922, with twenty-two branches, the CSCE had the most distinctive and extensive system of branches of any engineering society in the world.[38]

Generally, branches prospered when they served members' interests. As learned societies, however, they were less successful. They were usually in financial trouble, had difficulty attracting members, especially younger ones, and, like the national society, could not generate enough interest in the reading and discussion of papers.[39] The fate of the Toronto branch, the largest prior to 1911,[40] was typical. Organized in 1890 (largely through the efforts of Alan Macdougall), it was the CSCE's first branch. It lasted barely three years. Toronto members were uninterested and unwilling to support it financially.[41] Similar difficulties occurred after 1906, when the branch was revived and reorganized.[42] Less than 10 per cent of its members attended meetings, and, in 1913, no papers were presented.[43] By contrast, the Toronto Engineers' Club, founded 1899, prospered because, unlike the Toronto branch, it catered to the engineers' business and social requirements.[44] It was not until the Toronto branch combined with other Ontario branches to lobby for restrictive provincial licensing powers that it flourished, but only briefly. The newly formed licensing body soon eclipsed the branch, which had reverted to a learned society. A similar fate awaited the CSCE.

Clever management and pragmatic reforms, however, did not assuage indignation over the CSCE's deficiencies. Moreover, although the society had united engineers, it had failed to develop professional consciousness and to gain public recognition. Engineers were still recognized as individuals, not as a profession.[45] For nearly half a century, engineers had cultivated the trappings of professionalism – schools, societies, and journals – in order to rise above the status of tradesmen. But, by 1914, although engineers believed that they had substantially fostered Canada's material progress, their profession remained unrecognized.[46] The engineer's title was not protected by law (except in Manitoba and Quebec after 1898),[47] and anyone could – and many did – style himself 'engineer,' regardless of qualifications or experience.[48]

Engineers complained that other professionals, particularly lawyers and doctors, commanded undeserved measures of public esteem.[49] They resented even the attention lavished on geologists and envied the higher status enjoyed by engineers in other countries.[50] Although private corporations had begun to recognize engineers by promoting them to managerial positions, governments continued to appoint lawyers to railway commissions and inquiries (largely through party patronage) and excluded engineers from boards of health.[51] Moreover, while engineers played a crucial role at home and abroad during the First World War, they protested that they were not always effectively employed and that they were sometimes passed over in favour of other professionals, usually lawyers, for the command of engineering units.[52] Ignored by the press (except when it sensationalized the slightest controversy arising out of a public works department investigation),[53] engineers also felt that they were only indirectly recorded by historians.[54] An engineer, it was argued, could devote his life to furthering the progress and welfare of the community and never come to public attention, unless he made a mistake. '[The] Quebec Bridge,' commented Walter J. Francis, '[was] more widely known by its failure than it or any other bridge will be in its success.'[55]

Engineers deeply resented their low social status. In their view, their standing was not commensurate with their contribution to society. The First World War acted as a catalyst to this discontent, and engineers became fiercely determined to raise their status. At first, they blamed themselves for their misfortune, but, later, they reflected that their preoccupation with acquiring professional knowledge, to the neglect of social problems, may have been responsible for their low status.

In January 1916, in an attempt to increase the CSCE's prestige and influence, the general membership appointed a twenty-four-man committee on society affairs on an equitable and representative basis. The chairman was H.E.T. Haultain, professor of mining engineering, University of Toronto. This was the most important committee in the CSCE's history. Free of the Montreal clique's influence, it changed the society's thinking, and its recommendations had far-reaching consequences.[56]

Although a strong supporter of the CSCE, the irascible and outspoken Haultain was not a member of the Montreal clique. Like many engineering professors, he was more liberal than most engineers, but he was not a radical. He believed that the CSCE was fundamentally sound[57] and observed that engineers, in sharp contrast to doctors and lawyers, did not have a strong sense of professional identity or, as he put it, a 'tribal soul.'[58] Haultain had astutely identified the major factor inhibiting further professional development and public recognition.

Engineers were not a clearly defined and cohesive group. They were scattered over an immense, sparsely populated frontier and moved nomadically from job to job, absorbed in hectic, demanding, sometimes dangerous work. As such, they were isolated – almost strangers to each other[59] – and professed to have little time for or even interest in professional activities. They were difficult to organize and indifferent to organization. By nature, they were staunch individualists, self-reliant and independently minded. They were ambitious, fiercely competitive, and largely insensitive to the professional welfare and livelihood of fellow engineers. Already fragmented by specialization and torn by the conflicting demands of business and science, they were divided also by a professional class structure, founded on corporate hierarchy. These factors combined to blunt their enthusiasm for professional unity and to arrest the development of a professional identity.

Traditionally, engineers sought public recognition as individuals by building personal reputations. Unlike law and medicine, however, engineering offered little social distinction. Haultain recognized that the CSCE could not raise the engineer's status solely by improving his professional knowledge; only the community could confer higher social status. He argued that engineers had isolated themselves from the community by their preoccupation with the technical aspects of engineering: 'We have segregated ourselves and the great mistake of the engineers is we are paying so much attention to our work, we aren't thinking of anything else. We think in terms of copper and concrete etc instead of thinking in terms of the community. The community is of more importance to us than our profession and our work.'[60] To win public recognition, engineers must be more than technically competent; they must see their work in its context and develop a broad social consciousness. Engineering must become truly altruistic. To this end, Haultain advised engineers to develop 'the tribal instinct'[61] and seek recognition as a group through public service. Unless they changed their attitude and broadened their outlook, they would forever be regarded as tradesmen, not professionals. 'If we are going to bow down to wood and stone, concrete and copper,' Haultain warned, 'that is all we will amount to ... We will remain hewers of wood and drawers of water.'[62]

Haultain persuaded his colleagues that others would recognize the profession only when they served the public. Claims for recognition must be based on service rendered. A committee of the Toronto branch later explained:

The status of engineering can be improved, mainly by increasing its usefulness to humanity. It must be the aim of the engineer, therefore, to serve and guide the people and cultivate healthy, vigorous, and pronounced public opinion. It is coming to be realized more and more that engineers owe it to themselves and to the country alike to accept their duties as citizens of the community in which they live, and that they should use every effort to exert influence in the legislation of the country and the administration of public affairs wherever engineering principles or practices are involved.[63]

Thus public service, not technical excellence, was the crucial factor in the engineer's pursuit of greater social recognition. 'If we do not as a body serve the public,' commented R.O. Wynne-Roberts, 'we cannot legitimately expect its high esteem.'[64]

This dramatic shift in opinion within the CSCE may have been inspired partly by a 'revolt' of 'progressive' American engineers aiming to unite their profession and to use it as an instrument of social reform.[65] Although Canadian engineers were aware of this development, they were inspired more by opportunism than by altruism. They realized that they had received more public notice for their war service than for fifty years of professional development and assumed that economic benefits would accompany recognition. Technical excellence was of course essential, but public service was more rewarding. Engineers easily accepted this notion, since it was ideologically consistent with, and complementary to, their technocratic views. It seemed reasonable to them that the 'most valuable citizens in the community,'[66] those who built the modern world, should also solve modern social problems.

For the most part, the new principle of public service was derived from the older consultative professions and applied to a small minority of independent consulting engineers. Nevertheless, it was another major shift away from the CSCE's concern with educational matters. To this extent, it ran directly counter to the Montreal clique's conception of the CSCE as a learned society and represented a fundamental, almost revolutionary change in the society's outlook.[67]

On 30 October 1917, the CSCE's committee on society affairs submitted its recommendations to council, which later approved them and sent a letter ballot to members. The most important recommendations were complete revision of the by-laws, appointment of a full-time secretary, establishment of a monthly journal, and a change in the society's name.

The new by-laws introduced sweeping changes that not only redefined the society's objectives but fundamentally altered power relations within the CSCE. The society's original object was educational: 'To facilitate the acquirement and interchange of professional knowledge among its members and to encourage original investigation.' This was retained, but important new objects were added. The society would 'promote [members'] professional interests ... develop and maintain high standards in the engineering profession,' and, most significant, 'enhance the usefulness of the profession to the public.'[68] This last item would be implemented by the branches.

The committee believed that the branches were the most important factor in the CSCE's development.[69] They represented the society locally and were its 'sentinels,'[70] or the vital link between the profession and the public, as well as the means to serve the public. Originally, branch activities were limited, but by 1922 they were the most important centres of professional development.[71] While council set broad policy guide-lines, the branches were, according to Fraser S. Keith, 'the active energizing agents.'[72] The new by-laws increased local autonomy, accelerating decentralization – a trend initiated in 1908.[73] This was ironic, since the branches were originally intended to accommodate regionalist sentiment.

The undemocratic nature of the CSCE's electoral system continually prompted demands for reform. Prior to 1918, by-laws governing the election of the nominating committee and councillors encouraged disproportionate representation from Montreal-area engineers.[74] After 1918, under the new by-laws, electoral power was more equitably distributed. Montreal was guaranteed only two nominating committee members and two councillors. The other nominating committee members were elected mainly by the branches,[75] and the remaining councillors were nominated from eight 'electoral districts,' spread evenly across Canada. Although Montreal continued to have considerable influence, the new by-laws effectively broke the back of the Montreal clique and shifted power to younger, more aggressive engineers outside Montreal.

As early as 1904, Professor McLeod had called attention to his increasing work-load and recommended appointment of a full-time secretary.[76] Although few were openly critical of McLeod's performance,[77] it was generally accepted that the society urgently needed a full-time secretary. The Montreal clique concurred, but temporized, arguing that a qualified full-time secretary was difficult to find and beyond the society's means.[78] Nevertheless, in 1917, after McLeod's death, Fraser S. Keith, a thirty-nine-year-old McGill honours graduate in electrical engineering, with a career background in manufacturing and technical journalism,[79] became the CSCE's first full-time secretary. Keith was an important factor in the CSCE's transformation. He was energetic, articulate, and aggressive and a strong believer in raising the engineer's status through public service. He represented the younger generation of engineers which was impatient for improved status. Although the secretary's power had been reduced (he could no longer vote on council), Keith easily compensated by enthusiastically preaching the new orthodoxy of public service on frequent speaking tours to the branches and through the editorial columns of the society's new journal.

Until 1918 the CSCE did not have its own journal. Professional papers, together with proceedings, were published twice yearly in the society's *Transactions*. Occasionally, outstanding papers on railway nationalization, wartime munitions production, or the Quebec Bridge, for example, were published as monographs.[80] Before 1918, Canada's leading engineering periodical was the *Canadian Engineer*, published by Biggar-Samuel and later by the Monetary Times organization.[81] The *Canadian Engineer* was an independent, profit-making technical newspaper, comparable to the American *Engineering News-Record*, or even the British *Engineer*. But it was dissimilar to Canada's *Contract Record* and *Electrical News*: the former was concerned mainly with business and construction, while the latter represented the electrical industry. The *Canadian Engineer* was interested in civil, especially municipal, engineering and published a wide range of trade and professional news of interest to civil engineers and contractors. It had friendly relations with the CSCE[82] and served as a kind of unofficial surrogate journal, sympathizing with the CSCE's objectives and publishing its notices regularly.

By 1918, amid proposals in council to take over the *Canadian Engineer* as the society's official organ,[83] the CSCE founded its own periodical, the *Engineering Journal*. The new periodical provided the CSCE with the means to unite the profession and create a professional identity. It kept members informed of society business on a monthly basis, raised important professional issues, encouraged members to participate with written submissions, and published professional papers and practical information.[84] Under Keith's capable editorship, it became the leading engineering journal in Canada.

Changing the CSCE's name was undoubtedly the committee's most controversial recommendation. The CSCE, like the ICE and the ASCE, had been organized to include all branches of engineering. When the word 'civil' was adopted, it still had its original meaning – non-military – and mining, mechanical, electrical, and chemical engineering had not become distinct specialties.[85] Many members felt that the society's name was a misnomer, that it narrowed the society's scope and deterred many non-civil engineers from joining,[86] a condition inconsistent with the society's broadened outlook and its desire to consolidate the profession. Although the majority of members were civil engineers, they wanted to modernize the name by dropping the word 'civil.' This represented a significant change of opinion within the CSCE. Earlier, in 1903, a committee appointed to investigate changing the society's name recommended against any alteration, because the majority of members responding to its circular had been opposed.[87]

In examining this question, the committee on society affairs was motivated by the desire to create a single strong society, embracing all qualified engineers in Canada. In its view:

The engineering field in Canada is not and will not be for many years to come broad enough to support more than one large and successful professional association. It appears to us that an association embracing all classes of Canadian engineers would have a much wider and stronger influence in Canada than an association composed of Civil engineers with a small number of mechanical, mining, electrical or other engineers, and which would no doubt have in competition with it branches of other societies whose interests would naturally lie outside the interests of this Society.[88]

While many committee members at first opposed changing the name, they were persuaded that it was an impediment to the society's progress. Accordingly, they proposed what they considered a more dignified and professional name, acceptable to all engineers – The Engineering Institute Of Canada (EIC).[89] Following council's approval, a letter ballot was issued to members, along with a circular outlining the merits and demerits of the proposal. The membership unanimously endorsed the name change at the annual meeting in January 1918, and a special bill, amending the CSCE's charter, was passed by Parliament and was given royal assent on 25 April 1918.[90]

The change of name was more than a symbolic gesture. It had important implications. To the *Contract Record*, it signified 'an entire revision of character,'[91] and for H.H. Vaughan, the EIC's first president, it was an 'attempt to unite all engineers in Canada' with the EIC.[92] Mining engineers, however, were less impressed. The *Canadian Mining Journal*, for example, believed that the new name was imprecise and regressive,[93] and F.W. Gray, editor for the Mining Society of Nova Scotia, called the idea 'slightly grandiose and impractical.'[94] To other mining engineers, the name change concealed sinister and ulterior motives. Quoting the circular from the committee on society affairs, the CMI's *Monthly Bulletin* contended that the EIC's real intention was to become the sole engineering society in Canada, at the expense of the CMI.[95] According to H. Mortimer-Lamb, the name change revived an old plot to secure legislation compelling all engineers to belong to the EIC in order to practise.[96]

While mining engineers were ultimately proved correct in maintaining that the name change would lead to legislation restricting practice, that was not then official EIC policy. The committee on society affairs refused to deal with the issue,[97] and council, preoccupied with digesting the new organizational changes, had not yet committed itself to political action. The EIC, much to the CMI's annoyance, regarded the mining society as a trade body and did not consider it detrimental if the CMI's professional members also became EIC members.[98] Several prominent CMI members, notably Haultain, were members of both societies.

Although the EIC did not intend to take over the CMI, it had no reservations about absorbing branches of US engineering societies located in Toronto. The American Institute of Electrical Engineers (AIEE) had established a branch in Toronto before 1914. In 1917 a group of Canadian mechanical engineers went to New York to arrange for a Toronto branch of the American Society of Mechanical Engineers (ASME). No ASCE branch was organized in Canada. By 1918, the AIEE's New York office had received more membership applications from Toronto than anywhere else in North America, and the ASME attempted to take over the EIC's mechanical engineering sections.[99] These developments alarmed the EIC. Adhering to the recommendations of the committee on society affairs, it was determined to represent all engineers and establish itself as the only national society in Canada. The EIC considered the expansion of the American branches an unwarranted foreign intrusion into Canadian engineering affairs – a challenge to its prerogatives.

President Vaughan declared that, while it was acceptable for Canadian electrical and mechanical engineers to belong to foreign societies for legitimate professional reasons, it was their 'duty' to join first the national society of the country in which they earned their living. Foreign society membership, he maintained, should be complementary to, not a substitute for, Canadian membership. It should follow rather than precede EIC membership.[100] Using his influence as a former ASME vice-president, Vaughan, at a meeting in New York, secured a special agreement from the secretaries of the major American engineering societies, not to expand in Canada and to encourage their Canadian members to join the EIC. This agreement effectively stopped the expansion of American societies in Canada and formed the basis of a continuing 'understanding' between Canadian and American engineers.[101]

Having checked the spread of the American branches, the EIC then attempted to absorb them. Declaring that one large society could serve engineers better than several smaller ones, EIC officers tried to persuade ASME and AIEE members in Canada to form mechanical or electrical sections within EIC branches or to join an EIC branch as special 'affiliate' members.[102] Unfortunately, the American branches did not have the constitutional authority to affiliate with EIC branches, and most of their members preferred to retain their ASME or AIEE memberships, in order to keep informed of the latest American practices. Even the EIC admitted that it was not a substitute for specialized societies like the AIEE.[103] Many ASME and AIEE members in Canada probably feared the loss of their identity in a larger, predominantly civil engineering society.[104] Nevertheless, while the EIC did not absorb the American branches, it did contain them and reserved for itself the distinction of being a single national society with the potential to represent all fields of engineering. British and American engineers, the EIC boasted, had not achieved this. Ironically, in 1918, the EIC was in peril of being absorbed by the powerful American parent societies, centred in New York. These organizations were anxious to unite the profession and repeatedly attempted to involve the EIC in various schemes of international affiliation. The EIC, however, maintained its independence by scrupulously cultivating friendly relations with the Americans, while politely declining to join organizations such as the Engineering Council and, later, the Federated American Engineering Societies.[105]

Towards the end of the war, EIC members began to experience greater self-confidence and a heightened sense of purpose. According to Fraser S. Keith, engineers had entered a new era. 'The star of the engineering profession has risen above the horizon,' he declared; 'it is well started on its upward path of glory and eminence.'[106] Society was awakening to the engineer's potential. It was time for engineers to assert themselves and to assume their rightful place by playing an important social role with their unique expertise. The key was professional unity and collective action. The name change would broaden the new institute's professional appeal, build a strong, united body, and create a 'tribal soul.' While the dramatic changes initiated by the committee on society affairs stopped short of political action, that group had articulated the philosophical principles and laid the institutional foundations for more radical changes. Meanwhile, the EIC began to develop other strategies to raise the engineer's status by increasing public awareness of his contribution to society.

7

'The proper kind of publicity'

The quest for public recognition

Following the momentous 1917 report of the committee on society affairs, the EIC adopted limited social goals and tried to raise the profession's status through public service. This policy was attempted without government assistance and paralleled similar action by British and American engineering societies. The EIC hoped that public service would not only enhance its prestige but also help to solve engineers' economic problems and equip' them with an élite social role.

By 1914, many Canadian engineering leaders and thinkers had begun to realize that their lack of status arose, in part, from their failure to communicate with the public.[1] They believed that this stemmed from their inability to express themselves, as well as their aversion to publicity. 'Being engineers,' Haultain remarked, 'we are very poor hands at window dressing or publicity.'[2] While some engineers, such as T.C. Keefer, knew the value of publicity and were accomplished propagandists, others, particularly older engineers, were suspicious and distrusted the press.[3] They believed that it was morally suspect, the device of demagogues and radicals. They were certain that it ignored their achievements yet sensationalized the slightest mistake or controversy surrounding government engineering. In their view, this bias often distorted public perception of their work and sometimes ruined professional reputations.[4] Outstanding work, they contended, required no publicity.

In spite of this sentiment, some engineers believed that publicity could be beneficial. For Haultain, 'the proper kind of publicity,'[5] or balanced, unsensational press reports, could educate the public to the social importance of engineering and raise the practitioner's status. 'Engineering,' remarked the *Canadian Engineer*, 'is scarcely likely to command the place in the public esteem which its importance warrants until the public is brought to realize the far-reaching effect of the services rendered by technical men.'[6] Just as other professions, such as law, had effectively used publicity to increase their prestige, many engineers argued that they must use their superior powers of reasoning and learn to communicate with laymen.[7] Following the war, the EIC urged its members to publicize their work, in order to stimulate popular interest. They were encouraged, as private individuals, to supply newspaper and magazine editors with interesting popular articles and editorial material on engineering, in addition to giving public lectures.[8] They were also advised to seek public office and to join local business and service organizations as a means of presenting the engineering viewpoint.[9]

The resolve to stimulate popular interest was not a cynical attempt to manipulate public opinion. Engineers saw their task as public education, not propaganda. Viewing publicity from a narrow, élitist perspective, they believed that only engineers were capable of understanding and explaining technology.[10] They naively assumed that, once the public was credibly informed about their achievements, they would enjoy greater prestige.

Publicity, however, was only an essential first step to higher status; public service was the primary means. Enhancing the engineer's prestige through public service had become a well-established practice before the committee on society affairs recommended it as official policy in 1917.

During the First World War, one important public service initiative was to promote the need for industrial efficiency through research. Warning of the danger of German economic domination after the war, the CSCE stressed industrial research. Before the war, it argued, Germany aggressively established many science-based industries through the clever use of synthetics. These industries quickly became monopolies and left Britain and its allies dependent on certain German chemical, electrical, and glassware commodities.[11] As Germany's military subjugation would not necessarily destroy its formidable industrial potential, engineers predicted that a fierce economic struggle would follow the war. 'The present war,' asserted the Contract Record in 1916, 'is a mighty effort by Germany to gain not only a military, but also a commercial supremacy. Tomorrow the military struggle will end and then the real and permanent business of the nations will begin – industrial war.'[12]

The post-war struggle for commercial supremacy would be determined by industrial efficiency. The key to efficiency was research – Germany had proved that.[13] Canadian industry, engineers contended, was uncoordinated and inefficient. Little research was done[14] because conservative-minded manufacturers relied on tariffs and patent laws, instead of science, for industrial development.[15] Foreign competitors were fully committed to state-assisted industrial research.[16] The United States had not only established a Naval Consulting Board but was acquiring commercially useful German technology by confiscating German patents and industrial assets in the United States.[17] If Canada hoped to compete after the war and to take advantage of the wartime isolation of Germany, science, industry, and government must co-operate. Canada had no alternative.

As universities were viewed primarily as teaching institutions and industry was considered unwilling or unable to conduct research, the EIC concentrated its efforts on persuading the Dominion government to promote research. It recognized that the government was the only organization with the means to do so. Since 1894, the CSCE had urged Ottawa to establish laboratories to test Canadian building materials. This, it argued, would be in the public interest and benefit the government – the largest consumer of structural materials. Engineering professors, many of whom did private consulting work, would have benefited if the government had accepted the society's recommendations to subsidize university engineering laboratories, pending the construction of a national testing facility. The government was generally sympathetic, but the defeat of Laurier's Liberals in 1911 and the outbreak of war delayed implementation.[18] In the summer of 1916, five prominent CSCE members revived the idea and presented to Sir Robert Borden a memorandum on national industrial development that outlined the need for planned industrial development and recommended establishment of a national testing laboratory.[19] This initiative was followed by a meeting with Sir George Foster, minister of trade and commerce and acting prime minister.[20]

In late 1916, as the voluntary and private nature of Canada's war mobilization gave way, under the stress of war, to coercion and the intervention of the state in nearly every aspect of public and private life,[21] the government created a cabinet committee on industrial research. On 6 June 1916, in response to pressure from engineers, scientists, and some industrialists, a subcommittee of the privy council on scientific and industrial research was appointed by order-in-council, with provision for an advisory council. The members of the Honorary Advisory Council for Scientific and Industrial Research – including prominent engineers and scientists and some businessmen – were appointed on 29 November 1916[22] and given authority to study and co-ordinate research in Canada.[23]

The EIC's advocacy of industrial research was typical of its approach to public service; it was inclined to be more opportunistic than altruistic. In spite of genuine concern for industrial efficiency, the EIC was interested primarily in publicizing the need for industrial research for its prestige value to engineers. It was only partially committed to the idea and did comparatively little to advance the cause. Its arguments were superficial and unoriginal, mostly borrowed from British and Canadian scientists.[24] Apart from some representations to government, it followed the lead set by scientists – the real champions of industrial research.

By 1914, for example, the Royal Canadian Institute (RCI), Canada's oldest surviving scientific society,[25] founded a Bureau of Scientific and Industrial Research as a private research agency. Its purpose was to apply science to industry by means of 'Industrial Fellowships,'[26] modelled after the highly successful system of a Canadian, Dr Robert Kennedy Duncan, at the University of Kansas and the Mellon Institute of Industrial Research.[27] By 1916, senior RCI officers had assumed the leadership of the Honorary Advisory Council (later the National Research Council) to carry forward the bureau's work as a public enterprise.[28] At this point, the CSCE pledged its support,[29] while it continued to espouse the need for research as its own cause, in order to improve the CSCE's status. Referring to the memorandum on national industrial development, for example, Fraser S. Keith informed members that the society 'had an opportunity for publicity for the Society that does not often occur' and urged members to make it widely known.[30]

While engineers were as public spirited as most Canadians, when confronted with more immediate economic problems, they tempered their altruism with pragmatism. By 1918, civil engineers were in the midst of a developing crisis. Before the war, theirs was the dominant form of engineering in Canada; but, after the completion of major railway and public works, between 1908 and 1916, it was on the decline.[31] With the rise of new science-based industries during the war, electrical, chemical, and mechanical engineering displaced civil. By 1921, civil engineers comprised only 43 per cent of the professional engineers in Canada. By 1931, their ranks had declined to 38.4 per cent; by 1941, to 22.2 per cent.[32] These changes were soon reflected in course enrolments in the engineering schools. By 1922, for example, the civil engineering course at the Faculty of Applied Science and Engineering, University of Toronto, ranked fourth in number of students (130), behind electrical, chemical, and mechanical (totalling 625).[33]

Although employment prospects for industrial engineers were good, the future looked bleak for civils. The field was already overcrowded, and demand was decreasing while supply, in proportion to available jobs, was increasing. Wartime retrenchment by public works departments had already caused widespread unemployment. As well, the influx of nearly one thousand returned soldiers, combined with other engineers from domestic war-related engineering work, exacerbated the problem and generated anxiety among returning soldiers. 'You cannot realize the state of mind that men will get into,' Col. A. McPhail wrote in 1919 to H.H. Vaughan, president of the EIC, 'when they are sitting down here in France, waiting for orders to return to Canada ... without any information or prospects for the future.'[34] Towards the end of the war, the EIC attempted to relieve some of these anxieties.

As early as 1898, the CSCE had kept a register of engineers seeking employment. But it was not until 1918 that the EIC established a full-fledged employment bureau that served as a kind of 'clearing-house' for engineers and employers.[35] This development was welcomed by CSCE members. One Montreal engineer, for example, complained that he had to apply to Cleveland for a job located four blocks from where he lived.[36] The employment bureau operated efficiently through the *Engineering Journal* and branch secretaries and benefited primarily younger engineers. But, in spite of its popularity, it depended ultimately on the EIC's senior employing engineers.[37]

Engineers were often forced to use other methods to find jobs, sometimes by reviving public works–related activities, curtailed by the war and by the pre-war depression. One example was town planning. After engineers had overcome their suspicions that town planners were trying to monopolize the field at their expense, they became enthusiastic town planning supporters.[38] The Toronto branch became one of the most active town planning agencies in Canada, and, in 1919, engineers joined forces with architects and surveyors to found the Town Planning Institute of Canada. In these undertakings, engineers, like surveyors, were motivated primarily by the prospects of new employment opportunities.[39]

Similarly, the CSCE's promotion of industrial research was also partly an attempt to create professional employment. While supplying costly technical information to consulting engineers who could not afford laboratories, research facilities would provide regular work for some engineers. The same motives also prompted Canadian scientists to take up industrial research.

Few opportunities existed in Canada for ambitious young scientists. Some were underemployed; many were forced to seek work in the United States. Scientists, like J.C. McLennan, professor of physics, University of Toronto, chided apathetic manufacturers for not recognizing how science could improve productivity and repeatedly warned that Canadian-trained scientists, forced to work in the United States, were, in effect, strengthening competitive foreign industries at Canada's expense. They argued that

Canada could conserve its scientific talent only by establishing attractive career opportunities. Forced emigration aroused the RCI's nationalist indignation. As the University of Toronto had earlier established a PhD science program to help stem the flow of students to American graduate schools,[41] the RCI hoped that the Bureau of Scientific and Industrial Research would help to curb the loss of Canadian scientists to US research laboratories. By combining the resources of industry and learning under a centralized bureaucracy of experts, the RCI not only planned to promote industrial efficiency but also hoped to foster career opportunities for young scientists and engineers. 'The Bureau,' declared its secretary-treasurer, F.M. Turner, an industrial chemist, 'exists solely to try to get Canadian industrialists to avail themselves to a larger extent than they have in the past of the chemical and engineering talent we are developing in our universities.'[42]

The CSCE also attempted to create work by restricting competition and securing for its members exclusive access to all public works engineering in provincial and, particularly, Dominion governments. This was justified, usually, on the pretext of protecting the public. Unlike non-professionals and special interest groups, engineers could rationalize their self-interest in terms of defending the public interest.[43]

After the war, with the completion of major railway lines and the growing popularity of the automobile, road building became the most important public work in Canada. Although this was an excellent field for former railway engineers, much construction was handled by non-professionals or local men of influence, especially in eastern Canadian rural areas. Engineers argued that roads should be built scientifically by experts in order to prevent waste.[44] W.A. McLean, Ontario's deputy minister of highways and an EIC member, shared this view. Noting that 'narrow motives' might be imputed for this suggestion, he asserted that employing engineers would be in the public interest, 'a matter of public economy and efficiency.'[45] Other important EIC members, such as A.W. Campbell, Dominion highway commissioner, and George Hogarth, chief engineer, Ontario Department of Highways, were also naturally disposed to this idea. Thus, while the CSCE promoted scientific road construction by qualified engineers as a public service and developed road specifications and standards, its more influential members were endeavouring to create work by eliminating competition from rival non-professionals.[46]

Earlier, the CSCE also tried to create work in the Dominion government by restricting all aspects of government engineering to professionally qualified engineers – CSCE members. Between 1901 and 1918, the CSCE vigorously lobbied the government to raise the professional standards of its engineers by bringing them under the Civil Service Act. Ottawa should eliminate patronage by introducing the merit system and then organize a National Engineering Service, similar to the model Indian and Australian ones,[47] as a means of establishing high professional standards. Publicly, the CSCE argued that this would eliminate waste and save taxes. Observing that several government departments had their own independent engineering sections, the CSCE also maintained that the appointment of an all-engineer Board of Engineering Control, to advise the government on public works policy, would improve efficiency by co-ordinating work and eliminating overlapping and duplication.[48] Privately, engineers understood that this body would, in effect, give them control of government engineering. While the Laurier government was sympathetic, its defeat in 1911, and later the outbreak of war, blocked reforms. It was not until the end of the war that the Borden government, acting on a policy of civil service reform, made improvements.[49] At this point, the EIC focused its attention on the Public Service Commission and campaigned steadily for proper job classification and higher salaries.

In the mean time, the CSCE insisted that engineers should approve plans for public works[50] and be appointed to boards of health and railway commissions. These bodies, it contended, dealt with technical, as well as medical and legal problems.[51] It was necessary to protect the public from incompetent political appointees.[52] If high standards were not maintained, S.G. Porter, secretary-treasurer of the Calgary branch, warned, 'the interest of the public and the prestige of the profession [would] suffer.'[53] By 1917, the CSCE went so far as to question if it should press for amendments to existing legislation, in order to have engineers appointed to certain boards and commissions when, as one report stated, 'it feels that these amendments are for the general welfare of the community.'[54] The EIC was partially successful. An amendment to the Ontario Highway Improvement Act, for example, recognized EIC professional standards by stipulating that engineers, appointed under its provisions, be EIC members. Four engineers were appointed to the Lake of the Woods Control Board, and the wartime Fuel-Power Board consisted almost entirely of well-known EIC members.[55] But, aside from gaining these minor concessions,[56] the significance of the EIC's attempt to restrict competition lay in what that scheme revealed about its ambitions.

Restricting all aspects of government engineering to EIC members would eliminate competition from non-professionals and unqualified political appointees and, to a lesser extent, doctors and lawyers who dominated boards of health and railway commissions.[57] Thus, EIC members would monopolize government engineering without licensing. In turn, this would not only create work and upgrade the engineer's standing but would also improve conditions generally by setting the standard for other employers.[58] Moreover, the centralization of engineers from various departments, under a National Engineering Service, and the establishment of a Board of Engineering Control would have given engineers influence, perhaps even some political influence. Ultimately, however, these schemes revealed engineers' longing for a more orderly, rational, and bureaucratically structured environment, controlled by technicians. Engineers longed to function autonomously and advance by recognized stages, without competition or political interference, to assume eventually more prestigious positions of social leadership.

Protecting the public interest had other important advantages. It significantly raised the status of engineers and provided them with an élite social role. The CSCE's enthusiasm for industrial research was partly an outgrowth of the war effort.[59] Taking to heart David Lloyd George's 1915 remark that the war was a terrific contest between engineers of the warring nations,[60] engineers took up arms with patriotic zeal and soon earned distinction in rank and decoration. The CSCE was extremely proud of the fact that a third of its members (960 men, 943 of whom were officers before the end of the war) were on active service. These men were awarded with 116 decorations – including two Victoria Crosses – and, remarkably, suffered only seventy-five dead.[61] The war gave engineers an unprecedented opportunity to demonstrate their usefulness, not only at the front, providing fortifications and logistical support, but also at home, producing munitions and maintaining essential services. It brought them to public attention. For the first time in the history of the profession, they received the recognition they thought they deserved.[62]

The prospect of peace, however, threatened to deprive engineers of the source of their prominence. Their advocacy of industrial research, in many respects, was a means of extending the war effort into peace-time by postulating the threat of 'industrial war.' Engineers could then continue to play a socially useful role, since only they could apply science to industry and make science commercially viable.[63] As industrial research was the key to the emerging science-based chemical and electrical industries, engineers would become essential to national industrial progress and, ultimately, the national interest. Like Taylorites installing scientific management in American industry, engineers could attain independence, security, and even power by performing an essential service.[64] Acting as independent professionals, without share capital or managerial prerogatives, they could circumvent the traditional management structures and emerge near the top of industry, commanding authority and fees sufficient to preserve their middle-class status. By expanding the realm of their professionalism, as industry grew, they could even attempt to establish hegemony over industry.

Similarly, the CSCE's research on standardization[65] also offered engineers the same advantages. Before the First World War, most of the society's research was devoted to preparing specifications and standards. No other area of study had such a direct and crucial effect on engineering practice and the economy. By 1914, the CSCE had already printed and distributed various construction specifications, and by 1918 the EIC was participating in national and international organizations to standardize industrial components.[66] Much of this work was taken over and institutionalized by the Canadian Engineering Standards Association (later the Canadian Standards Association – CSA).[67] Several prominent EIC members were CSA directors.

EIC members undoubtedly recognized that the demand for engineers in an industrial economy depended on their expert services, which, in turn, rested on their exclusive possession of esoteric technical knowledge. It was essential for engineers to increase their knowledge through research, in order to enhance their usefulness to industry. Although EIC research on standardization was designed to improve engineering practice, it also gave engineers a competitive advantage in the market-place over non-engineers, since only engineers could facilitate standardization.[68] Because they had a monopoly of technical knowledge and expertise essential to industry, standardization, like industrial research, helped engineers to gain an élite role in a rapidly expanding industrial economy, especially when engineering standardization became the key to large-scale corporate consolidation.

But, as engineers contemplated their extraordinary potential in industry, their expectations were more realistic and pragmatic. The majority of CSCE members were civil, not industrial engineers. This fact precluded their participation in industrial research, except as publicists and promoters. Moreover, since the government was the only organization capable of conducting research, engineers saw themselves probably more in a bureaucratic context, with executive responsibility. Significantly, the memorandum on national industrial development recommended the appointment of an independent, non-partisan board of consulting engineers, consisting of two representatives from each branch of engineering, presumably nominated by the CSCE. According to the memorandum, the board's members would act 'as consulting engineers to the Dominion Government represented by the Prime Minister, independent of any department of the Government yet available through the Prime Minister to all, in precisely the same way that the general manager of a large corporation has consulting engineers at his call, not on his staff but available to take up independently of the working organization all such technical or economic problems as he may desire to have solved.'[69] Board members would act at the pleasure of the government. The choice of their replacement, however, would be at the discretion of the nominating engineering society.[70]

This plan was a bold, even presumptuous idea, which would have given non-elected technicians near-ministerial authority without electoral sanction or bureaucratic restraint. However, it revealed the kind of élite social role that engineers wanted to play. This was more clearly demonstrated, on a practical level, by the CSCE's efforts to assist city governments. Engineers supported urban reform and town planning, volunteered advice on special engineering problems,[71] and were of service in emergencies. During the Winnipeg General Strike of 1919, for example, they kept public utilities in operation and, later, performed a similar service in Montreal by operating the city waterworks with the help of 150 skilled tradesmen, drawn from local engineering firms.[72] But, looking at all its efforts to assist municipalities, the CSCE regarded two incidents as most significant.[73]

In July 1915, the Montreal members of the CSCE's council, with the support of the Montreal Board of Trade, urged the city to appoint an independent board of engineers to investigate a proposed aqueduct hydroelectric power scheme.[74] They were concerned because no engineer of standing had studied the entire project and contended that it would be economical neither in construction nor in maintenance. These misgivings were confirmed later by a comprehensive report published in the *Canadian Engineer*.[75] Caught up in a heated public ownership debate during an election year, city authorities at first adamantly refused to appoint investigators, but later, after the engineers' repeated urgings, they consented to the preparation of a gratuitous report.[76] The investigating committee, composed of seven of Montreal's most prominent engineers, acting as independent ratepayers, recommended immediate abandonment of the project in order to save money (and stressed the advantages of private ownership).[77] Unfortunately, this report did not impress city politicians.

Engineers had more success in Calgary. In 1915, the City Engineer's Department was sharply criticized by an alderman (the former city waterworks engineer, dismissed after his department was merged with the Engineer's Department) over the construction of a large, reinforced-concrete arch bridge over the Bow River at Centre Street. Fearing injury to the department, as well as to the prestige of the profession, if the attacks continued, the Calgary branch of the CSCE offered to make an impartial investigation. The city accepted. A three-man investigating committee, after a public hearing, concluded that there were no grounds for the charges. The city gratefully adopted the report. This ended the controversy and restored public confidence in the bridge and the City Engineer's Department.[78]

Although these incidents were unspectacular, they had special significance for engineers. They suggested an ideal role as independent consultants, possibly with some political influence. This would give them new prestige and authority from which they could aspire to social leadership.

Independent professional investigations revived the pre-war idea of expert commissions,[79] which had important advantages. Since engineers functioned as private citizens, the CSCE could avoid any appearance of being a special-interest pressure group, which would have compromised its members as impartial experts. Moreover, commissions gave engineers some immunity from political interference. Investigations were objective tribunals. Through rational and systematic analysis, engineers could publicly expose what they regarded as the partisan and political nature of attacks upon engineer-officials. They served as a kind of deterrent. Commenting on the Centre Street bridge controversy, Sam G. Porter, secretary-treasurer of the Calgary branch of the CSCE, maintained that members had performed a valuable public service by establishing the precedent that 'charges reflecting upon the ability of engineers in public office would have to pass the investigation of the local profession, that a great deal of unjust criticism would be avoided and the public relieved of a large amount of unnecessary worry.'[80]

Commissions also gave engineers the opportunity to mould public opinion. They enabled them to alter the context and premisses of public controversy by reducing it to its technical and economic elements, in order to appeal directly to the public, usually on the grounds of cost and efficiency. At the same time, while cloaking their biases in a scientific mystique, investigations gave many prominent engineers with close links to business – such as two CSCE past presidents, W. McLea Walbank, managing director of the Montreal Light, Heat and Power Company, and W.F. Tye, formerly chief engineer, CPR – a forum to expound their views. Predisposed to private ownership of municipal utilities (an outgrowth of their pro-business orientation),[81] they could, for example, transform the Montreal debate on public ownership from the alleged conspiracy of a private power interest foreseen by one city controller[82] to an indictment of municipal technical and financial mismanagement. Of greater importance, investigations enabled engineers to avoid the political process and play a dramatic part in public affairs. This enhanced their prestige and professionalism.

Referring to the Montreal and Calgary incidents, Secretary McLeod advised members that similar actions, 'judiciously taken,' would not only discharge their civic responsibility but also 'eventually increase the prestige and public appreciation of the profession.'[83] Such actions would bring engineers public attention. It would provide a base upon which to build their influence, in order to persuade the public how much society needed them. Trusting that the public would confer power and status in recognition of their importance, engineers could then assume more influential roles of social leadership.

Public service was a pragmatic response to the engineer's predicament – lack of status and jobs. But engineers were not motivated entirely by self-interest. Public service was also ideologically consistent with their technocratic idealism. Only qualified experts, for example, should undertake industrial research. Prestige and employment, engineers assumed, were merely just rewards for their social contribution. Ultimately, however, the EIC's attempt to improve its status by identifying the engineer's expertise with the public interest was only a qualified success. Public service undoubtedly increased the profession's prestige but did not materially improve the condition of the mass of ordinary, salaried engineers. Only élite consultants benefited directly from prestigious government appointments. As a learned society committed to limited social goals, the EIC could not solve the broader social and economic problems affecting the majority of its members. After the war, when confronted with more vexatious problems, these members would demand more pragmatic solutions.

8

Contemplating the 'unthinkable'

The EIC and unionism

In the years immediately following the First World War, engineers became alarmed about inadequate salaries. Inflation had seriously eroded their income and threatened their status. Unable to obtain assistance from the EIC, as individuals, they were forced to consider collective action.

'At best,' complained one engineer, 'engineering is a poorly paid occupation.'[1] This view was widely held. Opinions varied about why engineers were underpaid. Some believed that overcrowding and competition from incompetents and non-professionals tended to lower income. Others contended that engineers were simply too busy to secure better pay. Still others held that, unlike doctors and lawyers, engineers were unable to enforce standard fee tariffs and prevent unethical competitive practices.[2] Nevertheless all agreed on one point: inflation had significantly reduced their income.[3] Wartime inflation persisted after the Armistice. In June 1920, the Canadian cost of living index peaked at 201 (1913 = 100). Over a year later, in September 1921, while the index had fallen slowly to 162, it was still equal to the December 1918 level.[4] This substantially reduced purchasing power and forced some engineers to draw on savings.[5]

While organized labour received large wage increases during the war to keep ahead of inflation, engineers protested that their salaries had not improved. They claimed that they were paid little more, perhaps less, than tradesmen.[6] 'The average wage of the Canadian engineer,' observed a government engineer, 'is hardly more than the wage paid the most ordinary and uneducated class of mechanic or make-believe tradesman in practically all parts of the country.'[7] Government employment advertisements reinforced this belief. In a notorious 1918 *Canada Gazette* advertisement, cited by many as representative, a technical clerk with a degree in applied science, mathematics, or physics was offered an annual salary of $1,300. In the same issue, draughtsmen were offered $1,500, a law clerk $2,100, and a moving picture cameraman $2,400.[8]

For over half a century, engineers had struggled to rise above the status of tradesmen. Earning little more than mechanics and clerks had symbolic significance; it called into question their social progress. Most engineers believed that they were entitled to higher salaries because of their qualifications and responsibility.

Although many engineers thought they earned less than tradesmen, they actually earned substantially more. Between 1911 and 1921, electricians and plumbers, while they increased their earnings 70.3 per cent and 55.4 per cent respectively,[9] still earned less than engineers. At $40.33 a week in 1921, engineers, in some cities, averaged $13.27 a week more than electricians and $13.95 more than plumbers. They were also well ahead of federal and provincial government clerks, who averaged only $27.15 in the same year. (See Table A1; Tables A1–A8 are in the Statistical Appendix.) Engineers were also well above the Family Welfare Association's minimum weekly budget of $24.66, for a typical family of five.[10] Moreover, compared with other professionals in 1921, engineers were well paid. Although civil engineers earned about $500 a year less than the highest-paid professionals – professors and lecturers – they averaged more, in some cities, than architects, doctors, and dentists (see Table 3).

Engineers, like some other wage and salary earners, may not have appreciated their real earnings and imagined that inflation was lowering their standard of living.[11] As private citizens, they may also have believed that profiteers were manipulating prices; but, as professionals, their reaction was quite different. They did not succumb to hysteria, nor were they led astray by misinformed agitators. They were highly educated and approached most problems rationally. They had accurate first-hand knowledge of the industrial labour market. While they angrily protested low salaries, sometimes with unbecoming rhetoric, their grievances were real, not imaginary.

The apparent discrepancies between perceived and actual incomes arose from disparities in income distribution. Income varied according to field of specialization and age. Mining engineers, the highest-paid engineers in 1921, averaged $2,368.79 annually, while mechanical engineers, the lowest paid, received only $1,650.57. Although the average civil engineer's salary was relatively high[12] – about $103.24 a year more than the average for all professional engineers, $1,951.30 – most earned considerably less (see Table 4). As in other professions, older practitioners earned more than

TABLE 3
Earnings for selected professionals 1921

Occupations	Average annual earnings ($)*
Professors and lecturers	2,560.64
Lawyers and notaries	2,501.31
Civil engineers	2,054.54
Architects	2,019.55
Physicians and surgeons	1,969.10
Dentists	1,784.35

SOURCE: Calculated from: *Sixth Census of Canada*, 1921, Table 40, pp. 166–7, 182–5, 198–201, 218–19, 262–3, 284–7, 304–5, 318–21, 356–9, 382–5, 402–3, 436–9
*In certain cities of 30,000 and over

TABLE 4
Earnings for engineers 1921

Engineering specialization	Average annual earnings ($)*
All engineers	1,951.30
Mining	2,368.79
Civil	2,054.54
Electrical	2,005.52
Mechanical	1,650.57

SOURCE: As in Table 3
*In certain cities of 30,000 and over

younger colleagues. Engineers generally did not begin to receive higher salaries until they were at least 40 years of age.[13] Their salaries jumped as much as 85 per cent between the 20–24 and 35–49 age groups.[14] Although not all engineers over 40 earned high salaries,[15] statistically, their combined incomes weighted and thus distorted the 'average' engineer's salary. A more accurate picture emerges from the pattern of income distribution among engineers under 40.

For the first years after graduation, civil engineers usually worked at a variety of 'sub-professional'[16] jobs – as roadmen, chainmen, instrument-men, draughtsmen – that required only high school education, before advancing to professional positions.[17] These men furnished a plentiful supply of cheap skilled labour for large corporations – about 90 per cent of the staff of railway engineering departments, for example.[18] Competition for professional positions was fierce. In spite of their high educational qualifications, they were paid only slightly more than clerks and tradesmen. In 1921, engineers aged 20 to 24 averaged only $2.76 more per week than federal and provincial government clerks and $3.14 more than plumbers in the same age group (see Table A1). But even though they suffered hardship, even exploitation, they rarely complained. For the most part, they earned a 'living wage' and had few financial commitments. Young and ambitious, they were willing to tolerate low salaries and compete for more lucrative junior professional appointments.

Between 25 and 39 years of age, most junior professional engineers held low-ranking civil engineering posts. As associate members of the CSCE, they did not have enough professional experience (nor, often, the higher membership fee) to qualify as full members. Having fought their way out of the sub-professional ranks, they had not fully established themselves in secure corporate positions. They earned more than tradesmen: engineers 25 to 34 averaged $36.68 per week in 1921, while electricians and plumbers, in the same age group, earned only $28.49 and $25.78 respectively (see Table A1); but they were paid less than some skilled railway workers. Locomotive drivers, for instance, averaged 17 per cent more than engineers under 35 and even conductors received marginally more.[19] This was a constant irritation because many junior professional engineers worked for railways. Nevertheless, although they earned less than these workers, they could just afford some of the essentials of middle-class status. But, even though they earned more and possessed more than most tradesmen and younger sub-professional engineers, they felt impoverished.

Most sub-professionals were under 25 and single. Earning skilled tradesmen's wages, they could easily support themselves, when employed.[20] Junior engineers, however, were older and usually had families to support, in addition to incidental professional expenses. As well, they felt compelled, as one report noted, 'to maintain a standard of living commensurate with the general standards of the community for positions of similar dignity and responsibility.'[21] They could not live like tradesmen. Maintaining a 'respectable' standard of living was as much a condition of employment as a professional requirement, an expensive obligation not expected of sub-professionals.[22]

While junior engineers could withstand foreign competition, lack of public recognition and of control over their professional lives, even the humiliation of earning less than locomotive drivers and conductors, they could not tolerate the steady erosion of their standard of living. As prices continued to rise, they became increasingly anxious and complained bitterly of being unable to preserve their 'professional dignity.'[23] Although not reduced to poverty, they feared something worse: a fall from middle-class grace. They began to lose confidence in the old doctrine that individual initiative and professional excellence would be rewarded with status and security. They no longer felt responsible for their social progress and blamed others for their predicament.

Unlike some radical labour leaders, however, they did not fault the economy for their misfortune. Believing that capitalism was basically sound, they never developed a radical critique or saw their condition as part of a larger process. While they did not consider their problem unique, their analysis did not extend beyond the bounds of the profession; indeed, they viewed it as a 'family affair.'[24] As salaried employees of large corporations, they usually worked for other engineers. They held these men directly responsible[25] for their low salaries. 'Is not this state of affairs,' questioned J.C. Legrand, 'greatly due to the senior members of the profession who, when at the head of a department forget too easily the hardships through which they also passed?'[26] Accustomed to accepting authority, the junior engineers assumed that their dispute could be settled like a family matter through the sympathetic intervention of senior engineers. They were soon disappointed.

Management engineers were loyal primarily to business. The profit motive and career ambition usually took precedence over science and collegial loyalty. Their jobs depended on keeping costs down. 'Many of the so-called leading engineers,' declared N.C. Mills, managing director of a Montreal mechanical engineering works, 'are "leading" because they control the living of other engineers, and the leaders could not hold their jobs unless they kept wages down.'[27] As department heads, or middle-level technical administrators, they did not have the authority to grant the kind of pay increases younger engineers expected. The same principles applied, in a different way, to government engineering departments. Moreover, because their employers controlled the EIC, younger members received little help from their own professional society. 'When you elect as the president of the Engineering Institute one of the wealthiest men in Canada [Col. Leonard],' remarked William Snaith, a thirty-nine-year-old- production engineer, 'you will have a splendid president, but you should not expect too much in the way of increased salaries.'[28] Selecting its officers from among the prosperous and powerful, the 'capitalistic class of the profession,'[29] as one engineer put it, the EIC initially opposed agitating for higher salaries on the grounds that such action was undignified and inappropriate for a learned society. Thus, unable to obtain justice from their employers, or help from their professional society, the younger associate members were forced to consider other alternatives.

By 1918, the engineering press began to notice discontent among younger engineers. Unrest was widespread throughout North America.[30] In Canada, dissatisfied engineers abandoned the EIC in despair. They organized new engineering societies and even considered organizing trade unions to protect themselves.

In February 1919, for example, at a time when interest in the Vancouver branch of the EIC had waned, the British Columbia Technical Association (BCTA) was founded.[31] Its membership included engineers, as well as other related professional and non-professional technical workers. Unlike a learned society, the BCTA's purpose, in the words of its secretary-treasurer, was the 'protection and advancement of the material welfare of its members.'[32] Its activities included protesting the employment of aliens on provincial and municipal public works, preparation of a schedule of minimum salaries for civil engineers, and, most important, obtaining restrictive provincial licensing laws for engineers and architects. By 30 April 1920, with branches in Vancouver, Victoria, and Cumberland, the BCTA had 479 members, including practically all members of the EIC's Vancouver branch.[33]

The attempt to organize a chapter of the American Association of Engineers (AAE), in Toronto, was a more dramatic development. Originating in 1915 in Chicago, the AAE was a short-lived protest organization dedicated to advancing the economic interests of its members, predominantly young civil engineers. Under the able leadership of Frederick H. Newell, a University of Illinois civil engineering professor and an important national leader of the American conservation movement, the AAE grew spectacularly from a few dozen members in 1915 into the world's largest engineering society by 1921, before its rapid decline into relative obscurity by 1925.[34]

Even before the AAE had attained prominence, some Canadian engineers became excited about the prospect of organizing a similar association in Canada. In the spring and summer of 1918, two young EIC members, H.A. Goldman, assistant engineer, Toronto Harbour Commission, and F.B. Goedike, assistant engineer, Hydro-Electric Power Commission, Ontario, took the preliminary steps. Rather than establish an AAE chapter, however, they created an independent Canadian organization – the Canadian Association of Engineers (CAE). Professing aims similar to the AAE, the CAE attracted mostly younger engineers, and while it claimed to be complementary to, not a competitor of, the EIC, the EIC considered it a serious threat and later resolved to destroy it.[35]

Undoubtedly, the most important sign of discontent was the emergence of trade union sentiment. Some prominent engineers such as H.E.T. Haultain, as well as several junior engineers, asserted that unionization was the only solution to the engineer's economic problems. Haultain believed that engineers, even if licensed, would need some form of union, purged of 'objectionable features,' since they had no other means to protect themselves and raise their salaries.[36] The technical press discussed this idea, and in March 1920 the Toronto branch of the EIC even sponsored a lively debate on the subject.[37] Rejecting the notion of an orderly market governed by natural laws of supply and demand, unionization advocates used classic trade union arguments and rooted their case in the belief that the engineer was essentially a working man. His place was with labour, not capital. 'Our natural interest, as engineers,' declared Montreal engineer C.A. Mullen, 'is with those who "work" in industry, not with those who "own" industry.'[38] Continuing, he declared: 'The sooner we engineers ... come down from our self-erected mental pedestals and recognize the fact that we are but laborers in the common vineyard, along with the rest of struggling, sweating humanity, the better it will be both for us as a group of professionals and for the community at large.'[39] Contending that trade unions had benefited workers significantly, Mullen and others urged engineers to organize. Professional societies, they argued, could neither protect engineers nor raise their salaries. Unorganized, engineers were at the mercy of unsympathetic employers.[40]

On the surface, conditions appeared right for unions to flourish. Younger engineers seemed to constitute an alienated, class-conscious group of dissatisfied employees. Some prominent engineers had made unions more respectable, and potential leaders advanced persuasive arguments. However, while support for a union was growing, it had not developed into a positive movement. Unions were being discussed, not organized. There was no sense of urgency, no spontaneity, no grass-roots support, not even experienced organizers with a practical plan of action. At this point, only a minority of engineers supported the idea. Except for the 'Draughtsmen's Union,' no professional engineers' union was organized.

In March 1920, over one hundred engineering and architectural draughtsmen formed Local 40 of the International Federation of Technical Engineers, Architects and Draughtsmen, or, as it became known, the 'Draughtsmen's Union.' It had over five thousand members in the United States and was affiliated with the American Federation of Labor. A local had been organized in Montreal, and another was planned for Hamilton.

While the history of this union is obscure, it is clear that it was not highly regarded by professional engineers. They refused to join, probably because the union admitted non-professionals, as well as engineers ineligible for EIC membership.[41]

A number of factors inhibited union development. Engineers were difficult to organize and indifferent to organization. They were scattered throughout a multitude of remote industries across Canada and moved nomadically from job to job on short-term contracts. They lacked a common industrial base on which to organize a union. In spite of an outward appearance of occupational similarity, engineers were not alike. They worked in different industries, performed different technical and administrative functions, and occupied different positions in corporate hierarchies. Unable to organize across industrial lines, and aware of the implications of becoming involved in a sympathetic strike, they could neither bargain collectively nor threaten a strike. Strikes could always be broken by unorganized engineers who had no ethical reservations about sharp competition for scarce jobs in an overcrowded profession, especially during periods of high unemployment.

Other factors, such as the engineer's background and attitude, also curbed the growth of unionization. By the end of the nineteenth century, the era of the upper-class engineer, like T.C. Keefer, who used engineering to help preserve class privilege,[42] was over. Most Canadian engineers, like their American counterparts, were from humbler origins. In 1924, as part of a larger study on engineering education, the Society for the Promotion of Engineering Education discovered that most American engineers came from lower-middle-class, small-town, old-stock families.[43] Canada's most celebrated engineer-politician, C.D. Howe, for example, a ninth-generation New Englander, was from a comfortable, but not wealthy family. His father was a carpenter turned house builder[44] – a background typical of most Canadian engineers. Few had private-school backgrounds like Keefer; fewer still, like most Canadians, had working-class, union backgrounds. Many, including Howe, were raised on Horatio Alger. They were staunchly individualistic and thoroughly imbued with the spirit of enterprise. Fiercely competitive, they wanted to improve their individual status. Unions, they thought, thwarted this ambition and induced a 'levelling process'[45] which lowered their status. 'By unionizing,' Professor Peter Gillespie warned, 'engineers would prostitute an ancient, honorable and respected calling to the level of a trade.'[46] Engineers had struggled to rise above workmen. They had a strong middle-class bias against them and regarded unions as corrupt, irresponsible, and radicalized. Their main principle, according to Fraser S. Keith, was to 'demand and threaten, without assuming any responsibility either collectively or individually.'[47] The industrial strife of 1919, culminating in the Winnipeg General Strike, reinforced this prejudice. According to Keith, it was 'unthinkable'[48] that engineers should even consider union methods.

While unionization may have been in their immediate interest, engineers could not see themselves as class-conscious unionists, implacably arrayed against capital. Such a stance was alien to their thinking and contrary to their philosophy. Their social awareness had increased during the war, but their basic philosophy, especially their attitude to labour relations, had not changed. As late as 1919, in spite of their financial distress, the older conservatives continued to set the pattern of belief for the rest of the profession. Most engineers still assumed that, in a progressive liberal society, they could achieve success individually by serving, rather than opposing business. Above all, they believed that they were unique, that they occupied a neutral position between capital and labour (because they were salaried, not capitalists or wage earners)[49] and had a special mission to end class conflict. Although the ideal of the independent professional was sharply at variance with their status as salaried employees, engineers refused to abandon their aspirations for social leadership by embracing alien collectivist principles.

In turning away sharply from labour, however, engineers invariably moved closer to business. In spite of their reservations about business's unproductivity, they eventually became more closely allied, partly because of a pragmatic, perhaps cynical, realization that engineering depended on business and partly because of the conviction that business, in contrast to labour, was at least closer to the world's enlightened, progressive forces. Rather than fight for justice collectively with labour, they preferred to await better times and compete for success, as individuals, with business. This approach alarmed some union supporters. Recalling Aesop's fable about the bat who declined the offer of the mice to be their king – because he thought he was a bird – William Snaith cautioned: 'If the engineer feels that he is an ally of capital, is it not possible that he may be giving up his position as king of labor?'[50] Ultimately, however, engineers were content, as C.A. Mullen lamented, to be the 'Little Brother of the Rich' rather than the 'Big Brother of the Poor.'[51]

While it was unlikely that engineers would organize a union, the spectre of unionism terrified conservative EIC councillors. Caught up in the national hysteria arising from the Bolshevik revolution and 1919 domestic labour unrest, they saw unions as a major threat. They were convinced that unionization would destroy their carefully nurtured professionalism and ruin the EIC's prestige and credibility as a learned society. They did not fear younger engineers; what really frightened them was the growing support for unions among prominent and respected engineers.[52] It was imperative, they believed, that unions be firmly opposed. Although the AAE and the CAE had taken a strong anti-union stand,[53] the EIC seemed to regard the CAE as the spearhead of American engineering trade unionism in Canada.[54] It was less concerned about the BCTA, in spite of that group's aspirations to expand into other provinces and form a Canadian Technical Association.[55] Its immediate objective, therefore, was to crush the CAE.

The CAE was attacked on two fronts. To undermine it from within, Fraser S. Keith recruited prominent Toronto engineers to persuade CAE supporters to return to the EIC, on the grounds that their organization needlessly duplicated the EIC.[56] In spite of H.A. Goldman's scepticism about the EIC's pledges to assist younger engineers, the CAE found it increasingly difficult to resist the EIC's overtures. At a May 1918 meeting, for example, a *Canadian Engineer* reporter argued that the objectives of the two organizations were identical and urged that the EIC be given a chance to prove its good intentions. After a thorough discussion, F.B. Goedike, acting as chairman of the CAE during Goldman's illness, moved to suspend further meetings, except for the constitutional committee. This carried unanimously.[57]

A year later, the CAE was attacked indirectly, in Chicago, at the AAE's annual meeting. Assuming that the AAE was behind the CAE, Keith addressed the convention, stressing the EIC's similarity to the AAE. The meeting responded by passing a resolution prohibiting the establishment of AAE chapters in Canada. While this provision was rescinded the following year at the AAE's St Louis convention, the AAE and its imitators were finished in Canada. By this time, EIC branches had closed ranks and persuaded their members not to support the AAE.[58]

The CAE's destruction was a minor victory for the EIC. The CAE was in its infancy and had few supporters and perhaps little chance of success. It was not a trade union. The ferocity with which the EIC destroyed it demonstrated not only the institute's anti-union fervour but also its resolve to defend its prerogatives from outside encroachment, particularly from the United States. This was also evident in the EIC's attempt to contain the expansion of major American engineering societies, in Canada, through gentlemen's agreements secured in New York.[59]

As the imminent danger of unionism faded with the CAE's demise, the conservatives faced another, perhaps more insidious threat – collective bargaining. Although engineers would not organize a union, they had not rejected other forms of collective action to increase salaries.

Following the war, the main initiative to improve salaries came from EIC branches, not council. On 5 March 1919, for example, the Toronto branch appointed a committee to study salaries, in order to stimulate discussion and prod council into similar action. The committee's members included prominent Toronto engineers, as well as H.A. Goldman (secretary) and F.B. Goedike. On 16 October 1919, after careful study, it submitted its report. This remarkable study was the first of its kind in Canada. It was patterned after similar ones prepared by the ASCE and AAE and classified engineers employed by various industries into job categories, together with minimum qualifications and salaries. Following branch approval, it was forwarded to other branches, before its submission to council with a recommendation that the EIC officially adopt it.[60]

Ostensibly, salary schedules were merely guides to current professional levels.[61] But, while the conservatives could accept them as innocuous administrative aids, they feared that the schedules might be used to coerce, rather than assist employers. Developments in the United States and Canada made the conservatives suspect that the schedules were, in fact, the leading edge of collective bargaining. Salary schedules were a major priority for the AAE,[62] and the Toronto branch had brazenly recommended to local employers that its schedule be implemented.[63] A more alarming development was evident later in Manitoba. While Manitoba branch members pledged not to accept positions at a salary less than an agreed rate, the branch planned to negotiate with large corporate employers to have its salary schedule adopted. Members failing to receive an adequate salary would be helped to find other employment at an acceptable salary.[64] Although this was not collective bargaining, partly because of the absence of the strike threat, it could produce nearly the same effect.

This placed EIC conservatives in an awkward dilemma. If they ignored, or even encouraged, the development of salary schedules, they chanced precipitating collective bargaining; if they opposed them, they risked alienating the membership and undermining their own authority. Not only was there widespread support for salary schedules, but dissidents, such as H.A. Goldman, were not mollified by EIC promises to help improve salaries.[65] They demanded action. The conservatives, however, realized that helping members increase their salaries would have been an abrupt departure from EIC policy. In spite of its 1917 decision to help serve the public, the EIC was still primarily dedicated to facilitating the interchange of professional knowledge among its members. Serving the economic interests of individuals was contrary to its traditional educational role. Nevertheless, while undoubtedly moved by the financial distress of younger members, the conservatives also realized that unionization would be forced on the profession if they did not act.[66] Although they had crushed the CAE, they had not eliminated the threat of unionism. The underlying discontent remained and grew. To eradicate it, they decided to remove the source of unrest by helping younger engineers improve their financial position.

To a certain extent, this was already EIC practice before 1920. For example, the EIC had helped government engineers to increase their salaries. While most engineers were employed by private corporations, the institute believed that raising Dominion government engineers' salaries would indirectly help all engineers, because it would set the standard for other public and private employers.[67]

Following passage of the 1918 Civil Service Act, the Civil Service Commission (CSC) was directed to classify and reorganize the civil service. While the new act brought government engineers under the CSC's jurisdiction and extended the merit system of competitive examinations to the entire civil service, government engineers were still unhappy; they were apprehensive about receiving adequate pay increases. In the past, the CSC had not recognized their educational qualifications, and salary inequities persisted between technical and non-technical employees. Complaining that there were no technically trained men on the CSC, the EIC mounted a powerful lobby to influence the commission's recommendations. As influential councillors lobbied the CSC and government ministers, the branches approached local MPs. The Ottawa branch established close liaison with the government, while its publicity committee furnished the press and MPs with favourably inclined information.[68]

Although the EIC became involved in this lobby more by circumstance than by design, it effectively established an important precedent. As Fraser S. Keith observed: 'For the first time in the history of a purely professional organization an active concerted effort had been made to advance the material welfare of a section of its membership, and established a definite policy by *The Institute* from which it was never intended to recede.'[69] Thus by 1920 the EIC generally accepted that it should help improve the material welfare of individual members; but it had no official policy.

In April 1920, at the urging of Ontario members, the EIC appointed a committee on policy to define future objectives and policy.[70] The chairman was John Challies, the thirty-nine-year-old director of the Water Power Branch, Department of the Interior, and honorary secretary of the Honorary Advisory Council for Scientific and Industrial Research. After careful study, the committee recommended that the EIC broaden its objectives to 'promote the professional, the social and the *economic welfare* of the members.'[71] This and other recommendations institutionalized existing practice and laid the basis of EIC policy for many years.

Although the conservatives were pledged to promote the material welfare of individual members, they were not fully committed to the idea. They seemed to recognize its contradictory implications: the EIC could not promote self-interest and remain a learned society. They viewed the new policy recommendations as an unfortunate but necessary temporary expedient, a pretense designed to placate dissent, in order to preserve the institute as a learned society and protect their corporate interests. They would help, or at least appear to help, provided the EIC's professional status was not compromised. The same approach had been revealed a year earlier by the EIC's response to the CSC's recommendations.

The publication in June 1919 of the CSC's long report (*The Classification of the Civil Service of Canada*), prepared by the American consulting firm Arthur Young and Company, caused an immediate uproar throughout the civil service.[72] Surveyors were angry, and mining engineers characterized it as 'unfair and discriminatory.'[73] But the harshest criticism, from an engineer's viewpoint, came from the Engineering Council in New York. The council was keenly interested in Canadian civil service reform, because Arthur Young and Co. was implementing a similar classification plan for the US congressional committee on reclassification and compensation of government employees.[74] Arthur S. Tuttle, chairman of the council's committee on classification and compensation, concluded that the CSC's report failed to 'group engineering service along orderly lines, that it provides too narrow limits for promotions within a grade, and that the compensation proposed for all grades is inadequate for the service rendered.'[75]

This last criticism was the major source of complaint among engineers. Believing that wartime inflation was a temporary aberration, the consultants calculated salaries in relation to pre-war prices and proposed a cumbersome, *ad hoc* system of special 'war bonuses' to bridge the transition, pending the return of pre-war prices.[76] Prices, however, continued to rise, and government engineers were outraged. One important manifestation of this discontent was the formation of the Professional Institute of the Civil Service of Canada. Organized on the initiative of John Challies and the Ottawa branch, EIC, the institute was dissatisfied with inadequate salaries and inconsistent application of the classification to professionals.[77] In the mean time opposition to the report, from all quarters, grew so intense that the CSC decided to revise it.

In spite of strong opposition to the report among government engineers, and even 'considerable dissatisfaction'[78] in council, the EIC strongly endorsed it and tried to stifle criticism within the institute. Council argued that, while the report was not perfect, it had important advantages: it raised the government engineer's status, increased his pay, and provided for the review of individual grievances. Council also cautioned that if a new civil service bill – containing a revised classification – met concerted opposition, it might be defeated and lost. This raised the possibility of a return to patronage,[79] which had ravaged government engineering departments and discriminated against engineers. Warning that some politicians were scheming to re-establish patronage, council recommended acceptance of the bill and urged members to refrain from 'expressing any personal dissatisfaction.'[80]

While the conservatives had grounds to fear the return of patronage,[81] they had another, more compelling reason for endorsing the CSC's report. Feeling uneasy about the EIC's compromising role as a pressure group, they argued that they had already achieved their major objective: government engineers' salaries were improved without damaging the institute's status as a learned society. Later, when confronted with the threat of collective bargaining, the EIC undermined the immoderate branch salary schedules with the same methods it had developed earlier to block opposition to the CSC's recommendations.

On 23 March 1920, in response to mounting pressure within the EIC to improve salaries, council appointed a committee on remuneration to study salaries and to co-ordinate branch studies. One month later, council directed this committee to prepare a salary and fee schedule.[82]

Although traditionally opposed to salary schedules,[83] the conservatives were not opposed to increasing salaries. They had always maintained that engineers were underpaid. Believing that income often determined social status, they viewed the salary schedule as an opportunity to raise salaries and, thus, increase professional prestige – their long-term objective. Their immediate problem, however, was to check collective bargaining. The schedule was a means to that end. By establishing a national EIC schedule, the conservatives planned to supplant and, thereby, neutralize the potentially dangerous branch schedules. Thus, adopted by necessity, the salary schedule became the main defence against collective bargaining. The major tactical problem was to make it appear useful to appease young dissidents, while undermining it to render it harmless and thus protect the EIC.

Instead of preparing its own schedule, the committee on remuneration adapted a schedule prepared by the Engineering Council, New York.[84] The committee argued that this schedule was superior to others and maintained that preparation of another would be an unnecessary duplication. This choice was significant. Founded in 1917 by conservative American engineering societies, the Engineering Council's chief purpose was to forestall the AAE by blunting its initiatives with conservative counter-proposals.[85] Its salary scale was not only lower than the AAE's but significantly lower than some EIC branch schedules. The recommended salary minimum of the Toronto branch, for example, averaged $200 a year more than the AAE's minimums, and the Manitoba scale was even higher.[86] Adapting the Engineering Council's schedule, therefore, was a means to circumvent the radical branch levels, in order to impose a moderate scale. As well, on the pretext that high salary demands might alienate employers and encourage undercutting by non-EIC members, the committee substantially lowered the Engineering Council's modest salary scale[87] to render it almost completely ineffective. Even Fraser S. Keith was moved to condemn the action as a 'mistake.'[88]

Ultimately, time undermined the proposed salary schedule. The committee took over three and a half years to submit its final report. During this period it tactfully absorbed and stifled radical dissent, simply by outlasting it. As the cost of living dropped in September 1920, the salary dispute gave way to new controversies. Although engineers would continue to complain about inadequate compensation, the committee had shielded the EIC from collective bargaining, while appearing to serve ordinary engineers.

Perhaps the committee on remuneration's most significant achievement was to alter subtly the EIC's attitude to its members' economic problems. The branches looked to collective action to improve salaries. Although reluctant to form a union, they were prepared to use their collective strength, informally, through salary schedules, to confront, perhaps to coerce employers. By contrast, the committee on remuneration believed that engineers must improve their salaries as individuals, not as a group. It asserted: 'The larger part of any material improvement must come from the action of the members of the profession themselves. The value the individual member of the profession places upon his services and the remuneration he insists upon obtaining, must, in the long run, be the greatest factor in bringing about a financial improvement in the profession.'[89] The committee thus re-established the institute's traditional conservatism and repudiated the recommendations of the committee on policy. Moreover, in reasserting the principle that an engineer's financial welfare was an individual, not a collective responsibility, the committee effectively closed the door to union development in the EIC.

Manipulating the salary schedule was not a substitute for improving salaries, much less a credible alternative to collective bargaining. Although inflation declined, the financial condition of most salaried engineers did not substantially improve. The ineffective EIC schedule did not raise salaries, and younger engineers continued to feel insecure. They had recognized years earlier that the EIC was not serving their professional and economic interests, because it was still committed to the ideal of a learned society. Lacking alternatives, they began to reconsider Alan Macdougall's plan for licensing. Ironically, in protecting the EIC's professional dignity, the conservatives inadvertently weakened their position. While the EIC's assistance to members was more apparent than real, it helped to change the thinking and raise the expectations of ordinary engineers. Combined with the committee on policy's recommendations, the institute's assistance legitimized the novel idea that the EIC should promote the economic interest of individual members. When grass-roots pressure arose for political action to protect engineers, the conservatives would no longer have alternatives to, or convincing arguments against, licensing.

9

'A sort of trade union'

The EIC and licensing

'No single subject,' observed Fraser S. Keith in November 1918, 'is occupying the minds of engineers throughout Canada at the present time more than the question of securing legislation.'[1] During the war, the climate of opinion among rank-and-file CSCE members had begun to change in favour of political action. As more and more engineers complained of inadequate compensation, the technical press devoted increasing editorial space to the subject of licensing, and several CSCE branches passed resolutions in support of closing the profession. By 1918, the EIC was committed to an ambitious licensing campaign. Although the institute again encountered strong opposition from mining interests, the EIC was more united and determined, more adroit and politically sophisticated in its drive to overcome opposition and restrict competition by means of licensing.

In August 1918, the question of seeking restrictive licensing legislation was introduced formally at the CSCE's second annual professional meeting, in Saskatoon. In his paper 'Legislation Concerning the Status of Engineers,'[2] F.H. Peters, commissioner of irrigation, Department of the Interior, Calgary,[3] argued that legislation was the best way to improve the status of engineers. This suggestion, endorsed by the Calgary branch, met with the general approval of the meeting. Peters explained that the Calgary branch's decision to press for legislation developed from a 'general feeling of dissatisfaction' concerning the engineer's unsatisfactory financial situation.[4] Engineers, he said, had developed Canada's natural resources and industries but received 'neither the remuneration, nor the respect' they deserved.[5] By October 1918, major EIC branches in the west and east had endorsed Calgary's stand on legislation. Realizing that there was, as Keith observed, an 'insistent demand for legislation throughout Canada,'[6] on 1 October 1918 council endorsed the principle of obtaining restrictive licensing legislation, on condition that provincial legislation must include all qualified engineers (not just EIC members), be uniform from province to province, and allow registered engineers to practise in any province.[7]

While some EIC members strongly opposed licensing legislation, the majority was clearly in favour.[8] Consulting engineers viewed licensing as a means of regulating competition; government engineers believed that it would help to eliminate patronage and give them professional standing similar to Dominion and provincial land surveyors. For most salaried engineers, especially those in low-paying corporate or government positions, licensing would not only improve status but also increase salaries. Although all these engineers were motivated by pecuniary considerations, they did not expect licensing to improve their incomes immediately. Only unionization, some argued, could accomplish that. Instead, legislation was, as Peters cautioned, a 'means to an end';[9] it would improve salaries indirectly. While salary schedules and other devices might achieve short-term results, licensing was the only long-term, permanent solution. By eliminating 'unqualified' practitioners who discredited the profession, licensing would improve the engineer's status and thus, presumably, increase his salary.[10] C.C. Kirby, chairman of the Saint John branch, later explained that the object of licensing legislation, in addition to protection of the public, was to 'improve the status of the engineer ... and thereby obtain greater recognition and consequent better remuneration.'[11]

In their determination to increase salaries by licensing, engineers had not entirely forfeited their idealism or become obsessed with personal gain. The war had, if anything, revitalized their idealism and given them renewed purpose. Believing that they had saved civilization from destruction during the war, they wanted now to increase industrial production to help Canada survive in the great commercial struggle expected after the war.[12] Above all, after witnessing wartime inefficiency, they were more convinced of the need for engineers to lead the post-war world. However, while the war uplifted their spirits, it also disheartened them; wartime inflation forced them to consider the more immediate and mundane problems of jobs and salaries.

By 1918, one of the most serious problems faced by younger engineers in Canada, as well as in the United States and Britain, was increased competition arising from an over-supply of engineers.[13] In Britain, for example, during the first three years after the war, an unprecedented number of engineering school graduates, combined with older more

Figure 2
Differential growth of the professions 1881–1931
Source: Table A2 (in Statistical Appendix)

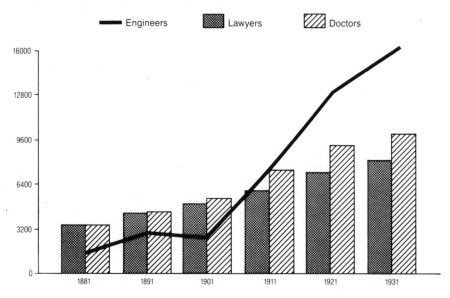

experienced men returned from former overseas possessions, created an over-supply.[14] In Canada, apprenticeships traditionally regulated supply. But a decade of unprecedented economic growth preceding the First World War substantially increased demand.[15] After 1904, the immigration of European and American engineers to build the transcontinental railways and, more important, the influx of engineering school graduates from expanded university faculties soon filled the demand but overcrowded the profession.

Statistical information on the growth of the engineering profession in Canada, during its crucial period of development before 1921, is incomplete. However, census reports and the CSCE's membership application files, although not strictly comparable, are useful.

In the forty-year period 1881–1921, the number of engineers in Canada grew from 1,459 to 12,814, a remarkable 778.3 per cent increase. Growth slowed in the 1891–1901 decade and even decreased, but the profession continued to expand after 1901, achieving its greatest percentage increase (188.5) of any decade, between 1901 and 1911, and, more important, its greatest numerical increase (5,475) of any decade, between 1911 and 1921

Figure 3
Number of engineers, lawyers, and physicians 1911 and 1921
Source: Table A2

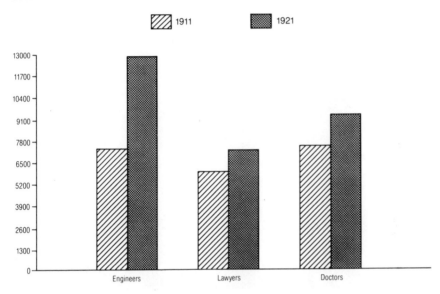

(see Figure 2). During this last, crucial decade, engineering grew faster than the general population, the labour force, and other professions, such as law and medicine, which engineers regarded as their professional models. Whereas these professions had grown by 31.1 and 25.1 per cent respectively, engineering had expanded by 74.6 per cent. By 1921, at 12,814, engineers outnumbered lawyers (7,209) and doctors (9,278) (see Figure 3). Much of this growth occurred in central Canada. Between 1911 and 1921, as Table 5 shows, the number of engineers increased by 2,415 in Ontario and 1,457 in Quebec. The eastern provinces had the next largest numerical (669) and percentage (136.5) increases, followed by the west and then British Columbia. And while mechanical engineers experienced the largest percentage increase (349.9), civil engineers, at 4,562, had the largest numerical increase (see Figure 4).

The CSCE also experienced similar growth patterns. Expanding to 4,879 members by 1921 (see Table A5), the society's largest numerical (2,157) and percentage (79.2) increases occurred in the decade 1911–21. Over half of this increase (55.8 per cent) took place in the four years after 1918 (see Figure 5). The membership increase for 1921 alone (830) was greater than

Figure 4
Number of engineers by specialization 1911 and 1921
Source: National Archives of Canada, Engineering Institute of Canada Papers,
MG 28, 1–277, Membership Files, 1887–1922

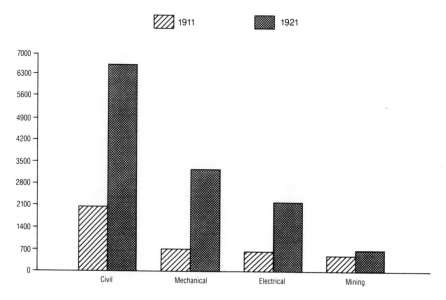

any previous year since the society's founding.[16] Between 1887 and 1922, two-thirds of all membership applications were from central Canada.[17] Slightly more originated from Quebec than Ontario, but after 1919 Ontario surpassed Quebec.[18] By 1921, Ontario had over one-third of all CSCE members, whereas Quebec had less than a quarter (21.5 per cent).[19]

Much of the engineering profession's growth came from two main sources: the immigration of European and American engineers and, more important, Canadian university engineering faculties. There is no accurate record of the number of immigrants who eventually practised engineering in Canada; however, on the basis of the ratio of foreign to native-born engineers, CSCE membership application figures (which were broadly representative of most qualified 'professional' engineers in Canada) offer some general indication.

Most CSCE applicants were Canadian born. Between 1887 and 1922, as Table 6 shows, about two-thirds of all initial CSCE applicants (65.0 per cent) were born in Canada. Less than a quarter (22.0 per cent) were born in Britain and the empire; only 7.9 per cent were American born. Excluding

Figure 5
CSCE membership growth 1887–1921
Source: Table A5

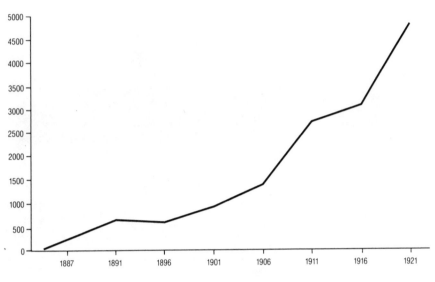

TABLE 5
Growth of engineering by region 1911–21

	Total Canada	East	Ontario	Quebec	Prairies	BC
Engineers and surveyors						
1911	7,339	490	2,032	1,548	1,322	1,947
1921	12,814	1,159	4,447	3,005	1,890	2,363
Increase (number)	5,475	669	2,415	1,457	568	416
Increase (%)	74.6	136.5	118.8	94.1	43.0	21.4

SOURCE: Calculated from: *Fifth Census of Canada, 1911*, Vol. VI, Table 5, pp. 66, 88, 110, 132, 154, 176, 198, 220, 242; *Sixth Census of Canada, 1921*, Vol. IV, Table 2, pp. 32–3

student and junior members, among practising engineers – full and associate members – Canadian born were just over half (57.7 per cent); British-imperial and American born, almost two-fifths (27.8 per cent and 10.5 per cent respectively). This pattern does not change significantly

Figure 6
Distribution of CSCE applicants by birthplace 1887–1922
Source: Table A6

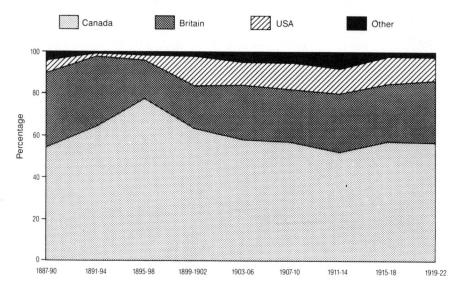

TABLE 6
Distribution of CSCE applicants by birthplace 1887–1922

Birthplace	All members		Full and associate members	
	Number	%	Number	%
Canada	2,582	65.0	1,263	57.7
Britain and empire	867	22.0	609	27.8
United States	314	7.9	230	10.5
Other	121	3.0	88	4.0
Unknown	89	2.1	0	0.0
Total	3,973	100.0	2,190	100.0

SOURCE: Calculated from: National Archives of Canada, Engineering Institute of Canada Papers, MG 28 1–277, Membership Files, 1887–1922
NOTE: Between 1887 and 1922, 108 applications came from engineers resident outside Canada

Figure 7
Apprentices and university students 1887–1922
Source: Table A7

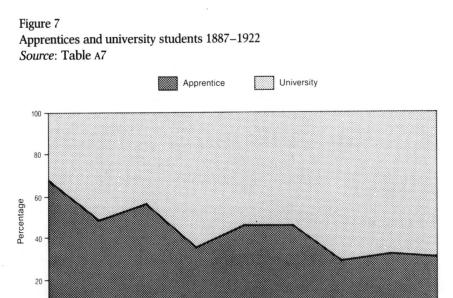

TABLE 7
Distribution of initial CSCE applicants by classification 1887–1922 and 1919–22

Membership classification	1887–1922			1919–22		
	No.	%	Av.	No.	%	Av.
Full member	626	13.5	17.4	119	9.1	29.8
Associate member	1,525	33.0	42.4	449	34.4	112.3
Junior	435	9.4	12.1	165	12.6	41.3
Student	2,041	44.1	56.7	573	43.9	143.3

SOURCE: As in Table 6

through time, except for American applicants. While the percentage of Canadian and British-imperial born remained fairly constant, at just over a half and quarter of all applicants, respectively, from 1887 to 1922, the percentage of American-born applicants rose from approximately 3 per cent in 1887 and 1898 to 12 per cent during 1899–1910 and 1911–22 (see Figure 6).

While immigrant engineers accounted for a relatively small portion of the increased post-war supply of engineers, engineering students counted for substantially more. Between 1919 and 1922, for example, 43.9 per cent of initial CSCE applications came from students; an annual average of 143.3 a year, twice the 1887–1922 average of 56.7 (see Table 7). Reflecting the decline in the apprenticeship system, the majority of these students were enrolled in university engineering faculties. Between 1887 and 1922, only 39.3 per cent of CSCE applicants received their professional training by apprenticeship. The number of apprenticed engineering students remained relatively high until the First World War. From this point, however, university students began significantly to outnumber apprenticed students (see Figure 7).

By this date, the universities already were graduating engineers in excess of demand, and some engineers were forced to seek work in the United States.[20] After 1918, Canadian engineering schools, like their British and American counterparts, expanded dramatically, graduating unprecedented numbers of engineers. Whereas 237 engineering degrees were granted in 1920, 629 were granted in 1923 (a number not surpassed until 1935).[21] Returned soldiers accounted for much of this growth. For example, of the total number of University of Toronto engineering students who wrote spring examinations in 1919 (772), half (394) were ex-soldiers.[22]

The unprecedented post-war increase in the supply of engineers created serious problems. Although the supply would decrease by the mid-1920s, the engineers' immediate welfare would depend on adequate demand for their services. In the 1921–31 decade, however, while supply of and demand for engineers were about equal,[23] the demand for civil engineers had declined sharply with the pre-war completion of major civil engineering works and with the rise of wartime chemical and electrical industries. In 1921, civil engineers constituted only 43 per cent of the professional engineers in Canada;[24] most CSCE members were civil, not industrial engineers. Employment opportunities for industrial engineers were good; but while the demand for civil engineers would improve, as the ranks of civil engineers became more crowded immediate prospects were poor.

Overcrowding depressed salaries and increased competition. With a large supply of engineers on hand, employers could lower salaries. When demand declined during a depression, or in the absence of large construction projects, competition for low-paying jobs became sharp. Emigration to the United States did not significantly reduce the over-supply, and few engineers were willing to foresake the profession after years of study and professional practice.[25]

All engineers were hurt by competition, but younger engineers, in their

Figure 8
CSCE membership classifications 1918 and 1921
Source: Table A8

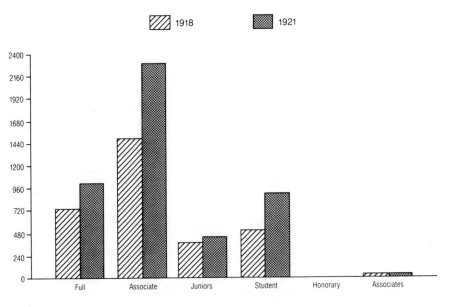

TABLE 8
Distribution of CSCE applicants by age group
1887–1922

Age group (years)	Number	Percentage
20–29	937	36.0
30–39	1,120	43.0
40–49	391	15.0
50–59	130	5.0
60–69	30	1.0
Total	2,608	100.0

SOURCE: As in Table 6
NOTE: Excludes student and junior members

thirties, were more directly affected. The majority of CSCE members, excluding student and junior members, were also in their thirties (see Table 8). Between 1887 and 1922, the average age was 34.0. Over half (61.0

TABLE 9
Average age of CSCE applicants
1887–1922

Classification	Average age
Full member	42.3
Associate member	32.9
Junior	26.7
Student	23.5

SOURCE: As in Table 6

TABLE 10
Average annual number of CSCE applicants 1887–1922, 1918–22

Classification	1887–1922		1918–22	
	Number	Average	Number	Average
Full member	626	17.4	130	26.0
Associate member	1,525	42.4	501	100.2
Junior	435	12.9	184	36.8
Student	2,041	56.7	593	118.6

SOURCE: As in Table 6

per cent) were associate members averaging 32.9 years, in contrast to full members, who averaged 42.3 years (see Table 9). Whereas associate members averaged 42.4 applications a year between 1887 and 1922, they averaged 100.2 in the 1918–22 period, substantially more than full member applicants (26.0) and slightly less than student applicants, at 118.6 (see Table 10). However, in terms of cumulative membership totals, recorded by the CSCE, in the same period, while the number of students grew by 400 (the largest percentage increase, 80.2), the associate member class, containing most of the younger professional engineers in their thirties, expanded by 799 members (53.8 per cent), to constitute the largest single membership class in the CSCE (see Figure 8). These engineers bore the brunt of increased competition within the profession after the war.

The ever-increasing number of younger engineers intensified competition for jobs and promotions. Although the supply of engineers would moderate in the mid-1920s, in the immediate post-war period the economic prospects of many young engineers must have appeared bleak. The recession would continue until 1924, and, although prices were falling, inflation still eroded purchasing power.

While other professions had strong organizations to protect their economic interests, younger engineers, such as thirty-five-year-old F.H. Peters, realized that the EIC, as constituted, would do nothing to help them.[26] Other strategies to raise the engineer's status – membership in an exclusive professional society, publicity, public service – had failed. Unlike lawyers and doctors, engineers did not have regulatory powers to limit the supply of practitioners or even fee tariffs to fix prices. As salaried employees, they had only one logical solution to their predicament, the traditional labour method – unionization. Having rejected this for social and philosophical reasons, younger engineers turned to licensing to achieve similar ends. They believed that they had no other alternative. Moreover, as the EIC had undergone fundamental structural changes during the war, it now seemed opportune to press for political action.

Although the public statements of Peters and others were vague about how licensing would benefit engineers financially, most EIC members understood. Opinions varied about the relative effects of licensing,[27] but all agreed on its implications: licensing would alter the supply-demand relationship in their favour. It would restrict competition, in order to limit supply and drive up wages. These were, of course, classic trade union tactics, and some prominent CSCE members described licensing as such. H.E.T. Haultain, for example, characterized closed professions, such as law and medicine, as 'a species of unionization,'[28] and consulting engineer R.O. Wynne-Roberts observed that licensing would make the profession 'a sort of trade union.'[29]

Licensing, in many respects, was better than unionization. As a private interest group, engineers could not lobby for what were, in effect, monopoly powers, on the grounds of self-protection. But, as professionals, posing as enlightened altruists, they could restrict competition on the pretext of protecting the public. Other professionals also had based their appeals for licensing and regulatory powers on the notion that the public needed protection, because it could not judge professional competence.[30] Thus, by rationalizing their self-interest in terms of serving the public interest, licensing could achieve the same results as unionization, in a 'dignified' way, without loss of professional prestige.[31] It would effectively confer monopoly powers on a private interest group, as a public service.

While the majority of EIC members favoured licensing, a small but important minority was staunchly opposed. These members tended to be older, well-established engineers who stood at the head of the profession and occupied senior management positions in government and industry. Many had served as CSCE councillors and presidents; most had been associated with the Montreal clique. Their opposition to licensing stemmed initially from their classical liberal attitudes towards the value of competition.

Conservative opponents of licensing saw competition as the matrix of professional achievement and material prosperity. In an expanding free market governed by natural law, they argued, competition eliminated incompetence and rewarded excellence. Licensing interfered with the natural order of things, stifled initiative, and encouraged mediocrity. Moreover, the conservatives asserted, it was ungentlemanly to combine for class advantage at the expense of the community, as well as against those less privileged, who honestly competed to become engineers. Engineering, like science, was classless. Licensing granted special privileges to an undeserving and unnaturally constituted élite. 'If an engineer cannot stand on his own feet in competition with brother members of the profession,' declared R.W. MacIntyre, a prominent BC engineer, 'we certainly have no right to bolster him up by Act of Parliament and drag our profession downhill by so doing.'[32] Licensing, conservatives argued, would not eliminate incompetents, but shield them; competence could not be legislated. The conservatives often observed that licensing had not prevented incompetents from practising law and medicine.[33] Echoing T.C. Keefer's assertion that engineers 'sought only a free field and asked no favors,'[34] the conservatives insisted that engineers must be free of all restraints in order to develop naturally. The market-place was the only real safeguard against incompetence and guarantee of efficiency and prosperity.

Consistent with their nineteenth-century views on the virtues of self-improvement, the conservatives maintained that the attainment of higher salaries was primarily an individual, not a collective responsibility. Engineers should be rewarded only for individual merit. Rather than adopt coercive trade union methods by organizing a 'closed shop,' engineers should emulate the Institution of Civil Engineers and improve the EIC's prestige as a professional society. This, in turn, would improve their prestige and, ultimately, their remuneration. Expanding on this idea, G.R.G. Conway, chairman of the Vancouver branch, CSCE, and chief engineer, B.C. Electric Railway, asserted:

The principal object of the leading national engineering societies is to raise the standards of the profession from time to time, so that only competent engineers shall be entrusted with the design and construction of engineering works, both public and private. Our object is not to attain that result by adopting the principles of trades unions ... but by increasing the value of our society so that it will be recognized that corporate membership has such a standing in the engineering world that our public authorities will appreciate the fact when entrusting the engineer to carry out public works.[35]

The conservatives conceded that engineers had not received the public recognition they deserved, in spite of their efforts to upgrade the EIC's professional stature. Rather than alienate public support by adopting trade union tactics, they suggested that engineers, to increase their prestige, had only to serve the public and publicize their achievements.[36]

In spite of their objections to licensing, the conservatives could not influence majority opinion and stem the demand for political action. Shortly after the second annual professional meeting, in Saskatoon, in August 1918, the CSCE took up, with determination and skill, the practical problems of drafting and promoting licensing legislation.

At the Saskatoon meeting, the legislation committee of the Saskatchewan branch presented a draft licensing bill for discussion. Intended as a model for other provinces, the bill was carefully studied but referred back to the committee for changes. A revised bill was later sent to council for approval, pending its introduction to the fall session of the Saskatchewan legislature. However, perceiving wide variations in licensing bills prepared by other branches, on 1 October 1918 council asked the Saskatchewan branch to withhold action. Another request, in December, to approve a draft bill, was also turned down for similar reasons.[37] While the branch was angered at what it considered unnecessary delay,[38] a consensus was emerging from other branches. Considering the need for uniform provincial legislation, many branches felt that draft legislation should be thoroughly studied by all branches before any legislature was approached. Following an earlier suggestion by the Montreal branch, a special legislation committee, chaired by C.E.W. Dodwell, consisting of one delegate from each branch, was appointed at the EIC's annual meeting in Ottawa, in February 1919, to draw up a sample licensing bill.[39]

In April 1919, the fourteen-member committee met for five exhaustive days in Montreal to draft a model act. Prepared as a standardized bill for all provinces, the model was more comprehensive than the Manitoba and Quebec acts. It prescribed stiff penalties for unlicensed people practising engineering or using the title 'Professional Engineer.' It also gave wide discretionary powers to governing councils, while making ample provision for licensed engineers of one province to practise freely in another.[40]

The outstanding feature of the model act was the provision for a separate licensing society, or provincial association. These bodies were designed to be independent from the EIC and equipped with full regulatory powers of professional self-government – administration, admission, discipline. Officially, formation of provincial associations was considered an 'unavoidable' expedient to forestall the CMI's opposition.[41] Twenty years had passed since the CSCE had last sought licensing powers, but memories were still fresh of the CMI's opposition. Unofficially, however, legal considerations may have been involved. The legislative committee's lawyer, Aimé Geoffrion, advised that the EIC could not obtain provincial legislation under its Dominion charter, as it had done earlier in Quebec.[42] Unlike the Manitoba act, which incorporated the CSCE as a separate body in Manitoba, Quebec's legislative assembly had merely recognized the CSCE's Dominion charter and granted the society special regulatory powers in Quebec. According to Geoffrion, the Quebec act was probably void, because, under the British North America Act, 1867, a provincial legislature could not impose obligations on a federal company.[43]

Although the legislative committee understood that the provincial associations, not the EIC, would effectively control the profession, it seems clear that the committee believed that the EIC could still maintain its power and influence. If the EIC took the initiative to create the associations, it could dominate and control them. Later, as Geoffrion hinted, the associations might be linked together by special Dominion legislation and then affiliated with the EIC.[44] This, however, never came to pass. Instead, creation of the provincial associations marked the beginning of a long and bitter struggle with the EIC for control of the profession.[45]

In May 1919, the model act was published in the EIC's *Journal*. Two months later, council issued a letter ballot to members, and in September the *Journal* announced that 77 per cent of the votes cast favoured the act.[46]

The conservatives responded pragmatically. While they were initially opposed to licensing for genuine philosophical reasons, the model act threatened some important vested interests. For instance, conservatives, such as G.H. Duggan and H.H. Vaughan, believed (somewhat prophetically) that establishment of provincial associations would ultimately harm and, possibly, destroy the EIC. Duggan, CSCE past-president and president of Dominion Bridge Company, contended that, because provincial association membership would be compulsory, engineers would drop their EIC membership rather than pay double dues. This would, according to Duggan, 'almost certainly destroy *The Institute*.'[47] This prospect must have been particularly distressing to successful men like Duggan and Vaughan, since one of the main benefits of EIC membership was prestige enhancement. At the same time, Duggan, Vaughan, and other corporate employers undoubtedly realized that licensing would be bad for business. It would drive up salaries, because only licensed engineers, not tradesmen or practical men, could sign plans. As well, provincial associations might act, directly or indirectly, as trade unions. Unlike the EIC, they were constituted mainly to protect the engineer's professional and business interests.

Rather than attack the model act directly, the conservatives at first preferred to undermine it tactfully. In an attempt to turn younger supporters against the act, Vaughan, Duggan, and others expressed the conviction, with some justification, despite disclaimers by some legislative committee members, that the model act would exclude most salaried engineers and benefit only consultants and chief engineers. (Under section 7[i], assistants working under the direct supervision of a professional engineer were not considered practising professional engineers.)[48] At the same time, Duggan and Vaughan also promoted the idea that, as an alternative to licensing, engineering legislation should only certify, or register 'civil' engineers employed on public works. This option would win public approval, they predicted, while avoiding the stigma of unionism.[49] It was also an ideal compromise for the conservatives. Registration would distinguish non-professionals from professionals (EIC members), without closing the profession. In turn, this would uphold the principle of competition, raise the professional status of all engineers, and, most important, relieve the emerging mechanical, chemical, and electrical industries of the obligation to hire only licensed engineers.

In spite of their efforts to undermine the model act, the conservatives seemed resigned to its introduction. They never mounted effective opposition or even argued their case forcefully and convincingly. Most, including Duggan and Vaughan, were compelled eventually to give qualified approval to legislation. Substantially outnumbered by younger men determined to close the profession, the conservatives realized that the EIC had been gradually drifting away from its traditional role. By 1920, the committee on policy would commit the institute to promoting the material interests of members and, thus, deprive conservatives of logical grounds to oppose licensing.

While the conservatives bemoaned restricting competition, they were more alarmed about unionism. During 1919, as the spectre of unionization loomed with the increase in the cost of living, many grudgingly accepted licensing as an unappealing alternative to unionization. Licensing, they rationalized, could achieve the same objectives as unionization, without sacrificing professional dignity.[50] It could also appeal to most younger engineers, even to some militant union supporters, as a positive measure.

The EIC recognized that the CMI was the biggest obstacle to licensing. Before it began its licensing campaign, the EIC attempted to pacify mining engineers. There were, as F.H. Peters remarked in Saskatoon, 'some old sores of long standing between the Civil and Mining engineers.'[51] The CMI had always suspected that the CSCE was attempting to lure its young professional mining engineers away from their society with the promise of higher status through membership in an exclusively professional society.

The CSCE's change of name, in 1918, to the Engineering Institute of Canada, also generated more suspicion. According to H. Mortimer-Lamb, CMI secretary and editor of the CMI's monthly *Bulletin*, the name change was part of a sinister plot to compel all engineers to belong to the EIC. A purely 'civil' engineering society, Mortimer-Lamb contended, could not obtain restrictive licensing legislation because of opposition from mining engineers and other technical men. Removing the word 'civil' from the society's name would overcome this opposition. It would first attract and then recruit enough non-civil engineers for the EIC, as a necessary prelude to closing the profession.[52] In this context, the EIC's renewed interest in licensing, combined with its public declarations that it was eager to unite all engineers and become a truly representative national society, aroused old suspicions. Mortimer-Lamb recounted that the society was accused of having 'ulterior motives,' that it had 'hegemonic aspirations which it hoped to satisfy by using the lever of legislation to force all engineers in Canada into its ranks.'[53] The EIC, he declared earlier, was 'smitten with megalomania.'[54]

Soon after the EIC's Saskatoon meeting, in August 1918, Fraser S. Keith wrote Mortimer-Lamb to allay CMI anxieties. Legislation, Keith explained, was essential not only to protect engineers but also to protect the public against the waste of public funds by unqualified practitioners. EIC licensing legislation, he pledged, would recognize all 'qualified' engineers, including CMI members, and licensing and regulatory powers would rest with an independent body appointed by government in conjunction with the universities.[55]

On 22 December 1918, senior EIC and CMI leaders, including Duggan and Mortimer-Lamb, met in Montreal to discuss the draft Saskatchewan bill. Mortimer-Lamb and his colleagues concluded that nothing in the bill was offensive to the CMI, and the meeting resolved that the question of legislation should be carefully studied before any action was taken. While the CMI remained opposed to legislation in principle, pending further study it agreed to co-operate with the EIC in framing an acceptable act.[56] In April 1919, Keith also promised that the EIC would not seek legislation that affected mining, without the CMI's approval.[57] These assurances, together with the publication of the model act in the CMI's June *Bulletin*, persuaded

CMI leaders that the EIC was acting in good faith. Sometime in August or September 1919, Mortimer-Lamb abruptly reversed himself and began to wax effusive about the merits of engineering fraternity and co-operation.

At this point, although less suspicious of the EIC's intentions, the CMI was still not well disposed to the idea of licensing. Unofficially, it was against legislation[58] but recognized that it could do little to oppose it. Lacking the EIC's extensive branch network, the CMI was not organized to fight provincial legislation. Moreover, there was some support for legislation within the CMI. By 1918, many members felt strongly[59] that something should be done to improve the engineer's status. Bogus mining engineers frequently wasted investment capital and consequently lowered the status of legitimate mining engineers. As a result, most CMI members favoured some form of regulation. 'Every member of the Institute,' Mortimer-Lamb concurred, 'will approve, without doubt, of the general proposition that legislation is needed for the better regulation of the practice of engineering in this country.'[60] Unfortunately, CMI members disagreed about what kind of regulation was needed.

Reflecting an old division within the CMI, professional and non-professional members differed over the relative advantages of self-, as opposed to government regulation. As well, a more important disagreement developed between young, professionally trained mining engineers and older professional and non-professional CMI members. Like the EIC's junior engineers, the young men in the CMI were also ravaged by wartime inflation and had similar anxieties about status.[61] Whereas older engineers would accept voluntary registration – to enable the public to distinguish between qualified and unqualified mining engineers, provided no hiring restrictions were placed on employers[62] – young engineers were prepared to accept more drastic measures. At the same time, there was also much indifference to licensing legislation among many other mining engineers in Canada.[63]

These two factors, disaffection and apathy, alarmed senior CMI members. They feared the imposition of a close corporation on mining engineers as a result of indifference, combined with the tacit acceptance, perhaps active support, of dissatisfied young mining engineers. Unable to stop licensing legislation, they resolved to render it harmless by removing the most objectionable feature: restrictions that might bar alien mining engineers from inspecting Canadian mine properties on behalf of foreign investors. Thus, apart from appointing committees to scrutinize provincial licensing bills and ensuring that no restrictions were placed on foreign investment in mining, the CMI reluctantly yielded to the EIC's legislative initiative.[64]

On 23 September 1919, the council of the EIC approved the model act and encouraged the branches to seek licensing laws from their provincial legislatures – much to the annoyance of Mortimer-Lamb, who felt that the EIC had thereby broken its promise to the CMI.[65] By spring 1920, all provinces, except Saskatchewan, Prince Edward Island (which had too few engineers to license), and Ontario, had passed engineering licensing laws. Ontario, possessing over a third of the EIC's membership, was central to the institute's legislation program. Legislative success in this province was essential to close the profession nationally.[66] At first, prospects appeared good. There was no foreseeable opposition; the CMI was neutralized and the Drury (United Farmers) government seemed receptive. However, unlike other provincial bills, Ontario's soon encountered delays and unexpected opposition.

Ontario EIC members realized that they could not agitate for licensing through their extensive branch network. By 1918, the province had eight branches. Some centralized umbrella organization was needed to co-ordinate legislative strategy and lobby the government in strength.[67] EIC members in British Columbia and Alberta had already organized provincially; most engineers in Saskatchewan and Manitoba already belonged to the Saskatchewan and Manitoba EIC branches. In August 1919, in response to a request from Ontario members, council approved the formation of an Ontario provincial division.[68]

Recognizing that the EIC did not include all the practising professional engineers in Ontario, the Ontario division urged that engineers from all branches of the profession be consulted about any legislation. On 22 November 1919, its first conference, in Toronto, decided that a joint advisory committee could best represent the views of all engineers. Accordingly, in December, Ontario's leading professional engineering and technical societies were invited to send two representatives each to form what was called the Advisory Conference Committee.[69] These organizations included: the American Institute of Electrical Engineers, Toronto branch; the American Society of Mechanical Engineers, Ontario section; the Canadian Institute of Mining and Metallurgy (formerly the CMI); the Canadian Society of Chemical Industry; the Association of Ontario Land Surveyors; and the Ontario Association of Architects, which later withdrew in order to pursue its own licensing legislation.[70]

These organizations, ostensibly divided by technical specialization and professional rivalry, eagerly responded to the EIC's invitation, not only to protect their own interests and watch over the EIC but also to fulfil a sense of social responsibility. The war effort had fostered a spirit of co-operation and joint action. 'Never was the time more opportune than at present,' declared Mortimer-Lamb, 'for the organization in Canada of the technical bodies for united endeavor for the advancement, not only of the special interests they represent, but for national service.'[71] Engineers and scientists joined forces in the Honorary Advisory Council for Scientific and Industrial Research (1916), later the National Research Council of Canada;[72] the Joint Committee of Technical Organizations (JCTO) (1917), formed to co-ordinate the work of scientifically and technically trained men in furtherance of the war effort;[73] and the Canadian Engineering Standards Association (1917, incorporated 1919), later the Canadian Standards Association.[74] The Advisory Conference Committee was founded in the best traditions of this wartime spirit of co-operation. It was part of an increasing tendency in Canada and elsewhere, during the war, towards the bureaucratization of science and technology.

Although the drafting of a complex bill by a large constituent committee was cumbersome and time-consuming, it had important advantages. As an independent advisory body, the committee was a practical demonstration of the EIC's good faith. This served to forestall a resurgence of opposition from mining engineers, while enabling the EIC to promote its licensing schemes through a broadly representative, non-partisan body. While the EIC had only two representatives, in spite of its numerical superiority, it easily dominated by its leadership and experience. Under Willis Chipman's chairmanship, the committee quickly rejected a draft licensing bill prepared by the JCTO, in which the different branches of engineering would be governed separately by a board of engineers acting under the direct control of a government department,[75] and adopted the EIC's model act. Thus, by involving potential opponents in the committee, ostensibly as equal participants, the EIC adroitly averted opposition, while conveying an impression of unanimous voluntary co-operation.

Between March and December 1920, the committee met to draft a bill. Overcoming the enormous difficulties of reconciling conflicting interests (a 'considerable achievement,' according to the *Canadian Engineer*),[76] the committee finally produced a bill that followed the general lines of the model act.[77]

In January and February 1921, committee representatives urged their societies to endorse the bill on its general merits. They explained that each branch of the profession would be regulated separately and given equal representation on the governing council. This provision would prevent any one branch from gaining control of the profession. After further revision, the bill was approved by the constituent societies. In March, Major A.W. Gray, associate member, EIC, the Ontario legislature's only practising engineer, who had twelve years of experience in municipal engineering and highway construction, in addition to two years of active service in the Canadian Railway Troops,[78] took charge of the bill, and the EIC began to lobby the cabinet and members of the legislature. The bill passed first and second readings by 20 April, but a lengthy House adjournment delayed third reading for a year. Meanwhile, before the House met on 14 February 1922, a special committee exempted all mining operations from the bill.[79]

By 10 May 1922, when the bill came up for third reading, no organized opposition had surfaced in the House. Suddenly, however, it became apparent that some influential members would oppose the bill unless changes were made.[80] On 16 May, the bill was referred back to the special committee, which struck out subsections (a) and (b) of clause 34. These unexpected last-minute deletions fundamentally altered the substance of the bill.

Originally, clause 34 read (deletions in italics):

Any person in the Province of Ontario who, not being registered as a member of the Association in the Province of Ontario, or licensed by the Association;
(a) *Practises as a professional engineer;*
(b) *Usurps the function of a professional engineer;*
(c) Uses verbally or otherwise the title of professional engineer, or makes use of any addition to or abbreviation of such title, or of any words, name or designation that will lead to the belief that he is a professional engineer or a member of the association, *or that he is a person specially qualified to practise in any branch of professional engineering;*
(d) Advertises himself as a professional engineer in any way or by any means.
(e) Acts in such manner as to lead to the belief that he is authorized to fill the office of or to act as a professional engineer;
shall be liable upon summary conviction by any court of competent jurisdiction to a fine of not less than $100 nor more than $200 for the first offence, and to a fine not less than $200 nor more than $500 for any subsequent offence.[81]

After 'further mutilation,'[82] as Willis Chipman recalled, such as the deletion of subsection 34(e), the bill was reintroduced, and it passed third reading on 5 June 1922.

The removal of the key penalty clauses reduced the bill to an ineffectual registration law similar to the 1896 Manitoba act. The engineering profession in Ontario remained 'open.' Anyone could practise; only the title 'Professional Engineer' was restricted to members of the new Association of Professional Engineers of Ontario (APEO). The act had established a system of voluntary certification, which regulated only the use of title, rather than licensure, which would have regulated practice.[83]

Although the EIC had tactfully forestalled opposition from mining engineers, it could not pacify the powerful northern Ontario mining industry. While professional mining engineers would accept some form of regulation, the mining industry unanimously opposed it. 'Not one mine operator in the Cobalt camp,' observed the *Northern Miner*, 'is in favor of the [licensing] bill.'[84] Licensing, owners believed, would interfere with the development of Canada's mineral resources and restrict their right to employ engineers of their own choice. It would not, moreover, guarantee the employment of the best engineers. Only employers who risked capital, not licensing bodies, could choose the best man.[85] Licensing bodies governed by engineers would simply promote the interests of engineers. According to R.E. Hore, consulting editor, *Canadian Mining Journal*, licensing bodies were 'Class organizations,' which became 'most dangerous when they conceal their activities under a cloak of professed public service.'[86] The *Canadian Mining Journal* contended that most mining engineers were indifferent to licensing and that, under ordinary circumstances, there would be little support for it. Advantage was being taken of the fact that licensing had become 'a popular fad.'[87]

To mine owners, licensing was a dangerous collectivist development, little different from unionism. Following the social and industrial upheaval in Canada and abroad after the war, they were probably as afraid of engineers forming a close corporation as of mine workers organizing a union. Deeply alarmed, they used their considerable influence at Queen's Park to have the special committee cripple the licensing bill before it became law.

By 1922, all provinces, except Saskatchewan and Prince Edward Island, had passed engineering licensing laws. Saskatchewan engineers would not overcome strong opposition to licensing from the public and the government until 1930. Some farmers believed that the bill would prohibit them from building small bridges and other similar works, and, while the government would support some form of registration, especially to protect the title 'Professional Engineer,' granting engineers exclusive powers to control the profession was strongly opposed in principle.[88] Prince Edward Island would not grant engineers full licensing and regulatory powers until 1955.[89]

The laws passed by 1922 differed in detail but generally resembled the model act. Quebec was an exception. The province merely transferred the 1898 act from the CSCE to the new Corporation of Professional Engineers of Quebec.[90] In British Columbia, Manitoba, Quebec, New Brunswick, and Nova Scotia, engineers succeeded in 'closing' the profession; no one could practise engineering, or use the title 'Professional Engineer,' unless he were a member of the local provincial association.[91]

In Alberta and Ontario, however, engineering was still an 'open' profession. Because of strong opposition in the Alberta legislature to the formation of a close corporation, the Alberta bill, like the Ontario counterpart, was also downgraded to an ineffectual voluntary registration measure. Only the title 'Registered Professional Engineer' was protected by law. Although licensing proponents, such as F.H. Peters, first president of the Association of Registered Professional Engineers of Alberta, remained hopeful that the act would be amended,[92] it was not until 1930 that registration was made compulsory. Penalties for illegal practice were not enacted until 1955.[93]

The Ontario bill disappointed many engineers. Although William Storrie, chairman, Toronto branch, EIC, believed that it was 'a step in the right direction,'[94] no immediate action was taken to improve it. The Ontario government was resistant to the formation of close corporations during the 1920s, and other groups, such as veterinarians and architects, could not obtain legislation to close their professions.[95] It was not until the 1930s that the Professional Engineers Act was amended. In April 1934, the APEO created an advisory committee on legislation that succeeded in drafting a bill acceptable to the government and mining interests. The draft was presented as a private measure, and it received royal assent on 25 March 1937. This amendment effectively 'closed' the profession, much like a medieval guild. It gave the APEO complete regulatory control over the practice of engineering in Ontario.[96]

Conclusion

Licensing did not solve all the engineers' problems. Like most middle-class professionals, they continued to complain about inadequate compensation and lack of recognition. Moreover, licensing did not entirely restrict competition. In most provinces, for example, qualified alien engineers could be licensed to practise temporarily, usually as consultants. Similar privileges were not permitted in the legal and medical professions. Nevertheless, licensing enabled scientifically trained engineers eventually to gain substantial control of the profession. This was a major step towards the monopolization of the practice of engineering in Canada.

Although engineers posed as altruists to obtain legislation, they did not believe that they were acting cynically. They viewed political action as a legitimate means of fulfilling their social responsibilities, while solving their own problems. No less public spirited than many other contemporary middle-class Canadians, the engineers had a social consciousness conditioned by pragmatism, as well as their technocratic outlook. Younger engineers regarded the short-term post-war crisis arising from overcrowding and inflation as an immediate and direct threat to their tenuous middle-class status. Though not abandoning their technocratic ideals, they were forced – more by circumstance than by design – to temper their idealism and act collectively like trade unionists, in order to protect themselves with licensing laws. They were convinced that they had no other alternative.

At the same time, however, engineering thinkers and spokesmen assumed that, as the creators of modern industrial civilization, they were already serving the public interest. Allowing only 'qualified' licensed engineers to practise would protect not only the public but also society's natural leaders – engineers. The engineers' outward pretense of professionalism was merely a pragmatic political ploy to acquire professional regulatory power for noble ends. This would elevate engineers to positions of greater prestige, from which they could aspire to their rightful place as leaders of a socially harmonious technocracy.

While engineers would not acquire full licensing and regulatory powers uniformly across Canada for another forty years, the decision to agitate for these laws marked the beginning of a long legislative process to close the profession. This represented a significant new collectivist initiative in Canada. Emerging during an era of dramatic social change accompanying rapid industrialization, the engineers' licensing associations were manifestations of the new urban-industrial order. They were part of a larger collectivist assault on the ideals of laissez-faire. Organized to restrict competition and monopolize practice, they were the middle-class counterparts to trade unions, business associations, and combinations. They represented the triumph of younger, protectionist engineers over older, free-market proponents and heralded the rise of an aggressive, self-confident 'new middle class' in Canada and the Western world. They also signalled the decline of traditional notions of professionalism.

The professionalism associated with doctors and lawyers represented the pre-industrial past. It was based on individual personal relations and governed by gentlemanly conduct and philosophical idealism. The new middle-class experts represented the emerging urban-industrial order. Their expertise was collective and impersonal. They were concerned with bureaucratic functionalism and the exact techniques of social management. They were singularly dedicated to the attainment of economy and efficiency for their own sake and impatient to bring the world into conformity with their values. They fostered the notion that society could be 'engineered'; that science, not common sense, should determine social policy; and, above all, that experts, not popularly elected amateurs, should manage the new urban-industrial order.

These ideas were élitist and anti-democratic, perhaps anti-humanitarian and authoritarian. Neither democrats nor aristocrats, philosopher kings nor even wilful Übermenschen, the middle-class experts assumed that they were above politics and conventional morality; that they functioned passively as the impartial servants of a higher scientific rationality in quest of an efficient and orderly new Jerusalem. They transvaluated the traditional national precepts of order and authority into a new order based on science, a new authority based on themselves. Although Canadian engineers never realized their goal of social leadership (except indirectly, perhaps, through C.D. Howe), by 1922 they had emerged as the pre-eminent middle-class experts. They were the quintessential technocrats – 'the master spirit of the age.'

Statistical appendix

TABLE A1
Average weekly earnings (dollars) for selected male wage earners 1921

Occupations	All ages*	20–24	25–34	35–49	50–64	65 and over
Engineers, professional	40.33	25.14	36.68	46.40	42.77	35.12
Electricians	27.06	22.33	28.49	30.16	26.84	25.42
Plumbers	26.38	22.00	25.78	28.65	25.69	20.98
Clerks, office (federal and provincial governments)	27.15	22.38	26.95	28.20	30.72	27.39
Locomotive engineers	42.41	32.74	39.65	42.55	46.47	42.15
Conductors (steam railway)	39.31	25.13	36.88	39.97	42.88	35.11
Brakemen and trainmen	31.82	26.62	31.68	33.20	32.11	27.11

SOURCE: Calculated from: *Sixth Census of Canada, 1921*, Vol. III, Table 37, pp. 142–7
*Does not include wage earners under 20. Figures cover certain cities of 90,000 and over.

TABLE A2
Growth of the engineering profession 1881–1931

	1881		1891		1901		1911		1921		1931	
	No.	% labour force	No.	% labour force	No.	% labour force	No.	% labour force	No.	% labour force	No.	% labour force
Gainfully employed (labour force)	1,377,585	100	1,606,369	100	1,782,832	100	2,723,634	100	3,173,169	100	3,927,230	100
Engineers and surveyors*	1,459	0.10	2,856	0.18	2,544	0.15	7,339	0.27	12,814	0.40	15,848	0.40
Lawyers and notaries	3,503	0.25	4,332	0.27	4,967	0.28	5,881	0.22	7,209	0.28	8,058	0.21
Physicians and surgeons	3,507	0.25	4,448	0.28	5,442	0.30	7,411	0.27	9,278	0.29	10,020	0.26

SOURCE: Calculated from: *Sixth Census of Canada, 1921*, Vol. IV, Table 3, p. xiii; Table 1, pp. 6–7. *Seventh Census of Canada, 1931*, Vol. VII, Table 40, pp. 72–3.
*Published census data for engineers, during this period, included surveyors.

TABLE A3
Growth of professions 1911–21

	1911	1921	No. increase	% increase
Population	7,169,650	8,775,853	1,606,203	22.4
Gainfully employed (labour force)	2,723,634	3,173,169	449,535	16.5
Engineers and surveyors	7,339	12,814	5,475	74.6
Lawyers and notaries	5,881	7,209	1,828	31.1
Physicians and surgeons	7,411	9,278	1,867	25.1

SOURCE: As Table A2

TABLE A4
Growth of engineering by specialization 1911–21

Specialization	1911	1921	No. increase	% increase
All engineers	7,339	12,814	5,475	74.6
Civil	2,036	6,598	4,562	224.0
Mechanical	732	3,293	2,561	349.9
Electrical	647	2,214	1,567	242.2
Mining	508	709	201	39.6
Other*	3,416	–	–	–

SOURCE: Calculated from: National Archives of Canada, Engineering Institute of Canada Papers, MG 28, 1–277, Membership Files, 1887–1922
*Includes surveyors

TABLE A5
CSCE membership statistics 1887–1921

Year	Total	Full members	Associate members	Others (non-voting)*
1887	251	–	–	–
1888	423	225	65	133
1889	542	259	87	195
1890	588	265	102	221
1891	633	277	105	251
1892	659	281	115	263
1893	647	280	124	243
1894	632	283	133	216
1895	657	286	141	230
1896	606	269	140	197
1897	591	271	145	175
1898	628	284	161	183
1899	716	294	232	190
1900	847	308	289	250
1901	900	318	314	258
1902	892	323	321	204
1903	981	338	341	302
1904	1,145	378	362	405
1905	1,261	386	390	485
1906	1,389	406	424	559
1907	1,521	422	471	628
1908	1,968	463	587	868
1909	2,331	488	692	1,151
1910	2,569	521	824	1,224
1911	2,739	548	949	1,242
1912	2,882	562	1,083	1,237
1913	3,008	585	1,186	1,237
1914	2,794	622	1,313	859
1915	3,059	674	1,372	1,013
1916	3,076	693	1,409	974
1917	3,047	709	1,434	904
1918	3,132	736	1,486	910
1919	3,439	818	1,706	915
1920	4,049	918	1,953	1,178
1921	4,879	1,018	2,285	1,576

SOURCES: 'President's Address' (G.H. Duggan) *Transactions of the Canadian Society of Civil Engineers*, 30 (1917) p. 80; 'Statement of Members,' *ibid.*, Vols. 2–31 (1888 to 1917); 'Statement of membership,' *Charter, By-Laws, List of Members and Roll of Honour of the Engineering Institute of Canada* (Montreal, 1918–21)
*Includes honorary members, associates (usually businessmen), juniors (after 1912), and students

TABLE A6
Distribution of CSCE applicants* by birthplace 1887–1922

Birthplace	1887–90 No.	%	1891–4 No.	%	1895–8 No.	%	1899–1902 No.	%	1903–6 No.	%	1907–10 No.	%	1911–14 No.	%	1915–18 No.	%	1919–22 No.	%
Canada	96	54.5	50	64.1	72	77.4	72	63.7	100	58.1	218	57.2	188	52.5	137	57.0	328	56.6
Britain and empire	63	35.8	26	33.3	17	18.2	23	20.4	45	26.2	96	25.2	100	27.9	67	28.0	172	29.7
United States	10	5.7	1	1.3	2	2.2	15	13.3	18	10.5	47	12.4	41	11.5	31	13.0	65	11.3
Other	7	4	1	1.3	2	2.2	3	2.6	9	5.2	20	5.2	29	8.1	5	2.0	14	2.4
Totals	176	100	78	100	93	100	113	100	172	100	381	100	358	100	240	100	570	100

SOURCE: As Table A4
*Excludes student and junior members

TABLE A7
Apprentices and university students 1887–1922

	Apprentices		University engineering students	
	No.	%	No.	%
1887–90	206	67.1	101	32.9
1891–4	53	48.6	56	51.4
1895–8	56	56.0	44	44.0
1899–1902	69	34.8	129	65.2
1903–6	177	45.7	210	54.3
1907–10	317	45.5	379	54.5
1911–14	150	28.4	379	71.6
1915–18	84	32.4	175	67.6
1919–22	303	30.0	710	70.0

SOURCE: As Table A4

TABLE A8
CSCE growth by membership classification 1918–21

Classification	1918	1921	No. increase	% increase
All members	3,152	4,879	1,747	55.8
Members	736	1,018	282	38.3
Associate members	1,486	2,285	799	53.8
Juniors	369	438	69	18.7
Students	499	899	400	80.2
Honorary members	9	10	1	11.1
Associates	33	38	5	15.2
Elected – acceptances pending	–	191	–	–

SOURCE: Calculated from: 'Statement of membership,' *Charter, By-Laws, List of Members and Roll of Honour of the Engineering Institute of Canada* (Montreal, 1918–21)

Notes

ABBREVIATIONS

MUA   McGill University Archives
NAC   National Archives of Canada, Ottawa
OA   Archives of Ontario, Toronto
UTA   University of Toronto Archives
UTL   University of Toronto Library

AS   *Applied Science*
BCMI   *Bulletin,* Canadian Mining Institute
CE   *Canadian Engineer*
CMJ   *Canadian Mining Journal*
CMR   *Canadian Mining Review*
CR   *Contract Record*
EJ   *Engineering Journal*
EN   *Electrical News*
ENGN   *Engineering News*
ENR   *Engineering News-Record*
JCMI   *Journal of the Canadian Mining Institute*
JEIC   *Journal of the Engineering Institute of Canada*
TCSCE   *Transactions,* Canadian Society of Civil Engineers
TEIC   *Transactions,* Engineering Institute of Canada

INTRODUCTION

1 For Macdougall's biographical details, see NAC, Engineering Institute of
Canada Papers, MG 28, 1–277, Membership Files (Alan Macdougall);

Minutes of the Proceedings of the Institution of Civil Engineers, 129 (1897) p. 375; *TCSCE*, 11 (1897) p. 191; 'The Late Alan Macdougall,' *Proceedings of the Canadian Institute*, new ser., pt. 3 (Sept. 1897) p. 94.

2 P.B. Waite, *Canada, 1874–1896: Arduous Destiny* (Toronto, 1978) pp. 74–8.

3 W.T. Easterbrook and Hugh G.J. Aitken, *Canadian Economic History* (Toronto, 1894) p. 294.

4 Reprinted in: *Philosophy of Railroads and Other Essays, By T.C. Keefer*, edited with an Introduction by H.V. Nelles (Toronto, 1972) pp. 3–59.

5 Easterbrook and Aitken, *Canadian Economic History*, p. 316.

6 'President's Address' (T.C. Keefer), *TCSCE*, 2 (1888) p. 17.

7 Gregory S. Kealey, 'Toronto's Industrial Revolution, 1850–1892,' in Michael S. Cross and Gregory S. Kealey (eds.), *Canada's Age of Industry, 1849–1896* (Toronto, 1982) p. 38. Also see Paul Craven and Tom Traves, 'Canadian Railways as Manufactures, 1850–1880,' *Historical Papers*, (1983) pp. 254–5.

8 Andrew Charles Gross, 'Engineering Manpower in Canada,' (PhD dissertation, Ohio State University, 1968) Appendix B, Table I, p. 370.

9 See Bruce Sinclair, 'Canadian Technology: British Traditions and American Influences,' *Technology and Culture*, 20 (Jan. 1979) pp. 110–11.

10 *Ibid.*, pp. 108–23.

11 Based on 'Notable Figures in the Institute's Past: Past Presidents,' *EJ*, 20 (June 1937) pp. 283–7; *TCSCE*, 6 (1892) pp. 262–5; *ibid.*, 11 (1897) pp. 192–3; *ibid.*, 13 (1899) pp. 365–6; *ibid.*, 24 (1910) pp. 33–4; *CE*, 5 (June 1897) p. 51; *ibid.*, 32 (19 April 1917) p. 344; *ibid.*, 34 (28 March 1918) p. 284; *EJ*, 4 (Dec. 1923) p. 542; W. Stewart Wallace, *The Macmillan Dictionary of Canadian Biography* (Toronto, 1963) p. 683.

12 See H.V. Nelles, 'Introduction,' to *Philosophy of Railroads*, p. xx.

13 Gzowski's biographers are not clear on this point. See Ludwik Kos-Rabcewicz-Zubkowski and William Edward Greening, *Sir Casimir Stanislaus Gzowski: A Biography* (Toronto, 1959) p. 7.

14 For an overview of Canadian engineering education see George S. Emmerson, *Engineering Education: A Social History* (New York, 1973) chap. 2; George Richardson, 'Early Schools Meet Local Needs,' *EJ*, 59 (July/Aug. 1976) pp. 49–50, and 'Engineering Schools Enter a New Era,' *ibid.* (Sept./Oct.) pp. 44–5; 'Engineering Education in Canada,' *ibid.* (Sept. 1962) pp. 60–98 and (Jan. 1963) pp. 42–66. For a concise analysis of the development of engineering education in the United States, see David F. Noble, *America By Design: Science, Technology and the Rise of Corporate Capitalism* (New York, 1977) pp. 20–3.

15 Frank D. Adams, 'The Universities and the Engineering Profession,' *JEIC*, 4 (Dec. 1921) p. 619.

16 Canada, Dominion Bureau of Statistics, *Statistical Report on Education in Canada, 1921* (Ottawa, 1923) p. 110.

17 C.R. Young, *Early Engineering Education at Toronto* (Toronto, 1958) p. 71.
18 *Ibid.*, p. 102.
19 See especially Edwin Layton, 'Mirror-Image Twins: The Communities of Science and Technology' in George H. Daniels (ed.), *Nineteenth-Century American Science: A Reappraisal* (Evanston, 1972) pp. 210–30.
20 Young, *Early Engineering Education at Toronto*, pp. 76–9, 114–20.
21 *Ibid.*, p. 101.
22 *Ibid.*, pp. 80, 135.
23 Macdougall, 'A Plea for a Close Corporation,' *TCSCE*, 6 (1892) pp. 106, lll.
24 T.C. Keefer, 'A Sequel to the Philosophy of Railroads,' in H.V. Nelles (ed.), *Philosophy of Railroads*, pp. 95–8.
25 For an analysis of British attitudes towards engineers, see Bruce A. MacFarlane, 'The Chartered Engineer: A Study of the Recruitment, Qualification, Conditions of Employment, and Professional Associations of Chartered Civil, Electrical, and Mechanical Engineers in Great Britain' (PhD dissertation, University of London, 1961) pp. 94–6.

CHAPTER 1: 'THE MASTER SPIRIT OF THE AGE'

1 Quoted in Pierre Berton, *The National Dream: The Great Railway 1871-1881* (Toronto, 1970) p. 46.
2 Some of Keefer's writings have been edited with an excellent introduction by H.V. Nelles, in *Philosophy of Railroads and Other Essays by T.C. Keefer* (Toronto, 1972). For a discussion of Kingsford, see 'Obituary – William Kingsford: A Tribute to His Memory,' *TCSCE*, 13 (1899) pp. 194–8; J.M. McConica, 'William Kingsford and Whiggery,' *Canadian Historical Review*, 40 (June 1959) pp. 108–20; and Carl Berger, *The Writing of Canadian History: Aspects of English Canadian Historical Writing, 1900–1970* (Toronto, 1976) pp. 2–3.
3 Although Canadian engineers drew inspiration from British engineering thought, they were exposed more to American ideas. They were avid readers of American engineering periodicals; heard addresses by prominent American engineers, such as George F. Swain, and came into contact with Americans in Canada, like C.D. Howe – Swain's student.
4 Edit. 'The Engineer's Opportunity,' *CE*, 15 (14 Aug. 1908) pp. 567–8.
5 St. George Boswell, 'The Engineer of Today,' *ibid.*, 3 (10 Feb. 1896) p. 257.
6 Edit. 'The Defeat of Reciprocity,' *ibid.*, 21 (28 Sept. 1911) p. 371.
7 C.M. Canniff, 'Retiring President, Toronto Engineers' Club,' *ibid.*, 20 (16 Feb. 1911) p. 327.
8 Sandford Fleming, 'Note on Electoral Representation and the Rectification of Parliament,' in *An Appeal to the Canadian Institute on the Rectification of Parliament* (Toronto, 1892) p. 24.

9 For a thoughtful analysis of the controversy over the meaning of the terms 'science,' 'applied science,' and 'technology,' see Maurice Adelman, 'Toward a Sociology of Technology' *Technology and Society* (Oct. 1974) pp. 123–7. Although mining engineers referred to themselves as 'technical men,' civil engineers rarely used the term. Occasionally they referred to engineering as 'applied science,' and they regarded their work as being more scientific than technical. The terms 'applied science' and 'engineering' were sometimes used interchangeably – even synonymously.

10 For background on the idea of progress in Canada, see L.S. Fallis Jr., 'The Idea of Progress in the Province of Canada, 1841–1867' (PhD dissertation, University of Michigan, 1966), especially chap. 4.

11 For an interesting analysis of the beneficial effects of the introduction of large-scale machine production to Canadian industry, see G.C. Cunningham, 'Energy and Labour,' *TCSCE*, 5 (1891) pp. 235–61.

12 UTL, Canadian Society of Civil Engineers, Toronto Branch Papers (hereafter Toronto Branch Papers) MS 102, Box no. 4, 'Meeting at Engineers' Club,' 5 Feb. 1917, p. 26.

13 Edit. 'Importance of Canada as an Engineering Field,' *CR*, 24, no. 38 (22 Sept. 1909) p. 31.

14 Canniff, 'Retiring President,' p. 327.

15 See, e.g., 'President's Address' (Henry T. Bovey) *TCSCE*, 15 (1901) p. 23.

16 R.W. Leonard, 'Presidential Address,' *TEIC*, 34 (Jan. 1920) p. 5.

17 *Ibid.*, pp. 18–19. Engineers were equally critical of corrupt and irresponsible business practices, which they believed created the conditions for labour disputes. See, e.g., 'President's Address' (W. McLea Walbank), *TCSCE*, 22 (1908) p. 47.

18 Leonard, 'Presidential Address,' pp. 5–14, *passim*; edit. 'Strikes and Lock-outs,' *CE*, 15 (23 Oct. 1908) pp. 749–50.

19 Leonard, 'Presidential Address,' p. 8.

20 Edit. 'Lenin on the Intellectuals and the Engineers,' *CMJ*, 41 (6 Aug. 1920) p. 635.

21 E.T. Clark, 'The Engineering Institute of Canada,' *Transactions*, University of Toronto Engineering Society, no. 36 (15 April 1922) pp. 29–30.

22 Although engineers liked to think that they were neutral in labour disputes, they lined up solidly with management and prided themselves on keeping public utilities running during municipal strikes. 'Vancouver Branch,' *JEIC*, 11 (July 1919) p. 520; 'Winnipeg Engineers' Achievement,' *ibid.* (Aug. 1919) p. 562; edit. 'Service to the Public,' *CE*, 38 (12 Feb. 1920) p. 217.

23 Engineers generally liked working men but did not accept them as their equals. Their attitude was apt to be paternalistic. See Eugene W. Stern's

remarks to the engineering students, University of Toronto, 'The Young Civil Engineer,' *AS*, new ser. 2 (Jan. 1909) p. 91.

24 Leonard, 'Presidential Address,' p. 14.

25 Engineers put great faith in the capacity of open discussion and arbitration to resolve labour disputes, provided, according to the *Canadian Engineer*, 'the parties are not extremists, prompted entirely by selfish motives.' The *Canadian Engineer*, for example, readily supported the Lemieux Act. See edit. 'The Arbitration of Labour Disputes,' *CE*, 20 (4 May 1911) p. 654.

26 Leonard, 'Presidential Address,' p. 11.

27 Edit. 'The Engineers' Opportunity,' *EN*, 25 (1 May 1916) p. 21.

28 H.V. Nelles, 'Introduction' to *Philosophy of Railroads*, p. xix.

29 Fleming, *An Appeal*, pp. 9–32; Sandford Fleming, *Parliamentary vs Party Government* (Kingston, 1891); Carl Berger, *The Sense of Power: Studies in the Ideas of Canadian Imperialism 1867–1914* (Toronto, 1970) pp. 199–200; T.L. Crossley, 'The Engineer in Politics' (abstract) *JEIC*, 4 (May 1921) p. 325.

30 Sam G. Porter, 'The Civil Engineer and His Relation to Society,' *CE*, 26 (12 Feb. 1914) p. 233.

31 Leonard, 'Presidential Address,' pp. 13–14; R.A. Ross, 'Retiring President's Address,' *JEIC*, 4 (March 1921) p. 198; Edit. 'Municipal Engineers,' *CE*, 31 (3 Aug. 1916) p. 99.

32 The young editor of the *Canadian Engineer* and town engineer for North Toronto, E.A. James, repeatedly drew attention to the abuse of city engineers by city councils. On James, see 'Our Representation in the Senate,' *AS*, no. 4 (Nov. 1910) p. 5; 'E.A. James, B.A.Sc.,' *ibid.*, new ser. no. 5 (March 1910) p. 4.

33 Edit. 'The Engineers' Opportunity,' p. 21; Edit. 'The Municipal Engineer,' p. 615; edit. 'Engineers and City Governments,' *EN*, 29 (26 April 1915) p. 311; edit. 'Municipal Engineer and Employer,' *ibid.*, 25 (21 Aug. 1913) p. 342.

34 Edit. 'Time for a Change in Municipal Government,' *ibid.* 28 (25 March 1915) p. 391; 'City Engineers and Civic Mismanagement,' *CR*, 25, no. 52 (27 Dec. 1911) pp. 38–9; Unsigned letter to Editor, *ibid.* no. 51 (20 Dec. 1911) p. 41. At least one engineer, however, had reservations about commission government; see Donald F. McLeod to Editor, *ibid.* 28, no. 6 (11 Feb. 1914) p. 162.

35 Ross, 'Retiring President's Address,' p. 199.

36 For background, see Paul Rutherford, 'To-morrow's Metropolis: The Urban Reform Movement in Canada,' Canadian Historical Association, *Historical Papers* (1971) pp. 204–24; 'Introduction,' *Saving the Canadian City: The First Phase 1880–1920*, edited with an introduction by Paul Rutherford (Toronto and Buffalo, 1974) pp. ix–xxiii.

37 John Weaver has suggested that W. McLea Walbank, managing director of

the Montreal Light, Heat and Power Company (and president of CSCE, 1907) endorsed municipal reform largely because his utility company could no longer profitably afford bribes to municipal politicians. John C. Weaver, 'Elitism and the Corporate Ideal: Businessmen and Boosters in Canadian Civic Reform, 1890–1920,' in *Cities in the West: Papers of the Western Canada Urban History Conference – University of Winnipeg, October, 1974,* eds. A.R. McCormack and Ian MacPherson (Ottawa, 1975) p. 53.

38 *Ibid.,* pp. 48–73; Alan F.J. Artibise, *Winnipeg: A Social History of Urban Growth, 1874–1914* (Montreal and London, 1975) chap. 3; *cf.* Samuel P. Hays, 'The Politics of Reform in Municipal Government in the Progressive Era,' *Pacific Northwest Quarterly,* 55 (Oct. 1964) pp. 157–69.

39 Edit. 'Engineers and City Government,' p. 311; edit. 'The Engineer and Public Service,' *CE,* 30 (9 Nov. 1916) p. 389.

40 Engineers pointed out, however, that medical progress was dependent on engineering for such things as fine surgical instruments and electrical appliances. The same argument was made in regard to architects concerning the application of reinforced concrete in buildings. See Walter J. Francis, 'Engineering as a Profession,' *AS,* new ser. 8 (Oct. 1913) p. 138; Walter J. Francis, 'Engineering in Canada,' *ibid.* 3 (March 1910) p. 217.

41 Francis, 'Engineering as a Profession,' p. 138.

42 Walter J. Francis, 'Address – The Engineer: His Character, Training and Personality,' *AS* (Nov. 1909) pp. 20–1; J.L.G. Stuart, 'Engineering among Other Professions,' *CE,* 26 (2 April 1914) p. 543; 'Cape Breton Branch' (Address by C.M. O'Dell) *JEIC,* 4 (July 1921) p. 425.

43 Francis, 'Address – The Engineer,' p. 20.

44 Edit. 'The Lawyer and the Engineer,' *CE,* 33 (16 Aug. 1917) p. 147; *cf.* Stuart, 'Engineering among Other Professions,' p. 542.

45 Edit. 'The Lawyer and the Engineer,' p. 147.

46 Stuart, 'Engineering among Other Professions,' pp. 542–3.

47 Edit. 'The Engineer and Public Affairs,' *CE,* 33 (27 Sept. 1917) p. 287.

48 Edit. 'Public Appreciation of the Engineer in Relation to His Work,' *CR,* 29 (15 July 1915) p. 696.

49 Edit. 'The Claim of the Engineer,' *CE,* 33 (12 Aug. 1917) p. 103. The *Contract Record* described the engineer as 'the pioneer of industrial and economic progress'; edit. 'The Epic in Engineering,' *CR,* 32 (14 Aug. 1918) p. 631.

50 Francis, 'Engineering as a Profession,' p. 137; Walter J. Francis, 'The Engineer and the Public,' *CE,* 26 (3 April 1914) p. 671; edit. 'The Engineer and Public Affairs,' p. 287.

51 Francis, 'Engineering as a Profession,' p. 138; *cf.* Francis, 'Engineering in Canada,' p. 218.

52 'President's Address' (Edward H. Keating), *TCSCE*, 16 (1902) pp. 27–8. Similar remarks were made by Canniff, 'Retiring President,' p. 326.

53 Walter J. Francis, 'The Engineer and the War,' *CE*, 30 (6 April 1916) p. 417.

54 See, e.g., Frederick B. Goedike to Editor, *CE*, 34 (23 May 1918) p. 469. In this context, John Murphy, quoting a speech by W.F. Tye, president of the CSCE, 1912, remarked that the engineer was 'the most important man in the world'; Toronto Branch Papers, Box no. 5, 'Minutes of a Special Meeting of the Ottawa Branch,' p. 4.

55 Edit. 'Reconstruction and the Engineer,' *CE*, 33 (5 July 1917) p. 19.

56 Edit. 'Engineers and City Government,' *ibid.*, 29 (26 April 1915) p. 311; edit. 'The Engineer and Public Service,' p. 389; edit. 'Reconstruction and the Engineer,' p. 19; edit. 'Present Representation and the Engineer,' *ibid.*, 33 (18 Oct. 1917) p. 349.

57 Edit. 'The Claim and the Engineer,' p. 103. Engineers were proud of their administrative achievements. They called attention to the growing number of engineers who were appointed city managers, proof of their ability to govern; edit. 'The Engineer and Public Service,' p. 309.

58 'Fifth General Professional Meeting' (Col. Leonard) *JEIC*, 11 (Oct. 1919) p. 672.

59 Haultain believed that the engineer's major characteristic was 'his persistent tendency towards honesty'; Toronto Branch Papers, Box no. 4, 'Meeting at Engineers' Club,' 5 Feb. 1917, p. 11.

60 Frederick B. Goedike to Editor, p. 469.

61 Edit. 'The Engineer's Opportunity,' p. 21. Ironically, one consequence of developing a self-image as unbiased thinkers, logical and objective, according to Edwin Layton, was to discourage engineers from solving the problems they had created. See Edwin Layton, 'Mirror-Image Twins: The Communities of Science and Technology,' in George H. Daniels (ed.), *Nineteenth-Century American Science: A Reappraisal* (Evanston, 1972) pp. 229–30.

62 Edit. 'Conscription and the Engineer,' p. 91.

63 Edit. 'Municipal Administration at Victoria, B.C.,' *CR*, 25, no. 44 (1 Nov. 1911) p. 35; see also edit. 'Expert Advice,' *CE*, 18 (16 June 1910) p. 604.

64 Thorstein Veblen, *The Engineer and the Price System* (New York, 1947) pp. 71, 134. Veblen predicted that engineers would lead a social revolution. For an excellent analysis of this aspect of Veblen's thought, see Edwin Layton, 'Veblen and the Engineers,' *American Quarterly*, 14 (Spring 1962) pp. 64–72.

65 The engineer's technocratic ideas, however, differed sharply from those of the technocracy movement that emerged briefly during the early 1930s in the United States and Canada. Canadian engineers, for example, never developed a radical anti-capitalist critique, advocating the abolition of the

price system. In style and outlook, they were closer to the technocrats later popularized by James Burnham and John Kenneth Galbraith. For background on technocracy, see William A. Akin, *Technocracy and the American Dream: The Technocrat Movement, 1900–1941* (Berkeley, 1977) and Henry Eisner Jr., *The Technocrats: Prophets of Automation* (Syracuse, 1967).

66 C.R. Young, 'The Rise of the Engineer,' *EJ*, 6 (Nov. 1923) p. 511.

67 Stuart, 'Engineering among Other Professions,' p. 553.

68 M.J. Butler, 'Success in the Engineering Profession,' *CE*, 8 (Feb. 1901) p. 224.

69 Engineers maintained that modern practice drew them increasingly into business – contracts, finance, labour relations, business law – and finally into management. Although they possessed a virtual monopoly of technical expertise, they also recognized that their professional lives were controlled by businessmen. The cultivation of business skills, they argued, would make engineers more competitive in an environment dominated by businessmen. Accordingly, engineering students were often counselled on the necessity of acquiring business, as well as technical knowledge. See R.A. Ross, 'A Plea for the Business Training of the Engineer,' *AS*, new ser. 2 (Dec. 1908) p. 57; edit. 'The Technically Trained Man in Business,' *CE*, 31 (3 Aug. 1916) p. 99; K.L. Aitken, 'The Commercial Side of Engineering,' *AS*, new ser. 1 (Feb. 1908) p. 190; E.T. Clark, 'The Engineering Institute of Canada,' pp. 30–1.

70 Edit. 'A Slack Time for Engineers,' *CE*, 27 (22 Oct. 1914) p. 573.

71 The 'success ethic,' especially in a developing colonial society like Canada, was generalized into a national cult. Its ideal was the entrepreneur, the self-made man who, by his own initiative, competed on an equal basis for wealth, power, and recognition. For a discussion, see Paul Rutherford, 'A Portrait of Alienation in Victorian Canada: The *Private Memoranda* of P.S. Hamilton,' *Journal of Canadian Studies*, 12 (June 1977) pp. 19–22. The success ethic was closely related to another Victorian ideal which W.L. Morton describes as 'The Cult of Manliness' – the 'expression of the drive to prove oneself in an individualistic competitive society and to do so with some style and *éclat*'; W.L. Morton, 'Victorian Canada,' in W.L. Morton, *The Shield of Achilles* (Toronto, 1968) p. 321. Engineers often liked to refer to theirs as the 'manly profession.' See, e.g., R.E.W. Haggarty to Editor, *CE*, 17 (22 Oct. 1909) p. 468.

72 Although Smiles's best-known work was *Self Help* (1859), engineers naturally preferred his *Lives of the Engineers* (1904), and Professor Peter Gillespie, University of Toronto, thought that a Canadian version of this book would be a great inspiration to engineering students; Toronto Branch Papers, Box no. 7, 'Biographies of Engineers,' pp. 1–2.

73 Gzowski combined all the right qualities for success in the eyes of engineers – engineering achievement, financial success, and social honours. For a

biography, see Ludwik Kos-Rabcewicz-Zubkowski and William Edward Greening, *Sir Casimir Stanislaus Gzowski: A Biography* (Toronto, 1959). For a brief popular study, see Norman Sheffe, *Casimir Gzowski* (Toronto, 1975).

74 Edit. 'The Engineer and Public Affairs,' p. 287. Also see Toronto Branch Papers, Box no. 4, H. Wickstead to E. Oliver, 17 Feb. 1917, pp. 2–3.

75 J.F.P. Tate to Editor, *CE*, 39 (25 Nov. 1920) p. 561.

76 St. George Boswell, 'The Engineer Today,' p. 258. Although engineers assumed that their outlook differed from that of businessmen in this regard, their reservations about success were similar to other philosophers of success who placed morality and character formation ahead of unrestrained acquisition. See Allan Smith, 'The Myth of the Self-Made Man in English Canada, 1850–1914,' *Canadian Historical Review*, 49 (June 1978) pp. 203–4; Michael Bliss, *A Living Profit: Studies in the Social History of Canadian Business, 1883–1911* (Toronto, 1974) p. 32; Timothy Travers, 'Samuel Smiles and the Pursuit of Success in Victorian Britain,' Canadian Historical Association, *Historical Papers* (1971) pp. 154–65.

77 Charles T. Harvey, 'The Conjunction of the Nineteenth Century from an Engineering Standpoint,' *AS*, no. 12 (1898–99) p. 168.

78 Boswell, 'The Engineer Today,' pp. 258–9; 'President's Address' (W.G.M. Thomson) *TCSCE* (1899) pp. 23–4. In this context, *cf.* T.C. Keefer's earlier views on the unsatisfactory professional relationship between contractors and engineers in 'A Sequel to the Philosophy of Railroads,' in Nelles (ed.), *Philosophy of Railroads*, p. 96.

79 Harvey, 'The Conjunction of the Nineteenth Century from an Engineering Standpoint,' p. 168.

80 J. Grant MacGregor to Editor, *CE*, 14 (4 Oct. 1907) pp. 367–8.

81 'President's Address' (E.H. Keating), p. 20.

82 *Ibid.*, p. 28.

83 C.E.W. Dodwell, 'Engineers and Engineering,' *JEIC*, 3 no. 3 (March 1920) p. 144.

84 Edit. 'The Survival of the Fittest,' *CE*, 33 (8 Nov. 1917) p. 409. Social Darwinism did not have as great an impact on Canadian engineers as it did on Americans. For an analysis of Social Darwinism and American engineers, see Edwin T. Layton Jr., *Revolt of the Engineers: Social Responsibility and the American Engineering Profession* (Cleveland, 1971) pp. 55–7.

85 See G. Baillairge, 'The Engineer, The Master Spirit of the Age,' *CE*, 8 (3 July 1900) p. 55.

CHAPTER 2: 'THE MONTREAL CLIQUE'

1 The Mining Society of Nova Scotia remained independent until its affiliation

with the Canadian Mining Institute in 1919. Although it admitted business-men, its members did not claim to represent an industry and aspired to be a professional society. Edit. 'Canadian Mining Societies,' *CMJ*, 35 (1 Nov. 1914) p. 894; F.W. Gray to Editor, *ibid.*, 39 (1 Dec. 1918) p. 401.

2 H. Mortimer-Lamb, 'The Institute in Its Relationship to Government,' *Bulletin of the Canadian Institute of Mining and Metallurgy*, no. 107 (March 1921) p. 231.

3 No scholarly history of the CMI exists. A few narrative accounts, however, have been written by CMI members: H. Mortimer-Lamb, 'Some Notes on the History and Recent Development of the Canadian Mining Institute,' *CMJ*, 30 (1 Oct. 1909) pp. 585, 588; John E. Hardman, 'Some Reminiscences of the Early Days of the Institute,' *BCMI*, no. 83 (March 1919) pp. 297–303; and W.M. Goodwin, 'The Institute – 1898–1948,' *Transactions of the Canadian Mining Institute and of the Mining Society of Nova Scotia*, 51 (1948) pp. 11–13.

4 UTL, Canadian Society of Civil Engineers, Toronto Branch Papers (hereafter Toronto Branch Papers), MS 102, Box no. 4, 'Meeting at the Engineers' Club' (Minutes) p. 25; Edit. 'Engineers and the Mining Industry,' *CMJ*, 39 (1 Nov. 1918) p. 363; Edit. 'The Canadian Mining Institute,' *ibid.* (1 Dec. 1918) p. 399.

5 The American Institute of Mining Engineers (AIME) was remarkably similar to the CMI. It admitted non-professionals: 'all persons practically engaged in mining, metallurgy, or metallurgical engineering'; quoted in John W. Lieb Jr., 'The Organization and Administration of National Engineering Societies,' *Transactions of the American Institute of Electrical Engineers*, 24 (Jan.–Dec. 1905) p. 287. The CMI considered itself a 'brother-in-arms' to the AIME; Hardman, 'Some Reminiscences of the Early Days of the Institute,' p. 303.

6 Edit. 'Canadian Mining Institute,' p. 400. The Canadian Electrical Associa-tion, founded 1891, was another trade society, organized along industrial, rather than professional lines. Its purpose was 'to foster and encourage the science of electricity and promote the interests of those engaged in any electrical enterprise.' Its members were connected mainly with electrical utilities and electrical manufacturing. 'The Founding of the C.E.A.,' *EN*, 49 (15 June 1940) pp. 64–7; 'The First Quarter Century,' *ibid.*, pp. 68–80, 87–8.

7 The council of the CMI was empowered to admit anyone whom it deemed 'eligible through connection with mining affairs.' *Bylaws of the Canadian Mining Institute* (originally adopted March 1905), printed in *BCMI*, no. 11 (June 1910) p. 217.

8 Edit. 'Canadian Mining Institute,' p. 413. Controversy over the status of the CMI was aroused by H.E.T. Haultain (a prominent member of both the CMI and the Canadian Society of Civil Engineers), who remarked that the CMI was

a 'trade association,' and by a Memorandum to Prime Minister Borden, from an unofficial committee of the Canadian Society of Civil Engineers, which disparaged the size of the CMI's professional membership. See Edit. 'The Canadian Mining Institute,' *CE*, 35 (7 Nov. 1918) p. 417; Edit. 'The Canadian Mining Institute,' *ibid.*, 36 (23 Jan. 1919) p. 173; *Memorandum Regarding National Industrial Development in Canada, Submitted to the Right Honourable Sir Robert Borden Prime Minister of Canada, May 1916, by certain members of the Canadian Society of Civil Engineers and Sir Charles Ross Bart*; NAC, Engineering Institute of Canada Papers, MG 28, 1–277, Scrap Books (hereafter Scrap Books), no. 6, R.A. Ross to R.L. Borden, 30 May 1917; Edit. 'Misrepresenting Canadian Mining Societies,' *CMJ*, 38 (1 May 1917) p. 190; Edit. 'That Memorandum of the Civil Engineers,' *ibid.* (15 May 1917) p. 207; R.W. Leonard to Editor, *ibid.* (1 June 1917) p. 228; John E. Hardman to Editor, *BCMI*, no. 80 (Dec. 1918) pp. 1012–13.

9 Mortimer-Lamb, 'Some Notes on the History,' p. 585. The CMI claimed to have prevented the imposition of an export tax on Sudbury Copper-Nickel and reduced the royalty on Yukon gold, in addition to achieving similar reforms in Quebec. It claimed also to have been instrumental in the establishment of a separate federal Department of Mines and to have virtually nominated its first minister; *ibid.*, p. 586; Goodwin, 'The Institute – 1898–1948,' p. 11; Mortimer-Lamb, 'The Institute in Its Relationship to Government,' p. 232.

10 Edit. 'The Engineer and the Canadian Mining Institute,' *CMJ*, 40 (29 Jan. 1919) pp. 49–50.

11 In 1918, the CSCE changed its name to the Engineering Institute of Canada (EIC). Only a few brief narrative histories of the CSCE exist. See, e.g., 'The Story of the Engineering Institute of Canada, 1887–1937,' *EJ*, 20 (June 1937) pp. 275–82; 'The Story of the Engineering Institute of Canada, 1887–1962,' *ibid.* (June 1962) pp. 74–8; W.G. Richardson, 'The Birth of the EIC,' *ibid.*, 59 (Jan.–Feb. 1976) pp. 54–7.

12 In 1887, most members of the CSCE were engaged in railway, contracting, or municipal work. Mechanical, electrical, chemical, and mining engineering were in their infancy, and the founders could not have foreseen the later degree of specialization. Nevertheless, they were far-sighted enough to have provided for their inclusion in the society: 'The Story of the Engineering Institute of Canada, 1887–1937,' *ibid.*, pp. 277–8; Edit. 'Broadening the Scope of the Canadian Society of Civil Engineers,' *CR*, 31 (28 March 1917) p. 274; Edit. 'An Engineering Society to Include All Canada's Technical Men,' *EN*, 26 (15 Feb. 1917) p. 19.

13 The formation of the Canadian Institute in 1849, by Sir Sandford Fleming and others, represented one of the earliest attempts to organize engineers.

This society, however, also included land surveyors and architects and, after a time, concentrated most of its attention on pure, rather than applied science. See W. Stewart Wallace, 'A Sketch of the History of the Royal Canadian Institute, 1849–1949,' in W. Stewart Wallace (ed.), *The Royal Canadian Institute Centennial Volume 1849–1949* (Toronto, 1949) p. 127. In 1860, the Association of Provincial Land Surveyors and Institute of Civil Engineers was incorporated in the United Province of Canada, but little is known about it. See 'Engineering Organization in Canada,' *Engineer*, 144 (30 July 1937) p. 130.

14 'President's Address' (T.C. Keefer) *TCSCE*, 2 (1888) p. 10. In Ontario, most city engineers were forced to obtain licences to practise as land surveyors, in order to carry out their responsibilities. See Alan Macdougall's remarks: 'Proceedings of the Toronto Summer Meeting,' *ibid.*, 10 (1896) p. 98.

15 'The Professional Status,' *ibid.* (1893) pp. 246–7.

16 'Personals: Enthusiastic Champion of Profession,' *JEIC*, 3 (July 1920) p. 370. Dodwell later headed the committee, which in 1919 drafted a model act that formed the basis of provincial legislation, establishing provincial licensing associations. He is somewhat inaccurately referred to as the 'father of engineering legislation in Canada'; *cf.* 'The Story of the Engineering Institute of Canada, 1887–1937,' p. 278.

17 Scrap Book, no. 1, Alan Macdougall, 'Circular,' 8 Jan. 1886. An earlier attempt to start a society was made by E.W. Plunkett, in 1880, when he issued a circular under the pseudonym XY. Plunkett advocated modelling a society after the Institution of Civil Engineers, but with certain modifications to meet Canadian needs. This initiative, however, was not successful. See *ibid.*, XY 'Circular,' 15 May 1880.

18 Macdougall personally financed the early organizational expenses and won praise and recognition from his colleagues. *Ibid.*, Macdougall to John Kennedy, 16 Feb. 1886; NAC, Engineering Institute of Canada Papers, MG 28, 1–277, Minutes (hereafter Council Minutes), Minutes of the First Annual Meeting, CSCE, 24 Feb. 1887, p. 10.

19 Council Minutes, Minutes of Meeting of Provisional Committee, 4 March 1886, enclosure, n.p.; *ibid.*, 11 Nov. 1886, Minutes First Annual Meeting, 24 Feb. 1887, pp. 3–4; 'President's Address' (T.C. Keefer) pp. 13–14.

20 In February 1881, An Act Respecting Civil Engineers, to regulate the qualifications of engineers through registration, was introduced as a private measure into the Ontario legislature. It divided engineering into branches and engineers into various grades. A board of engineers, appointed by the crown from a list of fourteen prominent engineers (cited apparently without the knowledge or consent of the engineers named), would be given broad powers to regulate all aspects of professional practice. This bill, however,

received little support and was thrown out upon second reading. See, OA, RG 8 1-7-H, An Act Respecting Civil Engineers.

21 In this respect, the views of the conservatives were more in accord with Plunkett's intentions; see above, note 17.

22 Keefer, 'President's Address,' p. 11.

23 Scrap Book, no. 1, quoted in Montreal *Gazette*, 25 Feb. 1887, clipping.

24 *Ibid.*

25 A majority (nineteen) of the CSCE's charter members were members of the ICE. C.H. McLeod, 'How Canadian Engineers Organize,' *CE*, 32 (19 April 1917) p. 341.

26 *Charter, By Laws and List of Members of the Canadian Society of Civil Engineers* (Montreal, 1905), hereafter *By-Laws* (1905), s. 3.

27 It was common practice for railway companies to give reduced or free passage to its employees to attend CSCE meetings. Other companies frequently entertained visiting engineers when they inspected their engineering works. See Minutes Ordinary Meeting, 3 Jan. 1889, p. 164; Council Minutes, 3 Feb. 1891, p. 57; 'Report of the Annual Meeting,' *TCSCE* 23 (1909) p. 85; *ibid.*, 25 (1911) p. 182.

28 NAC, Engineering Institute of Canada Papers, MG 28, 1–277, Correspondence (hereafter EIC Papers), P.K. Hyndman to H.T. Bovey, 18 April 1887.

29 The Engineers' Clubs were social clubs, which provided an informal setting for members to meet and entertain clients and business and professional associates. Their membership included prominent CSCE members, technically trained men, non-professionals, and businessmen. Among the oldest and most successful groups were the Toronto and Montreal engineers' clubs, incorporated in 1902 and 1903 respectively. The Toronto Engineers' Club, reorganized in 1911 in order to broaden its membership and social activities, was unique, because it served as the headquarters of all important engineering organizations in the city. 'The Engineers' Club of Toronto,' *CR*, 31 (7 Feb. 1917) p. 118; 'The Engineers' Club of Montreal,' *ibid.*, 26 (12 June 1912) p. 54; C.R. Young, 'The Engineers' Club of Toronto,' *AS*, new ser. 4 (3 Jan. 1911) pp. 107–10; 'Engineers' Club, Toronto: A Few Suggestions,' *CE* 15 (9 Oct. 1908) p. 728; 'Editorial Note,' *ibid.*, 19 (20 Oct. 1910) p. 517.

30 'President's Address' (Phelps Johnson) *TCSCE*, 28 (1914) p. 103.

31 Members of the CSCE were always concerned that this class would be confused, in the public mind, with the associate member class (a full-voting class, one grade junior to full membership) and attempted on several occasions to change its name. (See, e.g., Edit. 'E.I.C. Classifications,' *CE*, 40 [3 Feb. 1921] p. 197.) Officially, this class was intended for businessmen, managers, and even government bureaucrats, who were not civil engineers but whose work qualified them to co-operate with engineers to advance

professional knowledge; *By-Laws* (1905), s. 9. Unofficially, this classification was a means to exclude and prevent businessmen from dominating the society, without alienating powerful men, whose influence, prestige, and even business contacts, in some cases, the CSCE privately courted.

32 Students and honorary members (unless they were previously members) were also excluded from full membership. Honorary members were theoretically men eminent in engineering or related sciences but were usually university benefactors, governors-general, deans, railway magnates, and men (as in the case of Sir Sandford Fleming) who otherwise refused to join the CSCE as regular members. This class was never to exceed twenty members. NAC, Engineering Institute of Canada Papers, MG 28, 1–277, Letter Books (hereafter Letter Books), McLeod to F.O. McDonall, 9 Jan. 1896, p. 86; Council Minutes CSCE, 10 Feb. 1912, p. 87, 30 Oct. 1917, p. 74, 27 Nov. 1917, p. 81; McLeod to Fleming, 12 March 1896, NAC, Sandford Fleming Papers, MG 29, B 1; Fleming to McLeod, *ibid.*, 19 March 1896.

33 Minutes of Ordinary Meeting, 31 Jan. 1899, p. 181; Council Minutes, 24 Sept. 1889, p. 214; *ibid.*, 5 Nov. 1889, p. 224.

34 'Tenth General Professional Meeting: General Welfare of the Institute "Associates",' *JEIC*, 4 (Sept. 1921) p. 507. The fact that the associate class failed to grow could also be viewed as a testament to the professional standing of the CSCE.

35 The first discussion regarding the admission of women appears to have been prompted by the application of Mary O'Neil in 1920 (Council Minutes, 18 May 1920, p. 49; Toronto Branch Papers, Box no. 7, Copy Council Minutes, 18 May 1920, p. 5). The place of women seemed to have been confined to an auxiliary role at social functions as the wives and daughters of members; 'Thirty-Six Annual Meeting,' *EJ*, 5 (Feb. 1922) p. 93.

36 *By-Laws* (1905), s. 7. These requirements were remarkably similar to those of the ASCE: 'A Member shall be a Civil, Military, Naval, Mining, Mechanical, Electrical, or other professional Engineer, an Architect or a Marine Architect. He shall be at the time of admission to membership not less than thirty years of age and shall have been in the active practice of his profession for ten years; he shall have had responsible charge of work for at least five years, and shall be qualified to design as well as to direct engineering works. Graduation from a school of engineering of recognized reputation shall be considered as equivalent to two years' active practice. The performance of the duties of a Professor of Engineering in a technical school of high grade shall be taken as an equivalent to an equal number of years of actual practice.' Quoted in Leib, 'The Organization and Administration of National Engineering Societies,' pp. 286–7. Several years before the action was officially recognized in the CSCE's by-laws, council accepted as

equivalent responsibility service as a professor of engineering. Toronto Branch Papers, MS 102, Box no. 3, McLeod to Prof. Arkley, 7 June 1916; *By-Laws* (1919), secs. 7–8.

37 See H.H. Vaughan's remarks to the Commercial Club of Halifax, 'Luncheon at Commercial Club,' *JEIC*, 1 (Sept. 1918) p. 280. For an analysis of the significance of professional engineering membership standards, see Edwin T. Layton Jr., *Revolt of the Engineers, Social Responsibility and the American Engineering Profession* (Cleveland, 1971) pp. 26–8.

38 For a discussion of the need for trust and impartiality among professional engineers, see St. George Boswell, 'The Engineer Today,' *CE*, 3 (Feb. 1896) pp. 258–9.

39 'Report of the Annual Meeting,' *TCSCE*, 24 (1912) p. 134; 'Report of the Committee on Educational Requirements,' *ibid.*, 29 (1915) p. 71; 'Report of the Board of Examiners,' *ibid.*, pp. 83, 85.

40 *By-Laws* (1905), s. 10; 'Annual Report,' *TCSCE*, 4 (1890) p. 140.

41 'Annual Report,' *TCSCE.*, 3 (1889) p. 19.

42 'President's Address' (Galbraith), *ibid.*, 23 (1909) p. 109.

43 For a summary of the rather complicated procedure, see 'Procedure for Admission or Transfer,' *JEIC* (July 1918) p. 124.

44 'Preliminary Notice of Application for Admission and for Transfer,' *ibid.* (Aug. 1918) p. 172; 'Report of Annual Meeting,' *TCSCE*, 23 (1909) pp. 10, 120–1.

45 Many of these procedures were adopted directly from the ASCE. See Council Minutes, 3 Nov. 1891, p. 80; 17 June 1896, p. 272; 13 Oct. 1896, p. 279; 21 Dec. 1915, pp. 358–9.

46 Under the old rules, before 1918, a candidate could be excluded if 10 per cent of the votes cast were negative; *By-Laws* (1908), s. 13. Occasionally a cabal was struck and candidates were blackballed. In 1900, for example, six out of fourteen applicants were blackballed (Council Minutes, 19 June 1900, p. 158). As a rule, council rigorously scrutinized all applications before giving its approval. *Cf.* the case of J.N. Tyrell, who issued a misleading record of his professional career; *ibid.*, 13 Oct. 1896, pp. 278–9.

47 *By-Laws* (1905), s. 32.

48 Noting that the society lacked an executive head, since most presidents lived some considerable distance from headquarters, J.A. Jamison remarked that the president was looked upon 'as an honorary officer presiding at our annual meeting.' 'Report of the Annual Meeting,' *TCSCE*, 24 (1912) pp. 71–2.

49 On the importance of the secretaries, see H.E.T. Haultain's remarks, Toronto Branch Papers, MS 102, Box no. 4, 'Meeting at Engineers' Club' Minutes, 5 Feb. 1917, p. 15.

50 See EIC Scrap Book, no. 6, Newspaper clipping, Montreal *Herald*, 27 Dec. 1917, and especially MUA, McLeod Papers, Ass. 1640, Ref. 7 (1), Kirkland McLeod, 'Biography of C.H. McLeod,' unpublished ms; Malcolm M. Thomson, *The Beginning of the Long Dash: A History of Timekeeping in Canada* (Toronto, 1978) p. 8; 'The Story of the Engineering Institute of Canada, 1887–1937,' p. 280; 'Committee Report of the Canadian Society of Civil Engineers,' *CR*, 32 (23 June 1918) p. 63.

51 On McLeod's clandestine efforts to secure G.A. Mountain's election as a vice-president, after Mountain had emphatically declined the nomination, see EIC Letter Books, McLeod to Newton J. Kerr (Private), 12 Dec. 1900, p. 582. On another occasion, McLeod is reported to have kept McGill engineering student CSCE memberships up to date by observing, during his introductory lecture, that many students had let their memberships lapse and further remarking that this might have a bearing on whether they might pass their examinations. Interview: Dr John Sterling, 2 Aug. 1977, Montreal.

52 J.G.G. Kerry, 'The Past,' *EJ*, 30 (Aug. 1947) p. 369.

53 McLeod, for example, received only $300 (Council Minutes, 2 June 1891, p. 72) for a job, which, according to his son, Kirkland McLeod, took up a large portion of his time. McLeod Papers, Kirkland McLeod, 'Biography of C.H. McLeod,' p. 9.

54 Keith was paid $4,000 per annum. In 1925, he was succeeded by Prof. R.J. Durley, who had occupied the chair of mechanical engineering for many years at McGill and, also, had been in charge of gauges and standards for the Imperial Munitions Board, during the First World War. Council Minutes, 29 Feb. 1917, pp. 20–1; Kerry, 'The Past,' pp. 369–70.

55 See 'Report of the Annual Meeting,' *TCSCE*, 26 (1912) pp. 76–8. As early as 1887, members of the CSCE were aware of the American system of nominations. (See EIC Papers, T.C. Keefer to H.T. Bovey, 23 March 1887, Montreal.) While the CSCE adopted the American-style nominating committee, it did not adopt the American two-letter ballot procedure in electing the committee. *Ibid.*, p. 76; William H. Wisely, *The American Civil Engineer, 1852–1974* (New York, 1974) p. 35.

56 EIC Letter Books, McLeod to R. McColl, 2 Dec. 1899, p. 916.

57 See the remarks of H. Irwin and T.H. White: *TCSCE* (1898) p. 17, *ibid.*, 26 (1912) p. 80.

58 'President's Address' (G.H. Duggan), *ibid.*, 31 (1917) p. 66.

58 *By-Laws* (1905), s. 42.

60 'Report of the Annual Meeting,' *TCSCE*, 25 (1911) p. 163.

61 *Cf.* complaints of various members, 'Report of the Annual Meeting,' *ibid.*, pp. 163–4, *ibid.*, 26 (1912) pp. 79–80.

62 Unsigned Letter to Editor, *CR*, 28, no. 9 (26 Feb. 1913) p. 43.

63 R.A. Ross, 'Retiring President's Address,' *JEIC*, 4 (March 1921) p. 202. In many cases, the burden of travelling expenses was relieved, since several members of council were connected to railway companies and received free transportation. 'Report of the Annual Meeting,' *TCSCE*, 23 (1909) p. 85.

64 *Ibid.*, 26 (1912) pp. 77, 79–80; EIC Scrap Book no. 1, T.C. Keefer, 'Circular,' 9 Nov. 1897.

65 Council Minutes, 12 April 1904, p. 313; *TCSCE*, 25 (1911) p. 165.

66 *By-Laws* (1905), s. 37, p. 11.

67 *Ibid.*, s. 38, p. 11; *TCSCE*, 26 (1912) p. 76; *JEIC*, 11 (Oct. 1919) p. 681.

68 Scrap Book no. 1, 'Circular,' n.d. (1892). So strong was the authority of the nominating committee that, when it took the unprecedented action of nominating for president John Galbraith, who, unlike C.H. Rust (his opponent on an opposition ballot), had never been a vice-president, Galbraith's victory was ensured, in spite of fierce opposition from Rust's supporters. 'Copy of Anonymous Letter (confidential),' Jan. 1908; Scrap Books, no. 4, Circular to Corporate members, M.J. Butler, 21 Jan. 1908; *ibid.*, 'Reply to Mr. Butler's Circular,' 23 Jan. 1908.

69 The results were: Kennedy 133, Hannaford 67. Montreal *Gazette*, 14 Jan. 1892, p. 2. The following year, however, Hannaford succeeded to the presidency.

70 'Tenth General Professional Meeting: General Welfare of the Institute,' *JEIC*, 4 (Sept. 1921) p. 508.

71 Toronto Branch Papers, Box no. 1, Minutes of the Toronto Branch, CSCE, 12 Oct. 1916, p. 115. Also see H.E.T. Haultain's remarks, *ibid.*, Box no. 4, 'Meeting at Engineers' Club,' 5 Feb. 1917, pp. 7–8, 14.

72 MUA, Ass. 1640, Ref. 5, Dean Brown to W.H. Brittain, 8 June 1937, p. 3.

73 Unsigned Letter to Editor, *CE*, 15 (6 March 1908) p. 148.

74 Scrap Book no. 1, Circular regarding proposed Amendment to the By-Laws of the Canadian Society of Civil Engineers, 6 Nov. 1897. The council for 1897 appears to have had only three past presidents, or four if the current president, for that year, T.C. Keefer – who was serving yet another term – is included. *The Engineering Institute of Canada List of Officers for the Years 1887 to 1920* (Montreal, 1921) p. 43.

75 'Report of the Council,' *JEIC*, 1 (May 1918) p. 66.

76 See, for example, 'Report of the Annual Meeting,' *TCSCE*, 26 (1912) p. 70; *ibid.*, 27 (1913) p. 52.

77 See remarks by H.E.T. Haultain and Willis Chipman, Toronto Branch Papers, MS 102, Box no. 4, 'Meeting at Engineers' Club, Discussion,' 5 Feb. 1917, pp. 13–14, 22; Robt. W. King to Editor, *CE*, 8 (8 Dec. 1900) p. 162.

78 UTA, Haultain Papers, B 47 (B 72-005), H.E.T. Haultain, 'The Romance of Engineering' (Jan. 1922).

79 Many of these values originated in Britain. For a historical analysis of the evolution of the professions in pre-industrial and post-industrial Britain, see especially Phillip Elliott, *The Sociology of the Professions* (London, 1972) pp. 14–57.

80 Layton, *Revolt of the Engineers*, p. 32. By contrast, the American Society of Mechanical Engineers (ASME) was closely connected with business. On relations between the ASME and private American utility company interests, see, e.g., Bruce Sinclair, *A Centennial History of the American Society of Mechanical Engineers, 1880–1980* (Toronto, 1980) pp. 103–4.

CHAPTER 3: 'A SORT OF OUTCAST PEOPLE'

1 Edwin T. Layton Jr., *The Revolt of the Engineers: Social Responsibility and the American Engineering Profession* (Cleveland, 1971) p. 2.

2 'Toronto Engineers Framing New Code of Ethics,' *CE*, 39 (9 Dec. 1920) p. 597; Hyman Goldman to Editor, *ibid.*, 34 (9 May 1918), p. 409.

3 The percentage of consultants appears to have declined since 1922. In his study of the engineering profession between 1918 and 1971, A.R. Gordon discovered that, by 1951, only 3 per cent of engineers were self-employed; 2 per cent twenty years later. See Allan Ross Gordon, 'The Development of the Engineering Profession in Canada, 1918–1971' (MA thesis, Carleton University, 1981), p. 111.

4 After completing the Grand Trunk main line from Toronto to Sarnia (Gzowski's last venture in actual railway building, which laid the basis of his personal fortune), Gzowski and his partner, Sir David Macpherson, operated as railway contractors for a number of years. 'Obituary,' *TCSCE*, 13 (1899) pp. 192–3; Ludwik Kos-Rabcewicz-Zubkowski and William Edward Greening, *Sir Casimir Stanislaus Gzowski: A Biography* (Toronto, 1959) pp. 80–1.

5 One common cost-cutting practice among employers, for example, was to request job applicants to name their salaries and then hire the engineer who quoted the lowest. 'Classification and Remuneration of Engineers,' *CE*, 43 (20 Dec. 1922) p. 602; NAC, Engineering Institute of Canada Papers, MG 28, 1–277, Minutes (hereafter Council Minutes), 22 June 1920, p. 63.

6 Engineers had always clearly understood that engineering was, as H.A. Goldman put it, 'closely allied with economics.' H.A. Goldman, 'Rise and Fall in Prices,' *EJ*, 5 (March 1922) p. 140.

7 'President's Address' (M.J. Butler), *TCSCE*, 28 (1915) p. 107; Edit. 'Unemployment Situation,' *JEIC*, 4 (Oct. 1921) p. 546.

8 Alan Macdougall argued that one of the reasons why engineers were the first professional groups to feel the effects of bad times was that public improvements were regarded by authorities as 'luxuries' to be delayed as long

as the public purse was light. Alan Macdougall, 'Professional Prospects,' *Papers Read before the Engineering Society, School of Practical Science*, no. 7 (1893–4) p. 7.

9 The CSCE had always recognized the problem of chronic unemployment among its members and was lenient with members in arrears with membership dues during depressions. See, e.g., Council Minutes, 8 Dec. 1896, p. 296.

10 N.C. Mills to Editor, *CE*, 37 (23 Dec. 1919) p. 562.

11 'Discussion on the Law and the Engineer,' *TCSCE*, 30 (1916) p. 369.

12 *Ibid.*, pp. 367–8.

13 Edit. 'A Slack Time for Engineers,' *CE*, 26 (22 Oct. 1914) p. 573.

14 J.L.G. Stuart, 'Engineering among Other Professions,' *ibid.*, 26 (2 April 1914) p. 543.

15 Charles A. Mullen, 'Trade Unions and Engineers,' *CR*, 34 (28 Jan. 1920) p. 78.

16 'Employment Bureau', *JEIC*, 1 (8 Dec. 1918) p. 435.

17 NAC, Engineering Institute of Canada Papers, MG 28, 1–277, Scrap Books, 'Memorial to Sir Wilfrid Laurier,' 18 Nov. 1910.

18 'Report of the Annual Meeting,' *TCSCE*, 24 (1910) p. 83. Dodwell became the foremost advocate of upgrading the status of engineers in the public service.

19 *Ibid.*, p. 82; Edit. 'Work of the Can.Soc.C.E.,' *CR*, 24 (2 Feb. 1910) p. 31; C.E.W. Dodwell to Editor, *CE*, 34 (25 April 1918) p. 362.

20 See Robert MacGregor Dawson, *The Civil Service of Canada* (London, 1929) pp. 19–20. An important rejoinder to this pioneering study is Robert Borden, 'Problem of an Efficient Civil Service,' *Canadian Historical Association Annual Report* (1931), especially pp. 5–21. For a recent study, see J.E. Hodgetts *et al.*, *The Biography of an Institution: The Civil Service Commission of Canada, 1908–1967* (Montreal and London, 1972).

21 'Ottawa Branch News,' *JEIC*, 1 (1 May 1918) p. 61; C.E.W. Dodwell to Editor, p. 363.

22 'Report of the Annual Meeting' (1910) p. 83.

23 Canada, House of Commons, *Debates* (17 Jan. 1910) p. 2024. Warburton was the first MP to plead the cause of the government engineer in the House of Commons.

24 *Debates* (17 Jan. 1910) p. 2030.

25 Poor salaries were common throughout the civil services; Dawson, *Civil Service*, p. 76.

26 Edit. 'Salaries of Engineers,' *JEIC*, 11 (1 Jan. 1919) p. 18.

27 Edit. 'The Technical Man's Salary,' *CR*, 32 (9 Oct. 1918) p. 804; 'Memorandum presented to the Members of Parliament of the Lower Mainland of British Columbia by the Vancouver Branch of the Engineering Institute of Canada,' UTL, Toronto Branch Papers, MS 102, Box no. 6, n.p.; 'The Salary Situation,' *JEIC*, 11 (5 May 1919) p. 410.

28 'Report of the Annual Meeting' (1910) pp. 85–7; Dodwell to Editor, *CE*, pp. 363–4.
29 R.O. Wynne-Roberts to Editor, *CE*, 25 (10 July 1913) p. 151.
30 For a contemporary historical survey of municipal engineering, see R.O. Wynne-Roberts, 'Municipal Engineering,' *JEIC*, 4 (Feb. 1921) pp. 110–4.
31 Edit. 'Responsibility,' *CE*, 16 (26 March 1909) p. 415.
32 'A Supervising Engineer,' *ibid.*, 15 (31 July 1908) p. 520; Edit. 'Engineers and City Government,' *ibid.*, 29 (20 April 1915) p. 311; Frederick B. Goedike to Editor, *ibid.*, 34 (23 May 1918) p. 469.
33 'Report of the Annual Meeting,' *TCSCE*, 33 (1909) pp. 118–19; Edit. 'Expert Advice,' *CE*, 18 (16 June 1910) p. 604; Edit. 'Time for a Change in Municipal Government,' *ibid.*, 28 (25 March 1915) p. 391.
34 Edit. 'Untimely Interference with the City Engineer,' *CR*, 24, no. 18 (4 May 1910) p. 35; Unsigned letter to Editor, *ibid.*, 26, no. 37 (11 Sept. 1912) p. 41; 'The Rights of an Engineer,' *CE*, 111 (12 April 1896) p. 328. In the 1880s Toronto's medical health officer had similar misgivings about city politicians. See, e.g., Heather Anne MacDougall, '"Health Is Wealth": The Development of Public Health Activity in Toronto, 1834–1890' (PhD dissertation, University of Toronto, 1981) p. 353–5.
35 J. Grant MacGregor to Editor, *CE*, 14 (4 Oct. 1907) p. 367.
36 Edit. 'Municipal Engineers,' *ibid.* (23 Aug. 1907) p. 337; the *Canadian Engineer* praised engineers who were dismissed for maintaining their professional stand – 'Rights of the Engineer,' p. 338.
37 Commentators often pointed out that city engineers were forced to exercise political skills, apart from their varied duties, in order to survive and carry out their responsibilities. Edit. 'City Engineers and Their Difficulties,' *ibid.*, 20 (2 Feb. 1911) p. 253; 'Moncton Branch,' *JEIC*, 4 (Feb. 1921) p. 155; 'President's Address' (C.H. Rust), *TCSCE*, 26 (1912) p. 107.
38 Edit. 'Protection of the Municipal Engineer,' *CR*, 23, no. 26 (30 June 1909) p. 31.
39 Edit. 'Responsibility,' *CE*, 16 (26 March 1909) p. 415; Unsigned Letter to Editor, *CR*, 25, no. 46 (15 Nov. 1911) p. 38.
40 St. George Boswell, 'The Engineer Today,' *ibid.*, 3 (10 Feb. 1896) p. 258; Edit. 'The City Engineer and the City Council,' *ibid.*, 15 (13 Nov. 1908) p. 807; Edit. 'An Institute for Municipal Engineers,' *ibid.*, 25 (10 July 1913) p. 149.
41 Edit. 'Is Municipal Engineering on the Decline?' *CR*, 26, no. 14 (3 April 1912) p. 39; J. Antonisen to Editor, *ibid.*, 26, no. 18 (1 May 1912) pp. 41–2.
42 Edit. 'Wanted – Men,' *CE*, 15 (17 Jan. 1908) p. 48.
43 Edit. 'Status of the Engineering Profession,' *CR*, 27, no. 45 (5 Nov. 1913) p. 39; Edit. 'By What Authority Shall a City Engineer Be Tried?,' *ibid.*, 26,

no. 35 (28 Aug. 1912) p. 39; 'City Engineers and Civic Mismanagement,' *ibid.*, 25, no. 52 (27 Dec. 1911) p. 38.

44 'President's Address' (C.H. Rust), p. 112. One of the things that made an impression on a prominent English engineer, visiting Canada, was the intensity of press attacks upon city engineers in comparison with Britain. 'A Westminster Engineer's Impression of Municipal Work in Canada,' *ibid.*, 25, no. 48 (29 Nov. 1911) p. 35.

45 Provincial government engineers also appear to have experienced unjust treatment similar to that suffered by municipal engineers. Compare, for example, the case of J.W. Roland, chief engineer of the Highways Board, Nova Scotia, summarily dismissed without apparent reason. 'Halifax Branch,' *JEIC*, 4 (June 1921) pp. 381, 383.

46 Andrew F. Macallum to Editor, *CR*, 26, no. 36 (4 Sept. 1912) p. 41; J. Antonisen to Editor, p. 41; Edit. 'Engineers and City Government,' p. 311. Even the *Canadian Mining Journal* remarked that it was strange that very little was heard from municipal engineers. 'The Engineering Profession and Municipal Administration,' *CMJ*, 16 (May 1920) p. 138.

47 J.E. Hodgetts, for example, has observed an 'autonomous spirit' among such highly respected engineers as Samuel Keefer and noted how frequently these engineers assumed complete authority for works, believing that the politicians were too ignorant of the pertinent technicalities; J.E. Hodgetts, *Pioneer Public Service: An Administrative History of the United Canadas, 1841–1867* (Toronto, 1955) p. 204. City engineers also displayed 'an autonomous spirit.' This may account, in part, for their frequent clashes with politicians.

48 Unsigned letter to Editor, *CR*, 25, no. 46 (15 Nov. 1911) p. 38.

49 Harry Bragg, 'Engineers – and Engineers,' *CMJ*, 15 (Dec. 1919) p. 409.

50 Herbert J. Bowman, 'Municipal Engineering in Ontario,' *AS*, no. 10 (1896–97) p. 178; Edit. 'Counties and Their Engineers,' *CE*, 28 (20 May 1915) p. 587; A.N. Reed, 'Functions of Urban Municipalities in the North-West Territories: Public Works and Public Utilities,' *Saskatchewan History*, 10 (1956) pp. 88–9.

51 Edit. 'Question of Salaries,' *CE*, 19 (13 May 1910) p. 466; Edit. 'The Salaries of Engineers,' p. 607.

52 Edit. '"Wanted – A Cheaper Engineer,"' *CE*, 32 (29 March 1917) p. 281; 'Kitchener's New Engineer,' *ibid.*, 32 (17 May 1917) p. 425; 'How Kitchener Fired Its City Engineer,' *ibid.*, 32 (14 June 1917) p. 497.

53 Edit. '"Wanted – A Cheaper Engineer,"' p. 281.

54 J. Antonisen to Editor, *CR*, 26, no. 37 (11 Sept. 1912) p. 41.

55 Edit. 'Hamilton City Engineer's Suggestion,' *ibid.*, 27, no. 46 (12 Nov. 1913) p. 39; J.W.B. Blackman to Editor, *ibid.*, 27, no. 48 (26 Nov. 1913) p. 38; R.O. Wynne-Roberts to Editor, *CE*, 25 (10 July 1913) pp. 151–2. Wynne-

Roberts was the leading advocate of forming a distinct Canadian society. A provisional committee, consisting of a representative cross-section of Canadian municipal engineers, including eight prominent engineers, was formed to draft a constitution for the proposed society – the Canadian Institution of Municipal Engineers. Edit. 'The Proposed Municipal Engineering Organization,' *CR*, 27, no. 45 (5 Nov. 1913) p. 39.

56 The *Canadian Engineer* was the only critic of the proposal. It agitated against the proposed society, arguing that while a municipal organization was a good idea, it should be formed as a section within the CSCE. Most city engineers, the journal contended, were already CSCE members who could keep better informed of new engineering developments in all branches of the profession from inside the larger national society. Edit. 'An Institution for Municipal Engineers,' p. 150; Edit. 'Organization among Municipal Engineers,' *ibid.*, 25 (28 Aug. 1913) p. 374. The *Contract Record*, however, disagreed and asserted that the CSCE had 'not taken an active part in things of vital interest to municipal engineers' and that the society had neither the constitution nor the disposition to serve municipal engineers. Edit. 'Is Canada Big Enough for a Municipal Engineering Society?' *CR*, 38 (17 Sept. 1913) p. 41.

57 'Report of Annual Meeting – Discussion,' *TCSCE*, 22 (1908) p. 10; Council Minutes, 10 March 1908, p. 206. Engineers were particularly outraged by summary dismissals for frivolous reasons, such as a western city engineer who was fired for wearing kid gloves and attending afternoon teas. 'Report of Annual Meeting' (1908) pp. 59–61.

58 Edit. 'Municipal Administration,' *CR*, 25, no. 48 (29 Nov. 1911) p. 34. The editor of the *Contract Record* also took the initiative of writing the president of the CSCE to urge the society to intervene in a number of cases involving city engineers in the west. Council, however, declined to act, on the grounds that no representations had been made to the CSCE by individual members. Council Minutes, 9 Dec. 1911, p. 72.

59 City engineers sometimes had their work investigated by judges. Engineers had the same contempt for judges as they had for lawyers. In their view, judges were biased and ignorant of technical work and were, therefore, incompetent to pass judgment on engineering. Only engineers should judge other engineers. See, e.g., J. Antonisen to Editor, *ibid.*, pp. 41-2; Unsigned letter to Editor, *ibid.*, 26, no. 38 (18 Sept. 1912) p. 42. The *Contract Record* went so far as to suggest that city councillors were not qualified to choose their engineers and that a special board of engineers from the CSCE should recommend qualified candidates. 'City Engineers and Civic Mismanagement,' *ibid.*, 25, no. 52 (27 Dec. 1911) p. 38.

60 See 'Report of Annual Meeting,' *TCSCE*, 25 (1911) p. 157.

61 *Ibid.*, p. 158.

62 'Biography' (G.H. Duggan), *AS*, new ser. 6, no. 2 (June 1912) pp. 74–5.
63 'Report of Annual Meeting' (1911) p. 160.
64 *Ibid.*, pp. 175–6, 179; in a similar vein, Prof. E.P. Fetherstonhough argued that the society's effort to raise its status would be undermined by any action that would asociate the CSCE with trade unionism, in the eyes of the public. *Ibid.*, p. 179.
65 *Ibid.*, p. 176. Another motion to send a copy of a resolution regretting Vancouver city council's action in discharging Clement, without reasons, was defeated on the grounds that it was contrary to the society's precepts and would probably place the CSCE in 'a very undignified position,' since either it would be ignored or the CSCE would not receive a reply. *Ibid.*, pp. 177–9.
66 The *Canadian Engineer* saw the whole question as more 'a sentimental one than a practical one': Clement could declare that the CSCE supported him, in so far as he was discharged without a fair hearing. Edit. 'City Engineers and Their Difficulties,' *CE*, 20 (2 Feb. 1911) p. 253.
67 For example, the CSCE's attempt to discourage its members from applying for City Engineer Johnson's position in Kitchener – in effect, an *ad hoc* professional boycott – failed miserably. Toronto Branch Papers, MS 102, Box no. 4, Oliver to F.S. Keith, 30 March 1917; *ibid.*, Keith to Oliver, 2 April 1917; Edit. 'Wanted – A Cheaper Engineer,' p. 281.
68 Minutes, Ordinary Meeting, 23 April 1896, pp. 32–3. In 1900, when John Galt requested an investigation of his dismissal as city engineer, Ottawa, council advised him that such action was beyond the powers of the CSCE and suggested that he take legal action. Council Minutes, 9 Oct. 1900, p. 159.

CHAPTER 4: 'THE FOREIGN INVASION'

1 This act restricted the entry of aliens as contract labour (see 60–61 Vic., c. 11, s. 1). It was a reluctant response by the Laurier government to similar US legislation. Robert Craig Brown and Ramsay Cook, *Canada, 1896–1921: A Nation Transformed* (Toronto, 1974) p. 120.
2 In 1894, for example, McLeod observed: 'Montreal has been over run this winter by Engineers who have got out of employment in the United States owing to the financial depression.' NAC, Engineering Institute of Canada Papers, MG 28, 1–277, Letter Books (hereafter Letter Books), Letter from McLeod, 22 Jan. 1894, p. 314.
3 'The Royal Commission on the Alleged Employment of Aliens in Connection with the Surveys of the Proposed Grand Trunk Pacific Railway, Report of the Commissioner and Other Documents,' in Canada, House of Commons, *Sessional Papers* (1905) no. 36a (hereafter Winchester Report), pp. 6–13.
4 'Minutes of Evidence,' *ibid.*, p. 477.

5 See the remarks of C.B. Smith, *ibid.*, p. 527.

6 *Ibid.*, p. 491.

7 Winchester Report, pp. 15–29, *passim.* On Van Horne's practices, see Pierre Berton, *The Last Spike: The Great Railway, 1881–1885* (Toronto, 1971) pp. 94–7.

8 Winchester Report, pp. 15, 46.

9 *Ibid.*, p. 6.

10 *Ibid.*, pp. 37, 86, 135, 511.

11 *Ibid*, pp. 57, 48. Kyle also wrote to a number of American engineers offering positions at $175 per month, plus expenses, but a number of Canadian engineers were tendered only $150 and expenses. *Ibid.*, p. 58.

12 *Ibid.*, p. 18. Kyle later resigned on the grounds of embarrassing the GTP by exceeding his instructions in these letters. J. Castell Hopkins, *Canadian Annual Review of Public Affairs* (Toronto, 1904) p. 96.

13 NAC, Engineering Institute of Canada Papers, MG 28, 1–277, Council Minutes (hereafter Council Minutes), 8 Oct. 1903, p. 273; 13 Oct. 1903, p. 299; 8 Dec. 1903, p. 295.

14 See *Canadian Annual Review*, 1904, pp. 92–6.

15 J.J. Morgan, *The Canadian Men and Women of the Time* (Toronto, 1912) p. 1179.

16 Winchester Report, p. 55. Stephens weighted his averages with non-engineering employees; *ibid.*, p. 58.

17 Canada, House of Commons, *Debates*, 1904, pp. 3029–30.

18 Winchester Report, pp. 38–57.

19 *Ibid.*, pp. 64–5.

20 *Ibid.*, p. 5–6; *Debates* (18 July 1904) pp. 6884–5.

21 Winchester Report, pp. 53–5. Winchester was particularly angered with Stephens, since two of his division engineers, Kyle and George A. Knowlton, had dismissed staff for drunkenness.

22 The clearest expression of this idea was given by a New York consulting engineer and CSCE member in a letter to the *Contract Record*: Rudolph Hering to Editor, *CR*, 27, no. 13 (26 March 1913) pp. 44–5.

23 MUA, C.H. McLeod Papers, Ass. 1101, Ref. 48, 'Queen's 1907: The Profession 1908' (Speech to the Engineering Society, Queen's University) n.p.

24 *Ibid.*, 'Report of the Annual Meeting – Discussion,' *TCSCE*, 22 (1908) pp. 38, 43; *ibid.*, 23 (1909) p. 98.

25 These remarks were by the city engineer of Ithaca, NY. Donald F. McLeod to Editor, *CE*, 22 (8 Feb. 1912) p. 270.

26 In the mind of one engineer, the empire's greatness was the result of the 'open-door policy' of free access of talent. 'Report of the Annual Meeting – Discussion' (1909) pp. 116–17.

27 W. Murdock to Editor, *CR*, 27, no. 10 (5 March 1913) p. 67. Also see 'Report of the Annual Meeting – Discussion' (1908), p. 42 (Remarks of G.H. Frost).

28 'President's Address' (Phelps Johnson), *TCSCE*, 28 (1914) p. 105.

29 See Clipping, *Montreal Star*, April 1904, NAC, Engineering Institute of Canada Papers, MG 28, 1–277, Scrap Books (hereafter Scrap Book) no. 3; 'President's Address' (William Anderson), *TCSCE*, 19 (1905) pp. 23–4.

30 McLeod, 'Queen's 1907: The Profession 1908'; Edit. 'The Work and Opportunities of the Canadian Society of Civil Engineers', *CR*, 28, no. 5 (4 Feb. 1914) p. 125.

31 See remarks of G.H. Frost and W.J. Francis, 'Report of the Annual Meeting – Discussion' (1908) pp. 41-2.

32 Although some of these engineers may have been Canadian born, they constituted the largest single block of foreign engineers holding CSCE membership. Engineering Institute of Canada, *Charter, By-Laws, List of Members and Professional Engineering Acts* (Montreal, 1922) pp. 225–7.

33 'Report of the Annual Meeting' (1908) p. 42; W.F. Tye to Editor, *CR*, 27, no. 9 (26 Feb. 1913) p. 40.

34 W.F. Tye, 'The Present Status of the Engineer in Canada,' *ibid.*, 31 (11 April 1917) p. 334.

35 Winchester Report, 'Minutes of Evidence,' p. 527.

36 Commenting on two heavily subsidized railways, the Canadian Northern and the GTP, the *Canadian Engineer* maintained that these companies 'are not in a similar position to private corporations, as they are operating for the public good under public franchise'; Edit. 'Canadian Engineers,' *CE*, 21 (2 Nov. 1911) pp. 513–14. One prominent CSCE member from Ottawa believed that only CSCE members should be hired for all government and government-assisted works. See H. Victor Brayley to Editor, *CR*, 27, no. 9 (26 Feb. 1913) p. 41.

37 The other members of the commission were Sir Henry Drayton, chairman of the Board of Railway Commissioners, and Sir George Paish, who, because of illness, was replaced by the British railway authority W. Acworth. Brown and Cook, *Canada, 1896–1921*, p. 244.

38 Most of Swain's academic career, however, was spent at MIT; for background, see Robert Bothwell and William Kilbourn, *C.D. Howe: A Biography* (Toronto, 1979) pp. 20–1. Swain was best known to Canadian engineers through his presidential address, 'The Engineer and the Social Problems,' delivered at the Ottawa meeting of the ASCE in June 1913. Edit. 'The Engineer and the Community,' *CE*, 24 (26 June 1913) p. 915.

39 Swain, contrary to the CSCE's understanding, was not the commission's adviser. His job was merely to conduct the physical valuation. Scrap Book no. 6, Sir Henry Drayton to Sir Robert Borden, 19 Sept. 1916.

40 *Ibid.*, C.H. McLeod, 'Circular,' 7 Sept. 1916.
41 *Ibid.*
42 *Ibid.*
43 See, e.g., edit. 'The Canadian Municipality in Its Contact with an American Engineering Firm,' *CE*, 19 (6 Oct. 1910) p. 452; Council Minutes, 17 Oct. 1916, p. 434. According to the *Contract Record*, when plans were prepared by an American architect or engineer, it was 'almost a forgone conclusion that an American contractor will get the work'; Edit. 'Foreign Plans for Canadian Work,' *CR*, 24, no. 32 (10 Aug. 1910) p. 35. Architects were angered that American plans could enter Canada and easily escape duty. They lobbied for heavy import duties. Edit. 'Why Do Foreign Plans Escape Duty?' *ibid.*, 23, no. 6 (10 Feb. 1909) p. 29; Edit. 'Foreign Plans for Canadian Work,' *ibid.*, 24, no. 15 (13 April 1910) p. 37; Edit. 'Excluding Foreign Architects,' *ibid.*, 19, no. 9 (1 Sept. 1910) p. 253. For an American reaction, see Edit. 'The Canadian Import Duty on Engineers' and Architects' Drawings,' *ENGN*, 61 (19 March 1909) pp. 299–300.
44 Edit. 'The Persistent Practice of Employing Aliens,' *CR*, 32, no. 17 (24 April 1918) p. 321.
45 The Canadian Manufacturers' Association, for example, had previously said that it would support the architects' demand for a heavy import duty on plans, provided the architects specified only Canadian materials in their plans. Edit. 'Excluding Foreign Architects,' p. 253.
46 UTL, Toronto Branch Papers (hereafter Toronto Branch Papers), MS 102, Box no. 1, Minutes of Toronto Branch, 12 Oct. 1916, pp. 113–15; 16 Oct. 1916, pp. 115–16; *ibid.*, Box no. 3, L.M. Arkley to C.H. McLeod, 14 Dec. 1916; Edit. 'The Persistent Practice of Employing Aliens,' p. 321.
47 Council Minutes, 24 Nov. 1916, p. 443; 14 Dec. 1916, pp. 448–9; 9 Dec. 1916, pp. 1-2; 17 Jan. 1917, p. 6. The president and secretary of the Builders' Exchange and the president and secretary of the Architects' Association of Quebec also joined with the engineers and signed the Memorial (*ibid.*, 20 Feb. 1917, p. 26). The *Canadian Engineer* later reported that the cabinet was in general sympathy with the notion that Canadians should be given preference on Dominion public works. It also pointed out that the memorial did not mention private, municipal, or provincial contracts, since it was aimed chiefly at the award of the Lindsay Arsenal Contract to Westinghouse, Church, Kerr & Co. Edit. 'Memorial to the Government,' *CE*, 34 (25 April 1918) p. 357.
48 MUA, C.H. McLeod Papers, 1101, Ref. 58, McLeod to Laurier, 24 Nov. 1903, Scrap Book, no. 3, Clipping, *Montreal Star*, April 1904. Moreover, the CSCE decided that it was undesirable to make any representations to the government as to the composition of the Quebec Bridge Commission

(Council Minutes, 12 Dec. 1908, p. 253), and, beyond supplying basic information about a member's classification and record, the CSCE would not endorse or even recommend an engineer to the GTP (*ibid.*, 14 June 1904, p. 322). McLeod, almost to the point of being declared a hostile witness, stubbornly refused even to identify to the Winchester inquiry individual members of the CSCE who could have filled positions on the GTP survey. 'Minutes of Evidence,' Winchester Report, pp. 437–9.

49 McLeod 'Circular'; CSCE Toronto Branch Papers, MS 102, Box no. 3, McLeod to L.M. Arkley, 22 Sept. 1916; *ibid.*, 28 Sept. 1916.

50 Scrap Book no. 6, Drayton to Borden, 19 Sept. 1916. The American journal *Engineering News* viewed the CSCE's actions as a regrettable mistake with regressive implications, an abandonment of the society's professionalism. Edit. 'Canadian Engineers Object to Appointment of Aliens,' *ENGN*, 76, Pt. II (12 Oct. 1916) p. 711.

51 Edit. 'Employment of Alien Engineers,' *CE*, 31 (28 Sept. 1916) p. 261. The appointment of Morris Knowles of Pittsburgh to the Essex Public Utilities Commission was, according to this journal, 'a most flagrant example of the way in which competent Canadian engineers are ignored and aliens appointed to lucrative positions that could well be kept at home.' Edit. 'The Appointment of Alien Engineers,' *ibid.*, 31 (12 Oct. 1916) p. 303. Moreover, according to the *Canadian Engineer*, the problem was not confined to the Dominion government: for every alien appointed by the Dominion government, ten were hired by municipalities; *ibid.*

52 *Ibid.* Smith eventually submitted a minority report that took a stand against nationalization. The *Contract Record* rejected the *Canadian Engineer*'s arguments. Edit. 'Employing Alien Engineers,' *CR*, 30 (11 Oct. 1916) p. 973.

53 Scrap Book, no. 6, Drayton to Borden, 19 Sept. 1916, 'Minutes of Evidence,' Winchester Report, p. 439.

54 Edit. 'The Employment of Engineers,' *CE*, 22 (8 Feb. 1912) p. 269.

55 Edit. 'The Foreign Invasion,' *ibid.*, 18 (20 May 1910) p. 495.

56 Toronto Branch Papers, MS 102, Box no. 2, R.W. MacIntyre to Richard McBride, 4 Oct. 1912. In spite of assurances from McBride that Thompson would hire British subjects as his engineering assistants, Thompson contravened the premier's orders and hired Americans; *ibid.*

57 Conway, 'Legislation and the Engineer,' p. 109; Edit. 'The Foreign Invasion,' p. 496; Edit. 'The Employment of Alien Engineers,' p. 261.

58 'Report of Annual Meeting,' *TCSCE*, 19 (1905) p. 35. Also see remarks of W.T. Jennings and Sir Sandford Fleming in Winchester Report, p. 62. It was commonly believed by Canadian engineers that the designs of civil engineering works were governed by local climatic conditions, particularly ice, snow, and frost, and that the conditions of transportation and supplies

were different in Canada. Edit: 'Employment of Engineers,' *CE*, p. 269; 'Minutes of Evidence,' Winchester Report, p. 427.

59 For a colourful popular account of the rigours of railway building between Lake Superior and the Red River, see Pierre Berton, *The National Dream: The Great Railway, 1871-1881* (Toronto, 1970) pp. 282–9.

60 See Engineering Institute of Canada, Niagara Peninsula Branch, *History of Engineering at Niagara* (St Catharines, 1977) chap. 4.

61 Edit. 'The Foreign Invasion,' p. 496.

62 Winchester Report, p. 63.

63 'Minutes of Evidence,' *ibid.*, p. 590.

64 Toronto Branch Papers, MS 102, Box no. 3, A.E. Jennings to Prof. Arkley (27 Oct. 1910). Edit. 'Employment of Alien Engineers,' *CE*, 31 (28 Sept. 1916) p. 261; 'The Alien Labor Law and the Engineer,' *ENGN*, 61 (22 April 1909) p. 443. Considerable initial confusion existed about the status of the Canadian engineer in the United States, and the CSCE was even prepared to track down any discrimination: EIC Letter Books, McLeod to Boswell, 31 Dec. 1892, p. 983; 25 March 1893, p. 85; McLeod to the *Canadian Architect and Builder*, 15 March 1893, p. 68; McLeod to Sir Casimir Gzowski, 23 March 1893, p. 81; McLeod to W. Kerry, 23 March 1893, p. 89; McLeod to J.S. Hodgson, 3 April 1893, p. 94, 26 Oct. 1894, p. 536.

65 'Minutes of Evidence,' Winchester Report, p. 142; Edit. 'Appointment of a Health Commissioner,' *CE*, 22 (16 May 1912) p. 609; G.R.G. Conway, 'Legislation and the Engineer,' *ibid.*, 28 (7 Jan. 1915) p. 109; Edit. 'Employment of Alien Engineers,' *ibid.*, p. 261; 'At the Country's Service,' *CR*, 31 (May 1917) p. 430. W.F. Tye, however, held a contrary view: 'There are many more Canadians holding good positions and drawing good salaries in the United States than there are Americans doing work in Canada.' W.F. Tye to Editor, *CR*, p. 40.

66 'Form of Memorial to the Rt. Hon. Sir Robert L. Borden and to the Members of the Dominion Government concerning the employment of Alien Architects, Engineers and Contractors on large Public Works in Canada,' OA, MS Misc. Col. Box 1 no. 57, n.d., n.p. R.W. MacIntyre detected a 'stigma of unworthiness' attached to the whole business and stated that it was 'a tendency which casts very serious reflection and reproach on our rngineers [sic] and is diametrically opposed to the doctrines of anti-reciprocity and imperialism.' Toronto Branch Papers, MS 102, Box no. 2, R.W. MacIntyre to Richard McBride, 4 Oct. 1912.

67 Edit. 'Appointment of Alien Engineers,' p. 303.

68 C.E. Cartwright to Editor, *CR*, 27, no. 13 (26 March 1913) p. 46.

69 *Ibid.*

70 See, e.g., 'Report of Annual Meeting – Discussion' (1909) pp. 98–9, 117.

71 Edit. 'The Foreign Invasion,' pp. 495–6.
72 Edit. 'Work and Status of the Canadian Society of Civil Engineers,' *CR*, 28, no. 9 (26 Feb. 1913) pp. 37–8.

CHAPTER 5: 'INIQUITOUS' LEGISLATION

1 This bill called for a full measure of professional self-government, with complete statutory authority to control and regulate all aspects of professional practice by a board of engineers, appointed by the crown from a list of fourteen prominent engineers (listed apparently without the knowledge or consent of those named). Introduced as a private bill, it received little support and was thrown out upon second reading. See OA, RG 8 1-7-H, 'An Acting Respecting Civil Engineers'; 'President's Address' (T.C. Keefer), *TCSCE*, 2 (1888) pp. 11–13. The author of this bill is unknown. Keefer speculated that it was 'suggested by' E.W. Plunkett's May 1880 circular. (*Ibid.* See chapter 2.) J.L.P. O'Hanely, a charter member of the CSCE, may be the author. In a reminiscence, he claimed to have drafted a bill for the Ontario legislature which resembles the 1881 bill; *cf* NAC, J.L.P. O'Hanley Papers, MG 29 B11, Vol. II, 'Preface: The Ottawa Revelations – Civil Engineering,' p. 168.
2 See chapter 2.
3 For a concise analysis of the development of the regulation of the legal profession in Ontario, see appendix B to the Research Directorate's staff study, 'History and Organization of the Legal Profession in Ontario' (1978), prepared for the Professional Organizations Committee, Ministry of the Attorney General, Ontario, pp. 1–20.
4 D.W. Gullett, *A History of Dentistry in Canada* (Toronto, 1971) pp. 43, 283–6.
5 NAC, Engineering Institute of Canada Papers, MG 28, 1–277, Scrap Books (hereafter Scrap Book), no. 1, Alan Macdougall, 'Draft Report of the Committee on Professional Status,' 10 Oct. 1893.
6 *Ibid.*, 'Committee on Professional Status and Close Corporation,' n.d.: 'Discussion on a Plea for a Close Corporation,' *TCSCE*, 6 (1892) pp. 116–19; 'Report of Annual Meeting,' *ibid.*, 10 (1896) p. 12; Elizabeth Fisher, 'Professional Associations in Canada' (PhD dissertation, University of Toronto, 1932) p. 184.
7 As early as 1849, for example, An Act to Repeal Certain Acts Therein Mentioned and to Make Better Provision Respecting the Admission of Land Surveyors and the Survey of Lands in This Province (Provincial Statutes of Canada, 12 Vic., c. 35) set out the provisions for the qualification and examination of land surveyors.
8 See, e.g., W.C. Yates, 'Historical Review of the Association of Ontario Land

Surveyors,' Association of Ontario Land Surveyors, *Annual Report*, 82 (1967) pp. 149–53.

9 See Keefer's remarks: 'President's Address,' p. 10. Engineering was an 'open' profession; anyone could practise regardless of qualifications. Moreover, engineers had no legal status. They could not collect or sue for fees. The only recourse against an engineer was a civil action in negligence. Macdougall, 'Draft Report of the Committee on Professional Status'; Scrap Book, no. 1, 'Memorandum for the use of the Provincial Committee on Incorporation,' 3 July 1897; Research Directorate, 'History and Organization,' appendix D, p. 2.

10 *Statutes of Canada*, 57–58 Vic., c. 30.

11 'Report of Annual Meeting,' 9 (1895), pp. 44–5. The CSCE particularly objected to laws that designated surveyors as 'engineers' for distinctly civil engineering work. See, e.g., NAC, Engineering Institute of Canada Papers, MG 28, 1–277, Letter Books (hereafter Letter Books), Letter from McLeod, 14 March 1898, p. 30. Dominion land surveyors, however, had their own complaints about engineers encroaching on their domain. See Don W. Thomson, *Men and Meridians: The History of Surveying and Mapping in Canada*, Vol. 2 (Ottawa, 1967) pp. 64–5.

12 See, e.g., James T. Child's remarks, 'The Professional Status – Correspondence,' *TCSCE*, 7 (1893) p. 254. Keefer dated this agitation from the formation of the land surveyors into a close corporation. It is not clear, however, the exact date to which he was referring, since surveyors – at least in Ontario – did not become a close corporation until 1892 (*Ontario Statutes*, 55 Vic. c. 45). Perhaps he was referring to the organization of the Association of Provincial Land Surveyors of Ontario (1886) or the granting of exclusive survey privileges to Dominion land surveyors on Dominion lands under the Dominion Lands Act, 1874. See 'President's Address' (1888) p. 10.

13 'Discussion on the Professional Status,' *ibid.*, 6 (1892) pp. 114, 249–50; Letter Books, C.H. McLeod to C.E.W. Dodwell, 10 June 1892, p. 840. *Ibid.*, McLeod to D. Macpherson, 24 July 1901, p. 148.

14 'Association of Ontario Land Surveyors,' *CE*, 3 (April 1895) p. 342; 'Proceedings of the Toronto Summer Meeting,' *TCSCE*, 10 (1896) p. 98.

15 *CE*, 4 (May 1896) p. 16.

16 'Discussion on the Professional Status,' pp. 116–17; *CE*, 2 (Nov. 1894) p. 217; 'Report of the Annual Meeting,' *TCSCE*, 9 (1895) pp. 16, 83; Edit. 'Free Engineering Advice,' *CE*, 17 (4 Oct. 1909) pp. 367–8; Willis Chipman to Editor, *ibid.*, 8 (1 April 1901) pp. 254–5.

17 Willis Chipman to Editor, *CR*, 8 (1 April 1901) pp. 254–5; Robert W. King to Editor, *ibid.*, 14 (Dec. 1900) p. 162; 'Report of Annual Meeting,' *TCSCE*, 15 (1901) pp. 38–40; *ibid*, 16 (1902) p. 21.

18 See, e.g., 'Discussion on the Wielder of the Weapon,' *TCSCE*, 28 (1914) p. 509; Hyman Goldman to Editor, *CE*, 34 (9 May 1918) p. 409; 'Classification and Remuneration of Engineers,' *ibid.*, 43 (26 Dec. 1922) p. 662.

19 'President's Address' (W.T. Jennings), *TCSCE*, 14 (1900) p. 30.

20 'President's Address' (John Kennedy), *ibid.*, 7 (1893) p. 15. Not all engineers shared this lofty ideal. For some, economic conditions, as much as character, determined ethical conduct. In 1918, for example, H.A. Goldman asserted that increased competition, arising from occasional over-supply of engineers, accounted for the fact that some engineers were willing to take a colleague's job for less money. Hyman Goldman to Editor, *CE*, p. 409.

21 Alan Macdougall, 'The Professional Status: A Plea for a Close Corporation,' *TCSCE*, 6 (1892) p. 111.

22 See *ibid.*, p. 100.

23 Minutes, Ordinary Meeting, 20 May 1892, p. 125; 'Report of Annual Meeting,' *ibid*, 7 (1893) pp. 17, 19–20; Council Minutes, 11 Oct. 1892, p. 122.

24 Council Minutes, 6 Dec. 1892, p. 134; 'Report of Annual Meeting,' *TCSCE*, 7 (1893) pp. 18–19.

25 *Ibid.*, 8 (1894) p. 47; *ibid.*, 9 (1895) pp. 42–6, 49; *ibid.*, 10 (1906) p. 10; Council Minutes, 8 Oct. 1895, pp. 236–7.

26 NAC, Engineering Institute of Canada Papers, MG 28, 1–277, Minutes, Annual General Meeting, 14 Jan. 1896 (enclosure), 'Memorandum for the Committee of the Canadian Society of Civil Engineers Appointed to Consider and Secure Special Legislation' (strictly confidential) (hereafter 'Memorandum for Special Legislation').

27 A 1931 act established a registration board with licensing and regulatory powers, while the OAA was directed to perform the educational and administrative functions of a professional society. In 1935, the profession finally gained full self-governing and regulatory powers when the registration board and the OAA were integrated. See Raymond Card, *Ontario Association of Architects, 1890–1950* (Toronto, 1950) pp. 7–32, *passim*. As well, it was not until 1958 that veterinary surgeons finally acquired full regulatory powers to control their profession. See A. Margaret Evans and C.A.V. Barker, *Century One: A History of the Ontario Veterinary Association, 1874–1974* (Guelph, 1976) pp. 181, 254–68, appendix D.

28 'Report of Annual Meeting,' *TCSCE*, 7 (1893) p. 18. For a cogent analysis of the power of professional self-government, see Government of Ontario, Royal Commission, Inquiry into Civil Rights, *Report*, no. 1, Vol. 3 (Toronto, 1968) (hereafter McRuer Report) chap. 79.

29 'Report of Annual Meeting' (1893) p. 18.

30 Scrap Book, no. 1, 'Memorandum for the Use of the Provincial Committee on Incorporation,' 3 July 1897. Senior CSCE member E.H. Keating later asserted

that the CSCE 'embraces, with very few exceptions, all of the civil engineers in the Dominion of Canada from the Atlantic to the Pacific'; E.H. Keating to Editor, Toronto *Globe*, 6 March 1902, p. 7.

31 Letter Books, C.H. McLeod to Willis Chipman, 23 March 1899, p. 548.

32 This criterion was the same as the CSCE admission standards. See chapter 2.

33 Letter Books, Letter from Alan Macdougall, 31 August 1893, p. 189; Macdougall, 'The Professional Status: A Plea for a Close Corporation,' p. 244.

34 'Memorandum for Special Legislation.'

35 *Ibid.*

36 Minutes, Annual General Meeting, 14 Jan. 1896 (enclosure), 'Dominion Bill' (strictly confidential).

37 *Ibid.*, 'An Act Respecting the Profession of Civil Engineers' (strictly confidential).

38 'Report of Annual Meeting,' *TCSCE*, 10 (1896) pp. 9–11.

39 *CE*, 4 (July 1896) p. 80; Council Minutes, 11 Feb. 1896, pp. 250–1; 'Report of Annual Meeting,' *TCSCE*, 10 (1896) pp. 13–14.

40 *Ibid.*, p. 2.

41 'Civil Engineering a Close Profession in Manitoba,' *ENGN*, 36, no. 8 (1896) p. 123. On engineering licensing laws in the United States, see 'Licensing Laws for Engineers,' *Chemical and Metallurgical Engineering*, 28 (28 March 1923) pp. 588–9; 'Licensing and Registration of Engineers in the United States,' *Mining and Metallurgy* (Jan. 1945) pp. 22–7; James H. Schaub and Karl Pavlovic (eds.), *Engineering Professionalism and Ethics* (New York, 1983) chap. 8.

42 'Report of Council,' *TCSCE*, 11 (1897) p. 13; 'Report of Annual Meeting,' *ibid.*, 12 (1898) p. 4; Letter Books, McLeod to D. Macpherson, 24 July 1901, p. 149.

43 NAC, Engineering Institute of Canada Papers, MG 28, 1–277, Council Minutes (hereafter Council Minutes), 8 Dec. 1896, pp. 297–8; Letter Books, McLeod to Archibald, 27 Jan. 1897, p. 536.

44 Scrap Book, no. 1, Newspaper clipping, n.d. (13 Jan. 1897, ?).

45 'Report of Annual Meeting,' *TCSCE*, 12 (1898) pp. 14–15.

46 Letter Books, McLeod to M. Drummond, 9 June 1897, p. 730; *ibid.*, McLeod to Willis Chipman, p. 525.

47 *Ibid.*, McLeod to M. Murphy, 18 Jan. 1898, p. 932.

48 Letter Books, McLeod to St. George Boswell, 24 Nov. 1897, p. 836; *ibid.*, McLeod to St. George Boswell, 3 Dec. 1897, p. 853; McLeod to A. Duclose, 3 Dec. 1897, p. 855; *ibid.*, McLeod to G.A. Mountain, 13 Dec. 1897, p. 862; *ibid.*, McLeod to G.K. Addice, 13 Dec. 1897 (private and personal), p. 864.

49 Scrap Book, no. 1, 'Memorandum for the use of the Provincial Committee on Incorporation,' 3 July 1897.
50 'Civil Engineer's Bill,' *JCMI*, 2 (1899) p. 256.
51 Edit. 'Amazing Arrogance,' *CMR*, 16 (Feb. 1897) p. 37.
52 Scrap Book, no. 1, *Evening Mail*, 18 Feb. 1897, John Hardman to Editor (newspaper clipping). 'Canadian Society of Civil Engineers' Bill,' *CMR*, 16 (March 1897) p. 187.
53 Edit. 'Amazing Arrogance,' p. 37.
54 The history of this society is somewhat obscure. E.H. Keating confessed that he had never heard of it and, after inquiries with other engineers, even doubted its existence (E.H. Keating to Editor, Toronto *Globe*, 6 March 1902, p. 7). The DIAE's secretary, however, estimated that the society had approximately 2,000 members (twice the CSCE's membership), 500 to 600 of whom, he claimed, were 'civil' engineers. Although some prominent engineers, such as Sandford Fleming, were members, the DIAE admitted non-professionals. For this reason, the CSCE dismissed this organization as non-professional and refused its offer of affiliation. See 'The Royal Commission on the Alleged Employment of Aliens in Connection with the Surveys of the Proposed Grand Trunk Railway: Report of the Commission and Other Documents,' in Canada, House of Commons, *Sessional Papers* (1905) no. 36a, 'Minutes of Evidence,' pp. 149–51, 441–2; Council Minutes, 2 May 1902, pp. 266–7.
55 OA, Pamphlet, No. 37, Dominion Institute of Amalgamated Engineering, *Open Letter Regarding the Introduction into the Provincial Legislature of a Bill of the Canadian Society of Civil Engineers which has its Headquarters in the City of Montreal as Ordered by that Society's Council for Making All Branches of Engineering a Close Corporation* (hereafter DIAE, *Open Letter*) n.p.
56 *Ibid.*
57 'The Canadian Mining Institute,' *CE*, 8 (April 1901) p. 258.
58 Scrap Book, no. 4, 'Engineering Trust in Formative Stage,' *Halifax Herald* (newspaper clipping, n.d.). An official of the attorney general's office was reported to have described the 1902 bill as the 'most vicious piece of class legislation' he had ever seen; UTL, John Galbraith Papers, B 36 [B-70-001] Box no. 1 (hereafter Galbraith Papers), W.L. Goodwin to Galbraith, 28 Feb. 1907. These critics, as well as the DIAE and the CMI, recognized correctly that the legislation sought by the CSCE would give civil engineers virtually the right to determine who could earn a living practising engineering. (On the potential for the abuse of legislated power by self-governing professional societies, see McRuer Report, vol. 3, pp. 1163–6.) Other professionals had attempted to use legislation to restrict competition. In 1893, for example, a

front group for the Ontario College of Pharmacy attempted, unsuccessfully, to have the sale of patent medicines made a legal monopoly of pharmacists by having their ingredients classed as poisons. Michael Bliss, 'The Protective Impulse: An Approach to the Social History of Oliver Mowat's Ontario,' in Donald Swainson (ed.), *Oliver Mowat's Ontario* (Toronto, 1972) p. 185, n. 20.

59 'The Canadian Mining Institute,' *CE*, p. 259.

60 'Engineering Trust in Formative Stages' (clipping), n.p.

61 Scrap Book, no. 1, 'Kill This Bill,' Kingston, *Daily British Whig* (newspaper clipping), n.d.

62 *Ibid.*, Council Minutes, 11 March 1902, p. 218.

63 *Ibid.*, 12 April 1898, p. 61; Letter Books, McLeod to Willis Chipman, n.d., p. 272; 8 March 1899, p. 515; 9 Jan. 1900, p. 991; *ibid.*, McLeod to J.P. Mallarkoy, 21 Jan. 1899, p. 389; 'Report of Annual Meeting,' *TCSCE*, 16 (1902) p. 24.

64 Letter Books, McLeod to Carr-Harris, 25 March 1899, p. 559; McLeod to B.T.A. Bell, 3 Jan. 1900, p. 980; McLeod to Willis Chipman, 3 Jan. 1900, p. 982; Canadian Institute of Mining and Metallurgy, Montreal Council Minutes (hereafter Council Minutes, CMI), 17 Jan. 1900, p. 40; Letter Books, McLeod to Willis Chipman, 19 Jan. 1900, p. 32; Council Minutes, 13 Feb. 1900, pp. 137–8; Letter Books, McLeod to B.T.A. Bell, 18 Feb. 1900, p. 117; *ibid.*, McLeod to J. Galbraith, 6 March 1900, p. 166; Council Minutes, CMI, 10 March 1900, p. 45; Council Minutes (CSCE), 13 March 1900, p. 141; Letter Books, McLeod to Galbraith, 14 March 1900, p. 188; *ibid.*, McLeod to B.T.A. Bell, 23 March 1900, p. 208.

65 'C.S.C.E. Annual Meeting,' *CE*, 7 (March 1900) p. 295; 'Report of Annual Meeting,' *TCSCE*, 14 (1900) p. 9.

66 Letter Books, McLeod to Willis Chipman, 23 March 1899, pp. 547–8; *ibid.*, McLeod to G.M. Macdonell, 3 March 1902, p. 584; McLeod to W.R. Butler, 14 March 1902, p. 640; McLeod to C.B. Smith, 14 March, 1902, p. 645.

67 *Ibid.*, McLeod to L.W. Gill, 3 April 1902, p. 692.

68 Mining engineers were exempted from the bill; see 'An Act Respecting Civil Engineers,' sec. 8, printed in 'Report of Annual Meeting,' *TCSCE*, 16 (1902) p. 24. However, they could, as Dr Goodwin pointed out, be excluded from civil engineering related mine work, because only 'civil' engineers (not defined in the bill) could practise (section 2). 'Canadian Society of Civil Engineers Bill,' *JCMI*, 5 (1899) pp. 560–1.

69 *Ibid.*

70 See, e.g., DIAE, *Open Letter.*

71 Council Minutes, CMI, 7 April 1905, p. 167 (insert).

72 See especially Scrap Book, no. l, John E. Hardman to Editor, *Evening Mail*, 18 Feb. 1897 (newspaper clipping).

73 Galbraith Papers, Box no. l, W.L. Goodwin to Galbraith, 28 Feb. 1907. For the reaction of surveyors, see 'Ontario Land Surveyors,' *CE*, 18 (March 1902) p. 105.

74 Edit. 'An Objectionable Bill,' Toronto *Globe*, 4 March 1902, p. 6; Edit. 'The Engineers' Bill,' *ibid.*, 6 March 1902, p. 6.

75 NAC, Engineering Institute of Canada Papers, MG 28, 1–277, Minutes, Special General Meeting, 17 June 1896, p. 38.

76 *Ibid.*, Minutes Ordinary Meeting, 17 June 1896, p. 39; 'Proceedings of the Toronto Summer Meeting,' p. 102.

77 Michael J. Trebilcock, Carolyn J. Tuohy, Alan D. Wolfson, *Professional Regulation: A Staff Study of Accountancy, Architecture, Engineering and Law in Ontario Prepared for the Professional Organizations Committee* (Toronto, 1979) p. 26.

78 'Report of Annual Meeting,' *TCSCE*, 10 (1896) p. 8; EIC Letter Books, McLeod to C.E.W. Dodwell, 22 Nov. 1898, p. 271; *ibid.*, McLeod to N.E. Brooks, 14 March 1902, P. 344; 'The Status of Civil Engineering,' *CE*, 9 (April 1902) p. 87.

79 'Proceedings of the Toronto Summer Meeting,' p. 100.

80 'Memorandum for Special Legislation.'

81 *ENGN*, 36 (Aug. 1896) p. 120; Council Minutes, 5 Jan. 1897, p. 304; 'Report of Annual Meeting,' *TCSCE*, 12 (1898) pp. 13–14. Rutan also pointed out (p.14) that it was now possible for engineers to sue and recover fees for service.

82 'Report of Annual Meeting,' *ibid.*, 22 (1908) p. 38.

83 Letter Books, McLeod to Hon. Secretary, Centro Nacional de Ingenieros, Buenos Aires, 17 June 1902; *ibid.*, McLeod to S. Whinery, 6 March 1902, p. 602.

84 Both Chipman and McLeod complained of apathy among Ontario members. 'The real reason why our bill [1899] did not go through the Ontario Legislature,' McLeod asserted, 'was that the members of the Society resident in Ontario have not taken sufficient interest in this measure.' *Ibid.*, 11 April 1899, p. 590.

85 See J.G.G. Kerry's views: J.G.G. Kerry, 'The Past,' *EJ*, 30 (Aug. 1947) p. 370.

86 Council Minutes, 13 Jan. 1902, pp. 246–7; 21 April 1903, p. 262; 2 May 1903, pp. 265–8; 12 May 1903, p. 270. In the same year, the CSCE stopped the incorporation of the 'Manitoba Institute of Engineers and Architects'; 'Report of Annual Meeting,' *TCSCE*, 17 (1903) p. 4.

87 UTL, Toronto Branch Papers, MS 102, Box no. 2, A.C. Blanchard to C.H. McLeod, 11 May 1911; *ibid.*, A.C. Blanchard to A.B. Barry, 16 June 1911,

A.C. Blanchard to C.H. McLeod, 16 June 1911; Secretary, Toronto Branch, to E.H. Keating, 23 Oct. 1911; Secretary, Toronto Branch, to C.H. McLeod, 25 Oct. 1911; Council Minutes, 13 May 1911, p. 48; *ibid.*, p. 67.

88 Edit. 'Canadian Society of Sanitary Engineers,' *CE*, 21 (26 Oct. 1911) p. 486. 'It is a serious blow at the prestige and dignity of the engineering profession in Canada,' lamented the *Canadian Engineer* (2 Nov. 1911) p. 514.

89 Council Minutes, 8 Oct. 1910, pp. 358ff; 'Report of Annual Meeting,' *TCSCE*, 25 (1911) p. 121; Council Minutes, 8 Feb. 1913, p. 173.

90 *Ibid.*, 8 Oct. 1916, pp. 358f.

CHAPTER 6: IN SEARCH OF A 'TRIBAL SOUL'

1 President's Address' (John Galbraith), *TCSCE*, 23 (1909) p. 110.

2 NAC, Engineering Institute of Canada Papers, MG 28, 1–277, Scrap Books (hereafter Scrap Book), 'C.H. McLeod,' 10 Sept. 1903; UTL, Toronto · Branch Papers Box no. 4, 'Meeting at Engineers' Club – Discussion,' 5 Feb. 1917, p. 42; NAC, Engineering Institute of Canada Papers, MG 28, 1–277, Letter Books (hereafter Letter Books), Letter to Galbraith, 27 Feb. 1900, p. 154; *ibid.*, Letter from C.H. McLeod, 11 Dec. 1898, p. 482; 'Report of Annual Meeting,' *TCSCE*, 26 (1912) p. 72. Not all engineers believed that CSCE papers were below international standards. See, for example, the remarks of the city engineer of Hamilton: E.B. Barrow to Editor, *CR*, 28 (27 March 1913) pp. 46–7.

3 Unsigned Letter to Editor, *CE*, 15 (6 March 1908) p. 149.

4 See, for example, 'President's Address' (John Kennedy), *TCSCE*, 17 (1893) p. 14; Scrap Book, Circular by John Galbraith, 12 June 1908; 'President's Address' (Phelps Johnson), *TCSCE*, 28 (1914) pp. 103–4. Also see Letter Books, H. Macdougall to P. Gilpin, 2 March 1893, p. 46.

5 'Report of Council,' *TCSCE*, 11 (1897) p. 12; 'Report of Annual Meeting' (H.H. Vaughan), *ibid.*, 28 (1912) p. 53; Letter Books, Letter to Galbraith, 27 Feb. 1900, p. 154.

6 For example, between 1911 and 1914, an average of only one paper per 132 members was presented. See 'President's Address' (Phelps Johnson), (1914) p. 103.

7 'Report of Annual Meeting,' *TCSCE*, 22 (1908) p. 35; 'President's Address' (G.H. Duggan), *ibid.*, 31 (1917) p. 71.

8 Commenting on the standard specifications for Portland cement, compared with those issued by the American Society for Testing Materials, for example, the *Canadian Engineer* in 1908 lamented that the 'comparison does not reflect any great credit on the Canadian society.' 'The Canadian Society of Civil Engineers,' *CE*, 15 (23 Oct. 1908) p. 758. Also see Unsigned Letter to Editor, *CR*, 27, no. 9 (26 Feb. 1913) p. 43.

9 'Report of Annual Meeting,' *TCSCE*, 26 (1912) p. 71.

10 Scrap Book, no. 4, Circular by John Galbraith, 12 June 1908.

11 'Report of Annual Meeting,' *TCSCE*, 22 (1908) p. 9.

12 Toronto Branch Papers, Box no. 4, A.N. Worthington to E. Oliver, 19 Feb. 1917.

13 Andrew Charles Gross, 'Engineering Manpower in Canada' (PhD dissertation, Ohio State University, 1968) p. 50, Table 7b.

14 Scrap Book, no. 4, Circular by Committee on Society Affairs, 7 Nov. 1917.

15 'The British Columbia Engineer and His Problems,' *CR*, 27 (19 Oct. 1913) p. 39. Similar regional antagonisms also developed within the ASME. For an analysis of the 'New York' problem, see Bruce Sinclair, *A Centennial History of the American Society of Mechanical Engineers, 1880–1980* (Toronto, 1980) pp. 65–7, 85, 93, 184–6.

16 Of 663 civil engineers, approximately 300 were CSCE members. Canada, Department of Trade and Commerce, *Sixth Census of Canada, 1921*, Vol. IV (Ottawa, 1927) Table 4, pp. 158, 184; 'Retiring President's Address' (J.M.R. Fairbairn), *EJ*, 5 (Feb. 1922) p. 96.

17 'Report of Annual Meeting,' *CE*, 34 (7 Feb. 1918) p. 122.

18 See Dean Galbraith's remarks before the Winchester inquiry. 'Minutes of Evidence,' 'The Royal Commission of the Alleged Employment of Aliens in Connection with the Surveys of the Proposed Grand Trunk Pacific Railway, Report of the Commission and other Documents,' in Canada, House of Commons, *Sessional Papers* (1905) no. 35a, p. 513.

19 'Peterborough Branch,' *JEIC*, 4 (June 1921) pp. 371–3; UTA, Haultain Papers (hereafter Haultain Papers), B 47 (B-72-005) Box no. 4, Fraser S. Keith, 'Engineering Education,' 8 May 1924, p. 7.

20 F.W. Wetmore to Editor, *CR*, 27, no. 10 (5 March 1913) p. 67.

21 See chapter 2.

22 Edit. 'Protection for Engineers,' *CE*, 14 (14 Feb. 1908) p. 112.

23 *Ibid.*

24 In 1913, although the *Contract Record* observed that many prominent CSCE members had openly criticized the society in signed letters to the editor, there was also an unprecedented number of unsigned letters – presumably from engineers with career interests to protect – equally critical of the society.

25 See, e.g., Wm. P. Anderson to Editor, *CR*, 27 (12 March 1913) p. 48; 'Report of the Annual Meeting,' *TCSCE*, 28 (1914) pp. 112–13.

26 'Report of Annual Meeting,' *ibid.*, 22 (1908) p. 35; E.A. Stone to Editor, *CR*, 27, no. 15 (9 April 1913) p. 71. Apathy had developed to the point where a committee, charged with discovering means to increase the society's usefulness, in 1909, was unable to make recommendations, because it received only seventeen replies to a circular soliciting suggestions. 'Report of Committees,' *TCSCE*, 23 (1909) pp. 36–40.

27 'Report of Annual Meeting,' *ibid.*, 24 (1910) p. 41; 'President's Address' (Phelps Johnson) p. 105. Both the *Canadian Engineer* and the *Contract Record* were disappointed and scorned this position. Edit. 'C.S. of C.E.,' *CE*, 15 (10 July 1908) p. 489; Edit. 'Work and Status of the Canadian Society of Civil Engineers,' *CR*, 27, no. 9 (26 Feb. 1913) p. 37.

28 'Report of Committees,' *TCSCE*, 23 (1909) p. 41.

29 (Wm. Anderson), *ibid.*, 19 (1905) p. 24; Council Minutes, 9 June 1903, p. 274; C.H. McLeod, 'How Canadian Engineers Organize,' *CE*, 32 (19 April 1917) p. 342.

30 J.G.G. Kerry, 'The Past,' *EJ*, 30 (1947) p. 370.

31 See Canadian Society of Civil Engineers, *Constitution for Proposed Canadian Society of Civil Engineers* (Ottawa, 1886) secs. 33–7.

32 C.H. Mitchell, chairman, Toronto branch, for example, doubted that the Nova Scotia Society of Engineers would have been organized if the branches had been fostered earlier; C.H. Mitchell, 'Inaugural Address, Toronto Branch,' *CE*, 15 (6 March 1908) p. 151. For background on these societies, see 'Nova Scotia Society of Engineers,' *ibid.*, 14 (8 March 1907) p. 51; 'Nova Scotia Society of Engineers,' *CR*, 25 (25 Oct. 1911) pp. 51–2; 'The Engineering Society of Regina,' *ibid.*, 27 (15 Jan. 1913) pp. 64–6.

33 The differences were usually minor. In some branches, junior members could vote, and, in Vancouver, in order to give everyone a chance to hold office, the chairman and vice-chairman could hold office for one year only. See, e.g., 'St. John Branch,' *JEIC*, 4 (June 1921) p. 377; 'Tenth General Professional Meeting,' *ibid.*

34 'Formation of New Branches,' *JEIC*, 1 (May 1918) p. 63; F.A. Bowman, 'Engineering Progress in Nova Scotia,' *ibid.*, 3 (July 1920) p. 348; NAC, Engineering Institute of Canada Papers, MG 28, 1–277, Correspondence, Thomas A. Hay to H.T. Bovey, 12 April 1887; 'Engineering Gathering at Peterborough', *JEIC*, 2 (Dec. 1919) p. 779; 'Report of the Council,' *ibid.*, 3 (Feb. 1920) p. 72.

35 See, e.g., Toronto Branch Papers, Box no. 4, H.H. Vaughan to C.B. Hamilton, 26 June 1918; C.H. McLeod, 'How Canadian Engineers Organize,' p. 341.

36 Council, not the membership, approved of the formation of new branches, along with their by-laws. Although branches were permitted to increase revenue by the collection of branch dues and also through affiliate members' dues, the CSCE ultimately controlled branch finances – and thus the branches – through branch rebates. *By-Laws* (1905), s. 49.

37 See, e.g., 'By-Laws Toronto Branch Engineering Institute of Canada' in Toronto Branch, Engineering Institute of Canada, *Yearbook* (1919), sec. I, p. 13.

38 Since 1905, the ASCE periodically authorized the formation of 'Associations of
Members of the A.S.C.E.,' or 'local sections,' as they became known in 1921.
The local sections were designed to meet the professional needs of members on the local level and further the aims of the parent society. They were
given formal status in 1921. Although the associations held regular meetings and read papers, they were not full-fledged formally structured branches,
comparable to the CSCE branches. *Cf.* William H. Wisely, *The American
Civil Engineer, 1852–1974* (New York, 1974) pp. 48–51, 409; 'President's
Address' (Phelps Johnson) p. 105. CMI by-laws also made provision for the
establishment of 'local branches or sections,' in mining camps, towns, or
districts, wherever there were sufficient members. 'By-Laws of the Canadian
Mining Institute,' *BCMI*, no. 11 (June 1910) sec. 54, pp. 228–9.

39 Although branches found other means to augment their revenue, they were
usually in financial trouble. Toronto Branch Papers, Box no. 7, F.S. Keith
to W.S. Harvey, 3 March 1919; R.O. Wynne-Roberts, 'Questions of Policy for
Engineering Institute of Canada,' *CE*, 39 (7 Oct. 1920) p. 415.

40 With 157 members in 1911, the Ottawa branch became the largest in the
CSCE. 'President's Address' (G.H. Duggan) p. 78, Table 4.

41 'Annual Report,' *TCSCE* (1890) p. 46; Council Minutes, 5 May 1891, p. 68;
'Minutes Annual General Meeting,' 12 Jan. 1892, p. 82; 'Report of the
Annual Meeting,' *TCSCE*, 7 (1893) p. 4.

42 On the re-establishment of the branch, see 'First Annual Report of the
Toronto Branch Canadian Society of Civil Engineers, to 31 December, 1907,'
TCSCE, 22 (1908) pp. 31–2; Council Minutes, 13 Feb. 1906, pp. 74–5.

43 'Report of the Toronto Branch for the Year 1913,' *TCSCE*, 27 (1914) p. 96;
Toronto Branch Papers, Box no. 4, 'Meeting at Engineers' Club,' 5 Feb.
1917, p. 7.

44 See chapter 2. Relations between the Toronto branch and the Engineers' Club
were amicable. An attempt had even been made to establish the Engineers'
Club as a CSCE branch. 'Inaugural Address, F.L. Sommerville,' *CE*, 13 (2 Feb.
1906) p. 66; 'Report of the Annual Meeting,' *TCSCE*, 21 (1907) p. 6;
'Council Minutes,' 11 April 1905, p. 32; 'Engineers' Club of Toronto Will Not
Amalgamate,' *CE*, 12 (5 May 1905) p. 139.

45 Fraser S. Keith, 'Awakening Recognition of the Engineer,' *CR*, 31 (21 Nov.
1917) p. 953; Toronto Branch Papers, Box no. 5, 'Minutes of a Special
Meeting of the Ottawa Branch,' 21 Feb. 1918 (John Murphy quoting a speech
by W.F. Tye), p. 3.

46 Canadian engineers related their discontent to a larger world-wide feeling
of unrest among engineers over low status. Keith, 'Awakening Recognition of
the Engineer,' p. 953.

47 See chapter 5.

48 Edit. 'The Status of the Engineering Profession,' *CE*, 17 (12 Nov. 1909) p. 527; C.E.W. Dodwell to Editor, *ibid.*, 34 (25 April 1918) p. 362; C.E.W. Dodwell, 'Engineers and Engineering,' *JEIC*, 3 (March 1920) p. 143.

49 Walter J. Francis, 'Engineering as a Profession,' *AS*, new ser. 8 (Oct. 1913) p. 134.

50 'Engineers and Geologists' (H.E.T. Haultain), *CE*, 24 (3 April 1913) pp. 525–6; 'Discussion on Wielder of the Weapon' (P.A.N. Seurot), *TCSCE*, 28 (1914) pp. 514–15; 'Discussion on Canada's Railway Problem' (A.V. Robinson), *ibid.*, 31 (1917) p. 196. Engineers were jealous even of the alleged access that CMI members had to Dominion cabinet ministers. See Toronto Branch Papers, Box no. 4, 'Meeting at Engineers' Club,' p. 7.

51 Council Minutes, 8 March 1904, p. 310; Edit. 'Engineering Help Is Needed,' *CE*, 33 (23 Aug. 1917) p. 169; Toronto Branch Papers, Box no. 4, S.G. Porter to C.H. McLeod, 4 Jan. 1917; 'Engineers on Railway Commission,' *JEIC*, 4 (Jan. 1921) p. 34; 'Report of Annual Meeting,' *TCSCE*, 11 (1897) p. 33, *ibid.*, 25 (1911) p. 143; Edit. 'The Engineer and Boards of Health,' *CE*, 18 (21 Jan. 1910) p. 47; Edit. 'The Medical Health Officer and the Engineer,' *ibid.*, 23 (19 Sept. 1912) p. 484; Edit. 'The Public Health Act of Ontario,' *ibid.*, 24 (16 Jan. 1913) p. 180.

52 Edit. 'Need for Active Service at Home,' *CE*, 29 (22 July 1915) p. 193; Edit. 'Canadian Army Hydrographical Corps,' *ibid.*, (14 Oct. 1915) p. 482; Edit. 'Selection of Engineer Officers,' *ibid.*, 30 (9 March 1916) p. 337; Edit. 'Conscription and the Engineer,' *JEIC*, 1 (June 1918) pp. 91–2; Sapper to Editor, *ibid.*, 11 (March 1919) p. 226.

53 'Editorial Notes,' *CE*, 16 (12 March 1909) p. 348; Cecil B. Smith, 'The Relation of the Engineer and the Community,' *ibid.*, p. 545; 'Engineers and Newspaper Reports,' *ibid.*, 19 (27 Oct. 1910) p. 547; 'Discussion on Wielder of the Weapon' (F.B. Brown) p. 514.

54 Peter Gillespie, a University of Toronto engineering professor, believed that only an engineer could write sympathetic biographies of Canadian engineers, after the fashion of Samuel Smiths. Toronto Branch Papers, Box no. 7, 'Biographies of Engineers.'

55 Francis, 'Engineering as a Profession,' *AS*, p. 134.

56 For background on the formation of this important committee, see Toronto Branch Papers, Box no. 4, 'Meeting at Engineers' Club,' pp. 3–4; for Haultain's assessment, see Haultain Papers, Box no. 4, Haultain to F.M. Lyle, 22 April 1924.

57 As Haultain put it, the CSCE had 'magnificent foundations'; all that was required was 'to build the superstructure.' Toronto Branch Papers, Box no. 4, 'Meeting at Engineers' Club,' p. 15.

58 See especially Haultain Papers, H.E.T. Haultain, 'The Romance of Engineer-

ing: A Luncheon Address' (Jan. 1922) p. 7; H.E.T. Haultain, 'The Wielder of the Weapon,' pp. 494–502, 517–18; Toronto Branch Papers, Box no. 4, 'Meeting at Engineers' Club,' pp. 10–12, 16–17, 50. Engineers earlier had noted a decided lack of *esprit de corps* among Canadian engineers. Scrap Book, no. 3, Clipping *Montreal Gazette* (24 April 1905); 'Report of Annual Meeting,' *TCSCE*, 22 (1908) p. 10.

59 Edit. 'Communion of Engineers,' *CE*, 29 (11 Nov. 1915) p. 577; A. MacDonald to Editor, *ibid.*, 32 (18 May 1917) p. 432; Toronto Branch Papers, Box no. 4, 'Meeting at Engineers' Club – Discussion' (R.O. Wynne-Roberts) pp. 34–5; 'Cape Breton Branch,' *JEIC*, 4 (July 1921) p. 424.

60 Toronto Branch Papers, Box no. 4, 'Meeting at Engineers' Club,' p. 10.

61 *Ibid.*, p. 12.

62 *Ibid.*, p. 16.

63 'Toronto Engineers Suggest Means of Increasing Prestige of the Profession,' *CR*, 32 (24 April 1918) p. 326.

64 R.O. Wynne-Roberts, 'Engineering Prestige,' *CE*, 34 (18 April 1918) p. 332.

65 See Edwin T. Layton Jr., *The Revolt of the Engineers: Social Responsibility and the American Engineering Profession* (Cleveland, 1971).

66 Toronto Branch Papers, Box no. 4, 'Meeting at Engineers' Club,' p. 50.

67 The implications of this change were not lost on some CSCE members. See, e.g., Toronto Branch Papers, Box no. 4, H. Wickstead to E. Oliver, 17 Feb. 1917.

68 Engineering Institute of Canada, *By-Laws of the Engineering Institute of Canada* (1919), s. 1.

69 'Canadian Society of Civil Engineers Broadens Out under New Name,' *CR*, 31 (26 Dec. 1917) p. 1050.

70 C.H. McLeod, 'How Canadian Engineers Organize,' p. 341.

71 'Retiring President's Address' (J.M.R. Fairbairn) pp. 94–5.

72 Keith, 'Awakening Recognition of the Engineer,' p. 955.

73 J.G.G. Kerry, 'The Past,' p. 370.

74 The elective members of the nominating committee (six from Ontario and Quebec) nominated twenty-five councillors – ten of whom were Montreal residents and the remainder from anywhere in Canada. See chapter 2.

75 For each district in which no branch existed, the council appointed one member. *By-Laws* (1919), s. 6.

76 NAC, Engineering Institute of Canada Papers, MG 28, 1–277, Council Minutes (hereafter Council Minutes), 15 July 1904, pp. 325–6.

77 There were few exceptions; see, e.g., H.K. Dutcher to Editor, *CR*, 27, no. 13 (26 March 1913) p. 47.

78 W.F. Tye to Editor, *ibid.*, 27, no. 9 (26 Feb. 1913) p. 40; Wm. Anderson, *ibid.*, no. 11 (12 March 1913) p. 48.

79 'The New Secretary for the Canadian Society of Civil Engineers,' *CE*, 32 (8 March 1917) p. 222.

80 W.F. Tye's *Canada's Railway Problem and Its Solution*, for example, was a sophisticated polemic against railway nationalization by the wartime Borden government, while H.H. Vaughan wrote on Canadian munitions productions (*The Manufacture of Munitions in Canada*) and C.H. Duggan a study of the Quebec Bridge.

81 There were other technical periodicals published during this period. One of the most remarkable was *Applied Science*, published by undergraduates of the Faculty of Applied Science and Engineering, University of Toronto, under various titles since 1886. In addition to presenting student papers, this journal also published addresses by prominent Canadian engineers – usually alumni – on subjects related to engineering professionalism. For brief historical surveys, see T.H. Hogg, 'The Engineering Society University of Toronto,' *AS*, new ser. 2 (Feb. 1909) p. 169; Edit. 'Revival of an Undergraduate Engineering Publication,' *CE*, 40 (5 May 1921) p. 447; Peter Gillespie, 'Forty Years of the Engineering Society,' *University of Toronto Monthly*, 22 (5 Feb. 1922) p. 207.

82 Letter Books, C.H. McLeod to R.W. King, 17 Oct. 1900, p. 450; 25 Oct. 1900, p. 473; McLeod to E.B. Biggar, 25 Oct. 1900, p. 477; McLeod to E.H. Keating, 11 April 1902, p. 729.

83 Council Minutes, 31 Oct. 1917, p. 79; *ibid.*, 18 Dec. 1917, pp. 90–1.

84 Published on a monthly basis, this journal was originally entitled the *Journal of the Engineering Institute of Canada*. For a brief overview of its progress, see '40 Years of Publication, 1918–1958,' *EJ*, 41 (April 1958) pp. 135–6. Prior to its publication, the CSCE, for a number of years beginning in 1907, issued a monthly *Bulletin* which published the society's notices and similar business.

85 Edit. 'The Organization of Canada's Technical Men,' *EN*, 26, no. 6 (15 March 1917) p. 10. Letter Books, C.H. McLeod to R.W. King, 1 Nov. 1900, p. 499. The classification of courses by engineering schools and popular usage by corporate and government employers, and the growth of specialized engineering societies, were the general reasons cited for the specialized usage of the word 'civil.' See 'Report of Annual Meeting,' *TCSCE*, 16 (1902) p. 19; *ibid.*, 17 (1903) p. 71; Scrap Book no. 6, Committee on Society Affairs, 'Circular,' 7 Nov. 1917.

86 Toronto Branch Papers, Box no. 4, 'Meeting at Engineers' Club – Discussion,' pp. 17, 19. Some members had always believed that the term 'civil' engineer was too exclusive. See, e.g., Comments of J. Sproule, *CE*, 3 (2 June 1895) p. 43.

87 'Report of the Annual Meeting,' *TCSCE*, 16 (1902) p. 19; *ibid.*, 17 (1903) pp. 70–1.

88 Scrap Book, no. 6, Committee on Society Affairs 'Circular,' 7 Nov. 1917.
89 The committee favoured 'Engineering,' since it was broader in scope than 'Engineer' and less likely to confuse the public. 'Institute' was preferred to 'Society,' since it did not have the same fraternal or benevolent connotations. In short, the committee thought that the new name was more professional (*ibid.*). Some mining engineers, however, held the opposite view. Edit. 'Civil Engineers Change Name of Their Society,' *CMJ*, 39 (1 Feb. 1918) p. 32.
90 Edit. 'The New Name,' *JEIC*, 1 (May 1918) p. 60; Council Minutes, 13 Oct. 1918, pp. 78–9.
91 Edit. 'The Significance of the Engineering Institute of Canada,' *CR*, 32, no. 1 (2 Jan. 1917) p. 1.
92 'The President's Address' (H.H. Vaughan), *JEIC*, 1 (May 1918) p. 1. Some observers compared the EIC's new aspirations for professional unity with the formation of the Engineering Council in the United States. See Edit. 'Significance of the Engineering Institute of Canada,' *CR*, 32, no. 1 (2 Jan. 1917) p. 1; 'Canadian Society Becomes Institution,' *ENR*, 80 (21 Feb. 1918) p. 340.
93 Edit. 'Civil Engineers Change Name of Their Society,' p. 32.
94 Gray doubted whether the EIC had improved its prospects or status by attempting to combine all fields of engineering in one society, since one association could not serve the specialized needs of all engineers. Pointing out that a technical society existed for the advancement of learning, Gray asserted that the attempt to improve the status of engineers was a 'selfish ideal, and not in its essence distinguishable from trades unionism'; F.W. Gray to Editor, *CMJ*, 39 (1 Dec. 1918) p. 401.
95 Edit. 'A Rose by Any Other Name Etc.,' *BCMI*, no. 70 (Feb. 1918) pp. 83–4.
96 'Address by the Secretary,' *ibid.*, no. 76 (Aug. 1918) p. 721.
97 'Canadian Society of Civil Engineers Broadens Out under New Name,' p. 1050.
98 The CMI would have disputed this, since the majority of its members were professionals. Their suspicions about the name change were reinforced by memories of the CSCE's periodic attempts to obtain restrictive provincial licensing powers – a measure the CMI always believed would destroy its organization.
99 H. Elizabeth Fisher, 'Professional Asociations in Canada' (PhD dissertation, University of Toronto, 1932) p. 174. Council Minutes, 21 Nov. 1916, p. 441; 23 Nov. 1916, p. 443; Toronto Branch Papers, MS 102, Box no. 3, C.H. McLeod to L. Arkley, 30 Oct. 1916; *ibid.*, Box no. 7, Letter to F.B. Brown, 26 Feb. 1921; C.B. Hamilton to F.S. Keith, 3 June 1918; H.H. Vaughan to P. Gillespie, 26 June 1918.
100 *Ibid.*, Vaughan to Hamilton, 26 June 1918.

101 *Ibid.*, F.S. Keith to George Hogarth (confidential), 25 June 1918; Vaughan to Gillespie, 26 June 1918; Council Minutes, 26 June 1918, pp. 63–4. 'Report of Thirty-Fourth Annual Meeting,' *JEIC*, 3 (March 1920), p. 114; 'Retiring President's Address' (R.A. Ross), 4 (March 1921) p. 202.

102 Toronto Branch Papers, MS 102, Box no. 5, F.S. Keith to C.B. Hamilton, 6 June 1918; Vaughan to Gillespie, 26 June 1918; Vaughan to Hamilton, 26 June 1918; Gillespie to Vaughan, 2 Dec. 1918; Gillespie to E.V. Pannell, 21 Dec. 1918.

103 *Ibid.*, Box no. 6, Pannell to Gillespie, 12 Dec. 1918; (Copy), Council Minutes, 17 Dec. 1918, p. 1; 'American Engineering Societies in Canada,' *CE*, 36 (13 Feb. 1919) p. 221; Toronto Branch Papers, MS 102, Box no. 5, Vaughan to Hamilton, 26 June 1918; 'Report of Thirty-Third Annual Meeting,' *JEIC*, 2 (March 1919) p. 164.

104 Edit. 'A Canadian Institute of Electrical Engineers,' *EN*, 28 (1 May 1919) p. 25.

105 Toronto Branch Papers, MS 102, Box no. 6, Minutes of Council (copy), 17 Dec. 1918, p. 1; 'The Bon Entente,' *JEIC*, 1 (Dec. 1918) pp. 402–3; Edit. 'Joint Committee on International Affiliation,' *ibid.*, 2 (April 1919) p. 335; Committee on International Affiliation, 3 (Feb. 1920) p. 52; M.E. Cooley to F.S. Keith, *EJ*, 5 (Feb. 1922) p. 88; Council Minutes, 25 Sept. 1922, p. 78.

106 Keith, 'Awakening Recognition of the Profession,' p. 956.

CHAPTER 7: 'THE PROPER KIND OF PUBLICITY'

1 Edit. 'Publicity as an Asset,' *JEIC*, 1 (Oct. 1918) p. 291.

2 Haultain Papers B 47 (B-72-005) (hereafter Haultain Papers), Box no. 1, Haultain 'To Engineers,' 15 April 1918.

3 H.E.T. Haultain, 'Wielder of the Weapon,' *TCSCE*, 28 (1914) p. 500.

4 'Editorial Notes,' *CE*, 16 (12 March 1909) p. 348; Cecil B. Smith, 'The Relation of the Engineer to the Community,' *ibid.*, (23 April 1909) p. 545; Edit. 'Engineers and Newspaper Reports,' *ibid.*, 19 (27 Oct. 1910) p. 547; 'Presidential Address' (R.W. Leonard) *TEIC*, 34 (Jan. 1920) p. 18.

5 Haultain, 'Wielder of the Weapon,' p. 500.

6 'Community Service by Professional Engineering Society,' *CE*, 40 (26 May 1921) p. 515.

7 *Ibid.*; G.G. Moon to Editor, *JEIC*, 2 (March 1919) p. 224; Edit. 'The Engineer and the Community,' *ibid.*, 4 (May 1921) p. 313. Using publicity to upgrade status was not a new idea. See, e.g., Edit. 'Engineers and the Press,' *CE*, 14 (18 Oct. 1907) p. 386.

8 Edit. 'Engineers Extending Influence,' *JEIC*, 3 (Dec. 1920) p. 580; 'Saint John

Branch,' *ibid.* (June 1920) p. 318; 'Report of Council for the Year 1920,' *ibid.*, 4 (Feb. 1921) pp. 79–80.

9 'Presidential Address' (R.W. Leonard), p. 18; 'Tenth General Professional Meeting,' *JEIC*, 4 (Sept. 1921) p. 508; 'Victoria Branch,' *ibid.* (Nov. 1921) p. 585. Engineers were also encouraged to seek public office. See, e.g., 'Report of the Annual Meeting,' *TCSCE*, 23 (1909) p. 18.

10 C.D. Norton, 'The Education of the Public,' *CE*, 28 (25 Feb. 1915) p. 289; 'President's Address' (J. Galbraith), *TCSCE*, 23 (1909) pp. 111–12.

11 R.O. Wynne-Roberts, 'War and Its Relation to Engineering Work,' *CR*, 29 (3 Nov. 1915) pp. 1127–8; Frank D. Adams, 'The Work of the Advisory Council for Scientific and Industrial Research in Canada,' *BCMI* (May 1917) pp. 407–9. From the outbreak of war, Canadian manufacturers complained that they were unable to produce many articles essential to various trade processes, because of German monopolies. See, e.g., Edit. 'Development of Industrial Research,' *Industrial Canada*, 18 (May 1917) p. 54.

12 Edit. 'Industrial Research and Its Relation to Commercial Supremacy,' *CR*, 30 (22 Nov. 1916) p. 1101, italics added. This concept of a 'two fold war ... a war of arms and men' and a 'Trade war' was commonly held. See e.g., Edit. 'The War and the Engineer,' *AS*, 9 (Oct. 1914) p. 3.

13 Edit. 'Industrial Research a Mighty Factor,' *CE*, 28 (13 May 1915) p. 363; Edit. 'Industrial Reconstruction and Scientific Research,' *CR* 32 (26 June 1918) p. 499; Edit. 'Industrial Research and Its Relation to Commercial Supremacy,' p. 1101.

14 By 1918, only thirty-seven firms in Canada (less than 2 per cent) had research laboratories, compared with two thousand in the United States. Dr A.B. Macallum, of the University of Toronto, estimated that there were not more than fifty pure research scientists in Canada. See Mel Thistle, *The Inner Ring: The Early History of the National Research Council of Canada* (Toronto, 1966) p. 29; A.B. Macallum, 'The Canadian Honorary Advisory Council for Scientific and Industrial Research,' *CMJ*, 40 (8 June 1919) p. 28.

15 Edit. 'Research Work and the Manufacturer,' *CE*, 29 (7 Oct. 1915) p. 453; Edit. 'Canadian Research Bureau,' *ibid.*, 30 (13 Jan. 1916) p. 141; Edit. 'Need of Industrial Bureaus,' *CR*, 31 (20 June 1917) p. 531.

16 Edit. 'Industrial Research,' *CE*, 30 (29 June 1916) p. 689; Edit. 'Industrial Reconstruction and Scientific Research,' p. 499.

17 Edit. 'Competition after the War,' *CE*, 34 (6 June 1918) p. 319. A. Mitchell Palmer, US alien property custodian, seized and began selling all German-owned patents to the highest bidder, until smaller companies successfully opposed the practice. See David F. Noble, *America by Design: Science, Technology and the Rise of Corporate Capitalism* (New York, 1977) p. 16.

18 NAC, Engineering Institute of Canada Papers, MG 28, 1–277, Letter Books,

McLeod to Sir John Thompson, 21 May 1894, pp. 436–7; UTL, Toronto Branch Papers, MS 102 Box no. 2, G.H. Keefer to William Pugsley, 29 Oct. 1910; 'Report of the Annual Meeting,' *TCSCE* 24 (1910) p. 39; *ibid.* (1912) pp. 45–6; *ibid.* (1913) p. 41; *ibid.* (1914) p. 82; C.R. Young, 'The Engineering Institute of Canada and Research,' *EJ*, 30 (May 1947) p. 216.

19 'Memorandum Regarding National Industrial Development in Canada to the Right Honourable Sir Robert Borden, GCMG Etc., Prime Minister of Canada, by R.A. Ross, C.H. McLeod, Walter J. Francis, H.R. Safford, Members of the Canadian Society of Engineers and Sir Charles Ross Bart, Member of the American Society of Mechanical Engineers, May, 1916,' *TCSCE*, 31 (1917) pp. 341–8.

20 NAC, Engineering Institute of Canada Papers, MG 28, 1–277, Annual Minutes (hereafter Council Minutes) 20 March 1917, p. 26.

21 Various government control agencies, enacted under the government's emergency powers between 1916 and 1918, tended to centralize Canada's wartime economy. By 1918, charitable and semi-official social services, like the Military Hospitals Commission, were placed under government authority. As in other countries, these activities helped to undermine laissez-faire attitudes and prepared the way for the greatly expanded role of government in economic and social life. J.A. Corry, 'The Growth of Government Activities in Canada, 1914–1921,' Canadian Historical Association, *Report of the Annual Meeting* (1940) pp. 66–73; *Report of the Royal Commission on Dominion Provincial Relations*, 1940, Bk 1, pp. 101–3. For a discussion of the impact of the government's emergency powers on the economy, see David Edward Smith, 'Emergency Government in Canada,' *Canadian Historical Review*, 50 (Dec. 1969) pp. 432–5.

22 Privy Council 1266, 6 June 1916; *ibid.*, 2967, 29 Nov. 1916. The government, however, was not enthusiastic about the Honorary Advisory Council. Foster confided to his diary that most cabinet members were 'utterly indifferent or antagonistic.' Quoted in Thistle, *The Inner Ring*, p. 10.

23 For the scope and activities of the Advisory Council, see J. Castell Hopkins, *Canadian Annual Review of Public Affairs*, 1916 (Toronto, 1917) p. 445; 'The Research Council,' *BCMI*, no. 86 (June 1919) pp. 580–1.

24 Articles by British engineers were reprinted in the Canadian technical press; see, e.g., 'Germany's Preparations for the Industrial Struggle after the War,' *CR*, 29 (10 Nov. 1915) pp. 1153–5 and 'Engineering and Scientific Research,' *ibid.*, 30 (20 Sept. 1916) pp. 912–13. Many of their views resembled arguments advanced by Canadian scientists; *cf.* George Bryce, 'The Crying Need of Industrial Research in Canada,' *Transactions of the Canadian Institute*, 9 (1912) pp. 223–5; F.N. Turner, 'The Value of Research to Industry,' *CMJ*, 33 (15 Oct. 1915) pp. 617–21; J.C. Fields, 'Science and

Industry,' The Board of Trade of the City of Toronto, *Year Book* (Toronto, 1917) pp. 45-7; Frank Arnoldi, *Presidential Address at the Opening Meeting of 1915* (Toronto, 1915). Engineers do not appear to have elaborated on any of these ideas or even to have assimilated the arguments in detail.

25 Originally founded by Sandford Fleming and others as a professional society for engineers, architects, and surveyors, the Royal Canadian Institute had traditionally served as a centre for the professionalization of Canadian science and engineering. For a historical profile of the Canadian Institute (as it was called until 1914), see W. Stewart Wallace, 'A Sketch of the History of the Royal Canadian Institute, 1849-1949,' in W. Stewart Wallace (ed.), *The Royal Canadian Institute Centennial Volume, 1849-1949* (Toronto, 1949) pp. 121-67.

26 The Royal Commission on Industrial Training and Technical Education summarized the chief features of this system: (1) The University provides the laboratory accommodation and selects the Investigators ... (2) The Manufacturer, or the donor, indicates the specific subject or matter to be investigated and provides funds to support the fellowship for the purpose of such investigation. (3) Any discoveries become the property of the manufacturer ... subject to certain conditions, contained in the agreement between the donor and the University.' Canada, Report of the Royal Commission on Industrial Training and Technical Education, *Report of the Commissioners* (Ottawa, 1913-14) Pt. II, p. 379.

27 Royal Canadian Institute, *Co-operation between Science and Industry in Canada: The Royal Canadian Institute as an Intermediary for Its Promotion; Establishment of a Bureau of Scientific and Industrial Research* (Toronto, 1914); Royal Canadian Institute, *Bureau of Scientific and Industrial Research and School of Specific Industries of the Royal Canadian Institute* (Toronto, n.d.).

28 For background on the NRC, see Thistle, *The Inner Ring*, and Wilfrid Eggleston, *National Research in Canada: The NRC, 1916-1966* (Toronto, 1978). Although the Bureau of Scientific and Industrial Research did some minor research and disseminated useful technical information to various manufacturers, apart from an extraordinary offer from the Mellon Institute to administer five of its fellowships at the bureau, it could not obtain financial support after the appointment of the Honorary Advisory Council. See J.C. Fields to Editor, *CE*, 40 (23 June 1921) p. 4.

29 'Report of the Annual Meeting,' *TCSCE*, 31 (1917) p. 109. The CSCE was particularly useful in helping the Advisory Council distribute an industrial questionnaire. 'Committee Report of the Canadian Society of Civil Engineers,' *CR*, 32, no. 4 (23 Jan. 1918) p. 62; Thistle, *The Inner Ring*, p. 29.

30 NAC, Engineering Institute of Canada Papers, MG 28, 1-277, Scrap Book,

no. 6, Fraser S. Keith, 'National Industrial Development' (18 April 1916); Toronto Branch Papers, Box no. 4, F.S. Keith to L.M. Arkley, 14 April 1917.

31 C.H. Mitchell, 'The Future of Applied Science,' *JEIC*, 3 (Jan. 1920) p. 3; C.H. Mitchell to Editor, *CE*, 38 (13 May 1920) p. 472.

32 Andrew Charles Gross, 'Engineering Manpower in Canada' (PhD dissertation, Ohio State University, 1968) p. 50, table 7B.

33 'Hamilton Branch,' *JEIC*, 5 (Jan. 1922) p. 34.

34 Toronto Branch Papers, Box no. 7, Colonel A. McPhail to H.H. Vaughan, 2 Feb. 1919.

35 Council Minutes, 14 June 1898, p. 60; 'Employment Bureau,' *JEIC*, 1 (May 1919) p. 65.

36 Frederick B. Goedike to Editor, *CE*, 34 (23 May 1918) p. 469.

37 Edit. 'Employment Service Bureau,' *JEIC*, 3 (June 1920) p. 303; 'An Opportunity for Service,' *ibid.*, 4 (May 1921) p. 312.

38 See H.H. Vaughan's remarks, 'Discussion on Town Planning in Halifax,' *ibid.*, 1 (Sept. 1918) p. 269.

39 Walter Van Nus, 'The Plan-Makers and the City: Architects, Engineers and Surveyors and Urban Planning in Canada, 1890–1939' (PhD dissertation, University of Toronto, 1975) pp. 88–90; 'Ottawa Branch News,' *JEIC*, 1 (May 1918) p. 62.

40 See J.C. McLennan, 'Industrial Research in Canada,' *Transactions of the Royal Canadian Institute*, 11 (1916) p. 154; J.C. McLennan, 'Science in War and Peace,' *Addresses Delivered before the Canadian Club of Ottawa, 1916–17* (Ottawa, 1918) p. 142; J.C. McLennan, 'The Problem of Industrial Research in Canada,' *Industrial Canada*, 17 (July 1916) pp. 254–5; Royal Canadian Institute, 'Report of the Board of Governors of the Bureau of Scientific and Industrial Research,' *Year Book and Annual Report, 1916–1917* (Toronto, 1917) p. 14; Turner, 'The Value of Research to Industry,' p. 151.

41 Peter N. Ross, 'The Establishment of the Ph.D. at Toronto: A Case of American Influence,' *History of Education Quarterly*, 12 (fall 1972) pp. 358–80. McLennan was one of the earliest recipients of this degree. H.H. Langton, *Sir John Cunningham McLennan: A Memoir* (Toronto, 1939) p. 74.

42 OA, Royal Canadian Institute Papers, no. II, F.N. Turner to C.L. Burton, 23 Aug. 1915.

43 Edwin T. Layton Jr., *The Revolt of the Engineers: Social Responsibility and the American Engineering Profession* (Cleveland, 1971) pp. 6–7.

44 Report of Annual Meeting,' *TCSCE*, 25 (1911) pp. 152–3; Edit. 'Good Roads and Engineering,' *JEIC*, 2 (3 March 1919) p. 219; Edit. 'Message to Good Roads Congress,' *ibid.*, 2 (June 1920) p. 303.

45 Edit. 'Message to Good Roads Congress,' p. 304.

46 'Report of the Annual Meeting,' *TCSCE*, 25 (1911) p. 152; 'Report of Good

Roads Committee,' *ibid.* (1912) pp. 44–5; 'Good Roads Congress,' *JEIC*, 2 (May 1919) p. 407; Edit. 'Good Roads in Canada,' *ibid.*, 3 (April 1920) p. 198.

47 Scrap Book, no. 5, Memorial to Laurier, 18 Nov. 1910; 'Report of Annual Meeting,' *TCSCE*, 24 (1910) p. 88; Edit. 'Engineers in the Civil Service,' *CE*, 18 (4 Feb. 1910) pp. 95–6.

48 Scrap Book, no. 6, clipping, n.d.; Toronto Branch Papers, Box no. 3, clipping (Edit. 'National Engineering Service') n.d.; 'Report of Annual Meeting,' *TCSCE* (1910) pp. 82–3, 88; Edit. 'A National Engineering Service,' *CE*, 24 (23 Jan. 1913) p. 211. Similar arguments were advanced regarding government surveys. Without discounting the possibility of new employment opportunities, the CSCE urged that all government surveys (there were more than eight independent survey branches in the government) be co-ordinated and that a central registry bureau be established. 'Memorandum to the Right Honourable Sir Wilfrid Laurier, Prime Minister of Canada,' *TCSCE*, 21 (1907) pp. 29–31; 'President's Address' (William Anderson), *ibid.*, 19 (1905) pp. 25–7.

49 Scrap Book, no. 5, 'Memorial to Laurier,' 18 Nov. 1910; 'Report of the Annual Meeting' (1910) pp. 83–5, 88–9; Council Minutes, 11 Feb. 1911, p. 27; C.E.W. Dodwell to Editor, *CE*, 34 (25 April 1918) pp. 361–2; 'Ottawa Branch News,' *JEIC*, 1 (May 1918) pp. 61–2; Council Minutes, 24 Sept. 1918, p. 86; Edit. 'Salaries of Engineers,' *JEIC*, 2 (Jan. 1919) p. 18.

50 'Report of Annual Meeting,' *TCSCE*, 21 (1907) p. 41; *ibid.* (1908) p. 8; *ibid.* (1911) p. 137; Toronto Branch Papers, Box no. 5, 'Circular Resolutions,' 22 April 1918; 'Report of Council Meeting,' *JEIC*, 2 (Oct. 1919) p. 689.

51 Council Minutes, 8 March 1904, p. 310; *ibid.*, 10 March 1908, pp. 205–6; Edit. 'The Medical Officer of Health and the Engineer,' *CE*, 23 (19 Sept. 1912) p. 484; Edit. 'Public Health Act of Ontario,' *ibid.* (16 Jan. 1913) p. 180; Edit. 'Engineering Help Is Needed,' *ibid.*, 33 (23 Aug. 1917) p. 169; Toronto Branch Papers, Box no. 4, 'Report of the Committee on Sewage Disposal,' 18 Dec. 1918; 'Memorial to Borden,' *JEIC*, 2 (4 April 1919) pp. 337–8; Council Minutes, 21 Dec. 1920, p. 103; *ibid.*, 22 June 1920, p. 65.

52 Edit. 'Maintaining a High Standard,' *JEIC*, 3 (July 1920) p. 357.

53 'Alberta Engineers Discuss Engineer's Status and Proposed Legislation,' *CE*, 34 (24 May 1918) p. 463.

54 Report of the Sewage Disposal and Sanitation Committee,' *TCSCE*, 31 (1917) p. 105.

55 Edit. 'Improving the Highway Improvement Act,' *JEIC*, 3 (June 1920) pp. 302–3; 'Ottawa Branch,' *ibid.* (June 1921) p. 373; Edit. 'Practical Recognition for Engineers,' *ibid.*, (March 1919) p. 221; Edit. 'Government Commission Composed Entirely of Engineers,' *ibid.*, 1 (Nov. 1918) p. 336; 'Fuel-Power Board Created,' *ibid.* (June 1918) p. 92.

56 Engineers were still forced to compete with political appointees and other professionals – chiefly lawyers – and were sometimes excluded from important positions that required technical knowledge. Many EIC members, for example, were outraged that municipal engineers were not appointed to the Halifax Commission, which superintended reconstruction of the city after the 1917 explosion. Haultain Papers, Box no. 1, Letter to Haultain, 3 May 1918; Toronto Branch Papers, Box no. 5, S.G. Porter to Keith, 19 March 1918; Keith to Porter, 22 March 1918; Porter to Keith, 3 April 1918.

57 'Report of the Annual Meeting,' *TCSCE*, 25 (1911) p. 143; Council Minutes, 15 May 1917, p. 46; Toronto Branch Papers, Box no. 4, S.G. Porter to C.H. McLeod, 4 Jan. 1917; Edit. 'Engineers on Railway Commission,' *JEIC*, 4 (Jan. 1921) p. 34.

58 'Report of Annual Meeting,' *TCSCE*, 24 (1910) p. 101; *ibid.*, (1913) pp. 86–7; Edit. 'Federal Status of Engineers,' *JEIC*, 2 (Aug. 1919) p. 560.

59 For background on the engineers' war service, see 'The Engineer in Peace and War – The Increasing Value of Trained Men' (Walter J. Francis), *CR*, 30 (5 April 1916) pp. 324–5; 'The Work of the Canadian Engineers in France,' *ibid.*, 31 (21 March 1917) pp. 261–2; 'Ottawa Branch,' *JEIC*, 3 (Jan. 1920) p. 22; Arthur W. Currie, 'Engineering Battalions: Their Work in the War,' *CE*, 38 (12 Feb. 1920) pp. 201–10.

60 Walter J. Francis, 'The Engineer and the War,' *CE*, 30 (6 April 1916) p. 417.

61 'Victory,' *CE*, 35 (14 Nov. 1918) p. 237; H.H. Vaughan, 'The Manufacture of Munitions in Canada,' *TEIC*, 33 (1919) p. 1; 'Honour Roll,' Toronto Branch of the Engineering Institute of Canada, *Yearbook* (1919) p. 10; Council Minutes, 25 Feb. 1919, p. 24; 'Report of Honour Roll Committee,' *JEIC*, 2 (March 1919) p. 162; 'Personals,' *ibid.*, p. 237.

62 Edit. 'The Engineer and Public Service,' *CE*, 31 (9 Nov. 1916) p. 389; Edit. 'Recognition of the Engineer,' *ibid.*, 33 (22 Nov. 1917) p. 447; 'Tenth General Professional Meeting,' *JEIC*, 4 (Sept. 1921) p. 506.

63 Edit. 'Strategy of Research,' *CE*, 29 (18 Nov. 1915) p. 600. Engineers rarely acknowledged the paradox that engineering was, in turn, dependent on science. For an exception, see Edit. 'Canadian Research Bureau,' *ibid.*, 30 (13 Jan. 1916) p. 141.

64 It has been suggested that scientific management gave engineers autonomy and helped to preserve their middle-class status. See Samuel Haber, *Efficiency and Uplift: Scientific Management in the Progressive Era, 1890–1920* (Chicago, 1964) p. xii; Monte A. Calvert, *The Mechanical Engineer in America, 1830–1910: Professional Cultures in Conflict* (Baltimore, 1967) p. 243; and especially Layton, *Revolt of the Engineers*, p. 139. Although Canadian engineers were familiar with scientific management (in 1913, Taylor addressed the University of Toronto Engineering Society), apart from con-

demning labour's opposition to the system and contributing an occasional article to the technical press on its practical application, they did not appear interested in Taylorism, at least before 1922; Edit. 'Scientific Management,' *CE*, 21 (28 Sept. 1911) p. 372; 'The Principles of Scientific Management,' *ibid.*, 24 (13 Feb. 1913) pp. 295–6; J.S. Cameron, 'Industrial Relations,' *JEIC*, 3 (May 1920) pp. 243–50.

65 According to one report, the primary object of engineering standardization was to 'secure interchangeability of parts, to cheapen manufacture by the elimination of waste entailed in producing a multiplicity of designs for one and the same purpose, to effect improvement in workmanship and design and by concentration rather than by diffusion of effort to expedite delivery and reduce maintenance charges and storage'; 'Engineering Standards Committee,' *JEIC* (July 1918), p. 168. On the importance of engineering standardization to a modern industrial economy, see Noble, *America by Design*, chapter 5.

66 'Report of Annual Meeting,' *TCSCE*, 28 (1914) p. 14; 'Canadian Engineering Standards Committee,' *ibid.*, 3 (Feb. 1920) p. 53.

67 For the history, organization, and work of the Canadian Engineering Standards Association, see Canadian Engineering Standards Association, *Yearbook* (Ottawa, 1927) pp. 5–10.

68 Some engineers, such as W.J. Francis, even objected that some specifications were 'too educative in character' and could be used by mechanics and others to compete with engineers. W.J. Francis, quoted in 'Canadian Society of Civil Engineers Holds Momentous Annual Meeting,' *CR*, 32 (30 Jan. 1918) p. 77.

69 'Memorandum on National Industrial Development,' p. 347.

70 *Ibid.*

71 For example: 'Report of Annual Meeting,' *TCSCE*, 26 (1912) pp. 88–9; *Regina Morning Leader*, quoted in *JEIC*, 1 (May 1918) p. 66; 'Ottawa Branch,' *ibid.*, 4 (Feb. 1921) p. 78. McLeod advised members that, while it might be detrimental to the profession to give free advice, cases could arise, 'through the ignorance or apathy of officials, in which public interest and the prestige of the engineering profession may suffer grievously if gratuitous advice be not forthcoming.' Toronto Branch Papers, Box no. 4, C.H. McLeod, 'Memorandum for the consideration of the Branches of the Society,' 13 Jan. 1917.

72 'Vancouver Branch,' *JEIC*, 2 (July 1919) p. 520; Edit. 'Winnipeg Engineers' Achievement,' *ibid.* (Aug. 1919) p. 562; Edit. 'Service to the Public,' *CE*, 38 (12 Feb. 1920) p. 217.

73 McLeod, 'Memorandum for the consideration of the Members'; 'President's Address' (G.H. Duggan), *TCSCE*, 31 (1917) p. 74; 'Report of Annual Meeting,' *ibid.* (1917) pp. 18–19.

74 Council Minutes (McLeod to the Mayor of Montreal), 17 Aug. 1915, p. 355; *ibid.*, 5 Oct. 1915, p. 339; *ibid.*, 16 Nov. 1915, p. 350; 'The Canadian Society and the Montreal Commissioners,' *CR*, 29 (27 Oct. 1915) p. 1098. Montreal engineers had a special affection for the city waterworks, built by T.C. Keefer and expanded by many prominent Montreal engineers. For background, see John Irwin Cooper, *Montreal: A Brief History* (Montreal, 1969) pp. 27, 109–110; 'Engineers Condemn Montreal Aqueduct Scheme,' *CE*, 31 (23 Nov. 1916) pp. 424A–B.

75 'Montreal Waterworks Situation,' *CE*, 29 (11 Nov. 1915) pp. 569–72. This was an extraordinary move for this journal. It rationalized its actions by arguing that there was 'insufficient data upon which to base a proper judgment,' *ibid.*, p. 572.

76 'Report of Annual Meeting,' *TCSCE*, 30 (1916) p. 15; 'Montreal Rejects Advice of C.S.C.E.,' *CR*, 30 (12 Jan. 1916) p. 30; McLeod, 'Memorandum for the Consideration of the Branches of the Society.' Engineers deeply resented politicians making important technical decisions. 'It is unfortunate,' lamented the *Contract Record*, 'that a man [Controller Thomas Côté] without technical training should be at the head of the civic public works department, and should thus be in a position to decide matters involving engineering questions and millions of dollars'; Edit. 'The Montreal Aqueduct,' *CR*, 29 (10 Nov. 1915) p. 1149. They particularly resented Côté's statements that competent engineers had approved the project. The CSCE acknowledged that some engineers had examined parts of the project but held that no prominent engineer had studied all of it. *Ibid.*, Edit. 'Montreal Rejects Advice of C.S.C.E.,' p. 30.

77 'Engineers Condemn Montreal Aqueduct Scheme,' pp. 424A–B. The main points of the report are summarized in Hopkins, *Canadian Annual Review*, 1916, pp. 588–9.

78 The most detailed account of this incident was published in a letter to an American engineering journal. See Sam G. Porter to Editor, *ENGN*, 75 (15 June 1916) pp. 1148–9.

79 See chapter 3.

80 Porter to Editor, p. 1149.

81 Although in principle most engineers opposed any political involvement in commercial undertakings, because of the potential for corruption and inefficiency, they rarely argued in political terms, preferring to assess the issues on their technical and economic merits. They would accept some limited forms of government regulation but insisted on private ownership. See, e.g., W. McLea Walbank, 'Municipal Ownership of Public Utilities vs Private Enterprise,' *TCSCE*, 22 (1908) p. 55, and W.F. Tye, 'Canada's Railway Problem and Its Solution,' *ibid.*, 31 (1917) pp. 146–87. In 1917, five

CSCE members, including some who had served on the Montreal Aqueduct Power investigation, submitted a report commissioned by several Hamilton ratepayers, which opposed, on the grounds of cost, the construction of a provincially owned Hydro Radial Railway and recommended road construction instead. Council Minutes, 20 March 1917, p. 29; 'Ontario's Hydro Radial Railway,' *CMJ*, 12 (Feb. 1916) p. 60; H.V. Nelles, *The Politics of Development: Forests, Mines and Hydro Electric Power in Ontario, 1849–1941* (Toronto, 1974), p. 409.
82 'Montreal Rejects Advice of C.S.C.E.,' p. 30.
83 McLeod, 'Memorandum for the Consideration of the Branches of the Society.'

CHAPTER 8: CONTEMPLATING THE 'UNTHINKABLE'

1 R.E.W. Hagarty to Editor, *CE*, 17 (22 Oct. 1909) p. 468. *Cf*. W.H. Finley's remarks, years later: Edit. 'Toronto Engineers Discuss Salaries,' *ibid.*, 36 (6 March 1919) p. 288.
2 Hagarty to Editor, *CE*, p. 468; 'Report of Annual Meeting,' *TCSCE*, 22 (1908) p. 37; *ibid.*, 23 (1909) p. 147; 'The Pay of the Engineer,' *CE*, 35 (11 July 1918) p. 33; Edit. 'The Technical Man's Salary,' *CR*, 32 (9 Oct. 1918) p. 804; Hyman Goldman to Editor, *CE*, 34 (9 May 1918) p. 409.
3 UTL, Canadian Society of Civil Engineers, Toronto Branch Papers, MS 102 (hereafter Toronto Branch Papers), Box no. 7, J.C.N.B. Krumm, 'What the Institute Can Do,' 28 Feb. 1919, p. 4.
4 *The Canada Year Book, 1922–23* (Ottawa, 1924) p. 753.
5 'Branch News,' *JEIC* (May 1919) p. 421.
6 Edit. 'Salaries of Engineers,' *CE*, 22 (2 May 1912) p. 608; J.G. Legrand to Editor, *ibid.*, 34 (14 March 1918) p. 229; 'Pay of the Engineer,' *ibid.*, 34; Edit. 'The Salary Situation,' *JEIC*, 2 (5 May 1919) p. 410; 'Calgary Branch,' *ibid.*, 4 (May 1921) pp. 320–1; 'Tenth General Professional Meeting,' *JEIC*, 4 (Sept. 1921) p. 507; Toronto Branch Papers, Box no. 6, 'Memorandum Presented to the Members of Parliament of the Lower Mainland of British Columbia by the Vancouver Branch of the Engineering Institute of Canada,' n.d. Some engineers believed that salaries had fallen since completion of the CPR. See J.G. Legrand to Editor, p. 229.
7 Unsigned Letter to Editor, *JEIC*, 2 (Jan. 1919) p. 30.
8 'Civil Service Commission of Canada,' *Canada Gazette*, 51 (1 June 1918) pp. 4221–2. For reaction to this and similar advertisements, see Edit. 'Pay of the Engineer,' p. 33; 'Employment Bureau,' *JEIC*, 1 (July 1918) p. 137; 'Branch News,' *ibid.*, 2 (May 1919) pp. 421–2; Unsigned Letter to Editor, *ibid.*, 2 (June 1919) p. 468.
9 Calculated from: Canada, Department of Trade and Commerce, *Sixth Census*

of Canada, 1921, Vol. III (Ottawa, 1927) (hereafter *1921 Census* III),
pp. xix–xx, Table XI. 1921 was the first year that aggregate income data were
broken down and reported by individual groups. For more detailed data on
plumbers' wages 1901–19, see Canada, Department of Labour, *Wages
and Hours of Labour in Canada, 1901–1920*, p. 8.

10 For an analysis, see Terry Copp, *The Anatomy of Poverty: The Condition of
the Working Class in Montreal, 1897–1929* (Toronto, 1974) chap. 2.

11 Accounting for the outbreak of labour unrest preceding the Winnipeg General
Strike, David Jay Bercuson argues that not all workers were adversely
affected by inflation. The contract and railway shop machinists, for example,
who usually provided the most radical leadership and led the most militant
strikes, kept well ahead of inflation through large wartime wage increases.
Labour strife erupted not because these workers were becoming poorer,
Bercuson maintains, but because, through fear, panic, and prejudice, they
mistakenly thought that inflation was destroying their wage increases and
living standard. David Jay Bercuson, *Confrontation at Winnipeg: Labour,
Industrial Relations and the General Strike* (Montreal and London, 1974)
pp. 33–4.

12 Occasionally, inflated estimates of engineering salaries circulated. The
Christian Science Monitor concluded that engineers were the best-paid professionals in the United States ('Employment Bureau,' *JEIC*, 1 [Oct. 1918]
p. 317), and the ASCE estimated that the average American engineer's salary
was nearly $4,000 per annum. This figure was hotly disputed by the *Engineer-
ing Record* of New York, which observed that low-salary data were missing
and noted that the average salary of engineers employed in eastern New
York was only $1,775 (Edit. 'Compensation of Engineers,' *CE*, 32 [25 Jan.
1917] p. 93). This last figure was probably low, but more realistic. The
average salary in Alberta was estimated to be less than $2,100. ('Tenth
General Professional Meeting,' *JEIC*, 4 [Sept. 1921] p. 507). Nationally, it
was $1,951.30, for all professional engineers. See Table 4.

13 'Halifax Branch,' *JEIC* (June 1921) p. 382; J.C. Legrand to Editor,
p. 229.

14 See Table A1. For example, the total 1921 professional income of William
Snaith, thirty-nine-year-old production engineer, was $4,680, twice the
average civil engineer's salary. See UTL, William Snaith Papers, MS 42, Box
no. 1, 'Budget Book' (1921).

15 H.A. Goldman, an assistant engineer for the Toronto Harbour Commission,
contended that some older engineers, with twenty-five to thirty years of
professional experience, earned less than $1,500 a year; Hyman Goldman to
Editor, p. 409.

16 The EIC adopted this classification from the Engineering Council; 'Report of

Committee on Classification and Remuneration of Engineers,' *JEIC*, 5 (Nov. 1922) p. 541.

17 The career of one young Calgary engineer was typical. Beginning in 1903 as a $30-per-month tapeman for the CPR, J.H. Greenwood, twenty-one, advanced through a variety of sub-professional jobs, before his promotion, in 1906, to resident engineer at $125 per month. NAC, Engineering Institute of Canada Papers, MG 28, 1–277, Membership Files, J.H. Greenwood, Application to EIC, 'Details of Experience in the Field' (insert). Mining engineers also went through a similar kind of sub-professional apprenticeship, before they were considered qualified to hold a responsible professional position. See, e.g., D.R. Thomas to Editor, *BCMI*, no. 89 (Sept. 1919) p. 968.

18 Edit. 'Increased Salaries for Railway Civil Engineers,' *JEIC*, 1 (3 July 1918) p. 235.

19 Even locomotive firemen, brakemen, and trainmen averaged slightly more than engineers in the twenty to twenty-four age group. See Table 7.

20 Interview, E. Donald Grey-Donald, 19 July 1977, Montreal.

21 'Manitoba Engineers Pledged to Salary Schedule,' *CE*, 39 (11 Nov. 1920) p. 506.

22 While most engineers regarded middle-class status as a vocational obligation, some saw it as a right, or even a class privilege. Noting the engineer's difficulty in maintaining his social position, one engineer contended that the 'engineer feels that even though he is associated with the labouring classes during working hours, he should have the same privileges of any other liberal profession.' Romeo Morrissette to Editor, *ibid.*, 38 (8 April 1920) p. 357.

23 Frederick B. Goedike to Editor, *ibid.*, 34 (23 May 1918) p. 469; N.C. Mills to Editor, *ibid.*, 37 (23 Dec. 1919) p. 562; R.O. Wynne-Roberts, 'A Generation of Engineering in Canada,' *ibid.*, 38 (29 Jan. 1920) p. 170.

24 Edit. 'Toronto Engineers Discuss Salaries,' *ibid.*, 36 (6 March 1919) p. 288.

25 J.F.P. Tate to Editor, *ibid.*, 39 (25 Nov. 1920) pp. 501–2; 'Pay of the Engineer,' *ibid.*, 35 (11 July 1918) p. 33; UTA, Haultain Papers, B 47 (B-72-005) Box no. 4, Fraser S. Keith, 'Engineering Education,' 8 May 1924, p. 9.

26 J.G. Legrand to Editor, p. 229.

27 N.C. Mills to Editor, *CE*, p. 562.

28 'Should Professional Engineers Organize Union?' *ibid.*, 39 (11 March 1920) p. 284.

29 Fred Christie to Editor, *ibid.*, 37 (18 Dec. 1919) p. 551.

30 'Toronto Branch Committee on Prestige and Influence,' *JEIC*, 1 (June 1918) p. 100; 'Salaries and Fees Committee,' Toronto Branch, Engineering Institute of Canada, *Yearbook* (1919) p. 9; 'Remuneration,' *JEIC*, 3 (Dec. 1920) p. 578; Edit. 'Compensation of Engineering Services,' *ibid.*, 2 (Nov. 1919) p. 730;

Edwin T. Layton Jr., *Revolt of the Engineers: Social Responsibility and the American Engineering Profession* (Cleveland, 1971) p. 134.

31 NAC, Engineering Institute of Canada Papers, MG 28, 1–277, Council Minutes (hereafter Council Minutes), 7 April 1919, p. 43; 'Toronto Engineers' Policy Discussion,' *CE*, 39 (21 Oct. 1920) p. 447.

32 R. Snodgrass to Editor, *CMJ*, 41 (2 July 1920) pp. 540–1.

33 *Ibid.*, 'British Columbia Technical Association Active,' *CE*, 40 (12 May 1921) p. 459; 'Vancouver Branch,' *EJ*, 5 (March 1922) pp. 159–60; 'A Vocal Organization for B.C. Engineers,' *ibid.* (July–Aug. 1978) pp. 18–19; 'Toronto Engineers' Policy Discussion,' p. 447.

34 The best study of the AAE is William G. Rothstein, 'The American Association of Engineers,' *Industrial and Labor Relations Review*, 22 (Oct. 1968) pp. 48–72.

35 'Canadian Association of Engineers,' *CE*, 34 (7 March 1919) p. 198; 'Canadian Association of Engineers,' *ibid.*, 34 (25 April 1918) p. 376; Toronto Branch Papers, Box no. 5, H.A. Goldman to P. Gillespie (Personal), 6 March 1918; *ibid.*, Goldman to Gillespie, 22 March 1918.

36 'Toronto Engineers Demand Action on Salaries,' *CE*, 38 (11 March 1920) p. 285; 'Classification and Remuneration of Engineers,' *ibid.*, 43 (26 Dec. 1922) p. 662.

37 See 'Should Professional Engineers Organize Union?' *ibid.*, pp. 281ff.

38 Charles A. Mullen, 'Trade Unions and Engineers,' *CR*, 34 (28 Jan. 1920) p. 78; Fred Christie to Editor, *CE*, p. 551; 'Pay of the Engineer,' p. 34.

39 Mullen, 'Trade Unions and Engineers,' p. 76.

40 See William Snaith's argument: 'Should Professional Engineers Organize Union?' pp. 281–5; Fred Christie to Editor, p. 551; N.C. Mills to Editor, p. 562.

41 'Should Professional Engineers Organize Union?' p. 283; 'Toronto Draughtsmen Form Labour Union,' *CE*, 38 (1 April 1920) p. 336.

42 H.V. Nelles, 'Introduction,' to T.C. Keefer, *Philosophy of Railroads and Other Essays*, ed. H.V. Nelles (Toronto, 1972) p. li.

43 Layton, *Revolt of the Engineers*, pp. 9–10.

44 Robert Bothwell and William Kilbourn, *C.D. Howe: A Biography* (Toronto, 1979) p. 15.

45 'Toronto Engineers Demand Action on Salaries' (Prof. C.R. Young) p. 286.

46 'Should Professional Engineers Organize Union?' p. 283.

47 'Salaries and the Civil Service,' *JEIC*, 2 (June 1919) p. 463.

48 *Ibid.*

49 'Fifth General Professional Meeting' (President R.W. Leonard), *ibid.*, 2 (Oct. 1919) p. 645.

50 'Should Professional Engineers Organize Union?' p. 234.

51 'Trade Unions and Engineers,' p. 78.
52 Edit. 'EIC Committee on Policy,' *CE*, 39 (9 Sept. 1920) pp. 335–6.
53 Rothstein, 'The American Association of Engineers,' p. 59; Toronto Branch Papers, Box no. 5, H.A. Goldman to P. Gillespie (Personal), 6 March 1918, p. 2.
54 Toronto Branch Papers, Box no. 5, George H. Hogarth to Fraser S. Keith, 11 March 1918.
55 Council Minutes, 21 Dec. 1920, p. 105; Snodgrass to Editor, p. 541. The BCTA was expected to suspend operations shortly after the establishment of a provincial licensing association for professional engineers. It continued to function for a time, however, for the benefit of non-professional members who could not register under the BC Professional Engineers' Act. 'Vancouver Branch,' *EJ*, p. 160.
56 Toronto Branch Papers, Box no. 5, F.S. Keith to Hogarth, 12 March 1918; *ibid.*, Keith to Hogarth, 13 March 1918; *ibid.*, Keith to Hogarth, 3 April 1918; *ibid.*, Minutes: Toronto Branch, Vol. III, 12 April 1918, p. 195.
57 *Ibid.*, H.A. Goldman to P. Gillespie, 22 March 1918; 'New Association Suspends Meeting,' *CE*, 34 (23 May 1918) p. 472.
58 Council Meetings, 27 April 1920, pp. 34–5; 'Report of Council Meeting,' *JEIC*, 2 (June 1918) p. 470; 'A.A.E. Will Stay Out of Canada,' *CE*, 36 (12 June 1918) p. 535; 'Report of Council Meeting,' *JEIC*, 2 (Sept. 1919) p. 619; Toronto Branch Papers, Box no. 7, Council Minutes (copy), 18 May 1920, p. 3; *ibid.*, 20 July 1919, p. l; Council Minutes, 22 June 1920, p. 63; *ibid.*, 20 July 1920, p. 67; Edit. 'Co-operation for Mutual Benefit,' *JEIC*, 3 (July 1920) p. 357.
59 See chapter 6.
60 'Salaries and Fees Committee,' Toronto Branch, *Yearbook* (1919) p. 9; Toronto Branch Papers, Box no. 7, Letter from W.S. Harvey, 10 March 1919; 'Branch News,' *JEIC*, 2 (May 1919) p. 419; 'Toronto Branch Salary Schedule,' *ibid.*, 2 (Nov. 1919) p. 731.
61 Letter to Editor, *JEIC*, 1 (Nov. 1918) p. 364; Edit. 'Toronto Engineers Discuss Salaries,' *CE*, p. 288; Edit. 'Adopt the Institute's Scale,' *ibid.*, 38 (1 April 1920) p. 349; J.F.P. Tate to Editor, *ibid.*, p. 562.
62 Rothstein, 'American Association of Engineers,' pp. 59–60.
63 'Report of Council for the Year Nineteen Hundred and Nineteen,' *JEIC*, 3 (Feb. 1920) p. 70.
64 'Winnipeg Branch,' *ibid.* (Nov. 1920) p. 544; 'Recommended Salaries for Manitoba Engineers,' *CR*, 34 (3 Nov. 1920) p. 104; Edit. 'Manitoba Engineers Pledged to Salary Schedule,' *CE*, 39 (11 Nov. 1920) p. 505; 'Manitoba Engineers to Enforce Salary Schedule,' *ENR*, 84 (18 Nov. 1920) p. 1013.

65 'Toronto Engineers Demand Action on Salaries,' *CE*, 38 (11 March 1920) p. 286.
66 John H. Ryckman to Editor, *CE*, 38 (25 March 1920) p. 329; 'EIC Committee on Policy,' *ibid.*, p. 335.
67 P.E. Doncaster to Editor, *JEIC*, 1 (Dec. 1918) p. 435; 'Report of Council for the Year Nineteen Hundred and Eighteen,' *ibid.* (Feb. 1919) p. 60.
68 'Report of Council Meeting,' *ibid.*, 1 (Dec. 1919) p. 405; P.E. Doncaster to Editor, p. 435; 'Report of Council Meeting,' *ibid.*, 1 (Nov. 1918) p. 435; Edit. 'Government Considering Salaries,' *ibid.*, 2 (Feb. 1919) p. 121; 'Branch News,' *ibid.*, p. 132; Edit. 'Increasing Remuneration,' *ibid.* (April 1919) p. 335; Edit. 'The Salary Situation,' *ibid.* (May 1919) p. 410; 'Ottawa Branch,' *ibid.* (Aug. 1919) p. 512.
69 'Notable Engineering Conference,' *ibid.*, 3 (May 1920) p. 252.
70 Edit. 'Engineering Institute Council Discusses Salaries and Unionization,' *CE*, 38 (22 April 1922) p. 411; 'Notable Engineering Conference,' pp. 252–3; J.B. Challies to Editor, *JEIC*, 4 (Feb. 1921) pp. 65–6; 'Report of Committee on Policy,' *EJ*, 5 (June 1922) pp. 329–35.
71 *Ibid.*, p. 330 (italics added).
72 Edit. 'The Civil Service Bill,' *JEIC*, 2 (Aug. 1919) p. 561; 'St. [sic] John Branch,' *ibid.*, p. 572; J.E. Hodgetts *et al.*, *The Biography of an Institution: The Civil Service Commission of Canada, 1908–1967* (Montreal and London, 1972) p. 69.
73 Edit. 'Remuneration of Surveyors,' *CE*, 38 (18 March 1920) p. 314; 'Salaries of Mining Engineers in Government Service,' *BCMI*, no. 88 (Aug. 1919) p. 893; 'Salaries of Technical Officers in the Civil Service,' *ibid.*, p. 111.
74 'Criticizes Canadian Salary Ratings,' *ENR*, 83 (4 Sept. 1919) p. 486.
75 *Ibid.*, p. 487.
76 *Ibid.*; Edit. 'The Civil Service Bill,' *ibid.*, p. 561; Hodgetts, *Biography*, p. 70.
77 Hodgetts, *Biography*, p. 72; John Swettenham and David Kealy, *Serving the State: A History of the Professional Institute of the Public Service of Canada, 1920–1970* (Ottawa, 1970) pp. 7–8.
78 'Council of the Engineering Institute Supports Bill Classifying Civil Service,' *CE*, 37 (23 Oct. 1919) p. 407.
79 *Ibid.*; 'Presidential Address' (R.W. Leonard), *TEIC*, 34 (Jan. 1920) p. 16; 'Special Notes,' *JEIC*, 2 (July 1919) p. 524; Edit. 'Classification and Compensation of Engineers,' *ibid.*, 2 (Oct. 1919) pp. 680–1; Edit. 'Remuneration of Engineers,' *ibid.*, 3 (April 1920) p. 198.
80 Edit. 'Classification and Compensation of Engineers,' p. 681.
81 In 1921, for example, E.K. Spinney introduced a bill to remove a large number of civil servants, including all professional, scientific, and technical officers,

from the CSC's jurisdiction. For the EIC's official response, see Edit. 'Engineers and Patronage,' *ibid.*, 4 (June 1921) pp. 354–5.

82 'Remuneration of Engineers,' *ibid.*, 3 (April 1920) p. 198; Council Minutes, 27 April 1920, p. 33; 'Committee on Policy,' p. 65.
83 'EIC Committee on Policy,' p. 335.
84 'Classification, Remuneration and Tariff of Fees of Engineers,' *EJ*, 6 (Oct. 1922) p. 461.
85 See Layton, *Revolt of the Engineers*, p. 124.
86 'Classification and Salaries of Engineers,' *CE*, 37 (23 Oct. 1919) p. 398. The Manitoba branch recommended that $3,300 a year be set as the basic minimum salary for an engineer performing the lowest order of professional service. This was $1,000 a year more than the average civil engineer's salary in Canada. 'Recommended Salaries for Manitoba Engineers,' p. 1046.
87 'Classification, Remuneration and Tariff of Fees of Engineers,' p. 463.
88 'Tenth General Professional Meeting,' *JEIC*, 4 (Sept. 1921) p. 509.
89 'Classification, Remuneration and Tariff of Fees of Engineers,' p. 463.

CHAPTER 9: 'A SORT OF TRADE UNION'

1 Edit. 'Legislation,' *JEIC*, 1 (Nov. 1918) p. 335.
2 F.H. Peters, 'Legislation Concerning the Status of the Engineer,' *ibid*, 1 (Aug. 1918) pp. 217–20.
3 Peters was a distinguished RMC graduate and ICE and ASCE member. For a career profile, see John William Leonard, *Who's Who in Engineering: A Biographical Dictionary of Contemporaries, 1922–1923* (New York, 1923) p. 987.
4 Peters, 'Legislation Concerning the Status of the Engineer,' p. 217.
5 *Ibid.*
6 Edit. 'Legislation,' p. 335.
7 Fraser S. Keith, 'Engineering Legislation in Canada,' *ENR*, 86 (Jan. 1921) p. 21.
8 C.H. McLeod, 'How Canadian Engineers Organize,' *CE*, 32 (April 1917) p. 342; Peters, 'Legislation Concerning the Status of Engineers,' pp. 219–20; R.O. Wynne-Roberts, 'Engineering Prestige,' *CE*, 34 (April 1918) p. 347.
9 F.H. Peters to Editor, *CE*, 34 (Feb. 1918) p. 141.
10 'Message from Councillors' (Arthur Surveyer), *JEIC*, 1 (June 1918) p. 110; Peters, 'Legislation Concerning the Status of Engineers,' p. 218.
11 C.C. Kirby, 'Legislation in New Brunswick,' *ibid.*, 3 (July 1920) p. 341.
12 See chapter 7.
13 Other professions, such as dentistry, also discovered that the supply of practitioners had far outstripped demand. See D.W. Gullett, *A History of*

Dentistry in Canada (Toronto, 1971) pp. 96–7. Overcrowding, however, was not necessarily a problem for Ontario lawyers. See Curtis Cole, 'A Developmental Market: Growth Rates, Competition and Professional Standards in the Ontario Legal Profession, 1881–1936,' *Canada-United States Law Journal*, 7 (1984) pp. 231-45.

14 See E.J. Mehren, 'Engineers and Their Societies in Britain,' *ENR*, 93 (Sept. 1924) pp. 380–1.

15 Elizabeth Fisher, 'Professional Associations in Canada' (PhD dissertation, University of Toronto, 1932) p. 298; C.H. Mitchell to Editor, *CE*, 38 (May 1920) p. 472; 'Classification and Remuneration of Engineers,' *ibid.*, 43 (Dec. 1922) p. 661.

16 'Retiring President's Address' (J.M.R. Fairbairn), *JEIC*, 5 (Feb. 1922) p. 95.

17 See Table 2, chap. 6.

18 NAC, Engineering Institute of Canada Papers, MG 28, 1–277, Membership Files, 1887–1922.

19 'President's Address' (Fairbairn), p. 97.

20 UTA, H.E.T. Haultain Papers, B 47 (B-72-005), Box no. 4, Fraser S. Keith, 'Engineering Education,' p. 5. By 1920, the Faculty of Applied Science and Engineering, University of Toronto, alone had over 800 students. By 1924, there were 2,091 engineering students in Canada. ('Hamilton Branch,' *JEIC*, 2 [Jan. 1919] p. 34; Keith, 'Engineering Education,' p. 6). Some engineers believed that misinformation about career prospects accounted for the increase. See, e.g., Edit. 'Matriculation Standards,' *CE*, 15 (Feb. 1908) p. 122; Hyman Goldman to Editor, *ibid.*, p. 409.

21 Andrew Charles Gross, 'Engineering Manpower in Canada' (PhD dissertation, Ohio State University, 1968) appendix B, Table 2, p. 371.

22 A.M. Reid, 'The Twenties,' in R.S. Harris and I. Montagnes (eds.), *Cold Iron and Lady Godiva: Engineering Education at Toronto, 1920–1972* (Toronto, 1973) Table I, p. 53.

23 Gross, 'Engineering Manpower in Canada,' p. 45.

24 *Ibid.*, Table 7B, p. 50.

25 R.E.W. Haggarty to Editor, *CE*, 16 (Oct. 1909) p. 468; 'Classification and Remuneration of Engineers,' p. 661; 'Discussion on the Law and the Engineer,' *TCSCE*, 30 (1916) p. 369.

26 Peters, 'Legislation Concerning the Status of Engineers,' p. 218.

27 R.O. Wynne-Roberts thought that licensing would attract, not limit, the number of practitioners. Wynne-Roberts, 'Engineering Prestige,' p. 349.

28 H.E.T. Haultain to Editor, *JEIC*, 3 (May 1920) p. 261.

29 R.O. Wynne-Roberts to Editor, *CR*, 29 (Oct. 1915) p. 1040.

30 See, e.g., Michael Bliss, 'The Protective Impulse: An Approach to the Social History of Oliver Mowat's Ontario,' in Donald Swainson (ed.), *Oliver*

Mowat's Ontario (Toronto, 1972) pp. 184–5; A. Margaret Evans and C.A.V. Barker, *Century One: A History of the Ontario Veterinary Association, 1874–1974* (Guelph, 1976) p. 63; Gullett, *A History of Dentistry in Canada,* p. 137.

31 Edwin T. Layton Jr., *The Revolt of the Engineers: Social Responsibility and the American Engineering Profession* (Cleveland, 1971) pp. 6–7.

32 R.W. MacIntyre to Editor, *JEIC,* 2 (March 1919) pp. 226–7; *cf.* C.B. McColl to Editor, *ibid.* (Jan. 1919) p. 32.

33 Edit. 'Would the Licensing of Engineers Raise Their Professional Status?' *CR,* 29 (Jan. 1915) p. 27; Houston, 'Troubles in the Engineering Profession,' p. 380.

34 'President's Address' (T.C. Keefer), *TCSCE,* 2 (1888) p. 11.

35 G.R.G Conway, 'Legislation and the Engineer,' *CR,* 29 (Jan. 1915) p. 47.

36 Wynne-Roberts, 'Engineering Prestige,' p. 349; 'Branch News,' *JEIC,* 1 (Nov. 1918) p. 343; R.O. Wynne-Roberts, 'A Generation of Engineering in Canada,' *CE,* 38 (Jan. 1920) p. 172.

37 'Branch News – Saskatchewan,' *JEIC,* 1 (Oct. 1918) p. 296; 'Branch News – Saskatchewan,' *ibid.* (Nov. 1918) p. 344; 'The Second Professional Meeting,' *ibid.* (Sept. 1918) p. 225; Edit. 'Legislation,' *ibid.* (Nov. 1918) p. 335; 'Branch News – Saskatchewan,' *ibid.* (Dec. 1918) p. 409; UTL, Toronto Branch Papers, MS 102, Box no. 6 (hereafter Toronto Branch Papers), 'Minutes of Council, Special Meeting' (copy), 4 Dec. 1918; Edit. 'Summary of Legislation Situation,' *JEIC,* 2 (Feb. 1919) pp. 120–1.

38 'Branch News – Saskatchewan,' *JEIC,* 2 (Feb. 1919) p. 129.

39 Toronto Branch Papers, Box no. 7, 'Resolution,' Montreal Branch, 7 Jan. 1900; *ibid.,* W.S. Harvey to F.B. Brown, 4 Feb. 1919; 'Report of Special Legislation Committee,' *JEIC,* 2 (March 1919) p. 173; Fraser S. Keith, 'Engineering Legislation in Canada,' pp. 21–2.

40 Keith, 'Engineering Legislation in Canada,' pp. 21–2; see 'An Act Respecting the Civil Engineering Profession,' *JEIC,* 2 (May 1919) pp. 411–14.

41 Toronto Branch Papers, Box no. 7, 'Report, Committee on Legislation' (confidential), 11 April 1919; 'Niagara Peninsula Branch,' *JEIC,* 2 (July 1919) p. 528; C.E.W. Dodwell, 'Engineers and Engineering,' *ibid.,* 3 (March 1920) p. 144.

42 Toronto Branch Papers, Box no. 5, Aimé Geoffrion to Arthur Surveyer, 8 May 1918; *ibid.,* 'Report on Legislation Committee' (confidential), n.d.

43 *Ibid.,* Geoffrion to Surveyer, 8 May 1918.

44 *Ibid.,* 'Report of the Legislation Committee.'

45 See especially 'The Engineering Institute of Canada and the Provincial Associations of Professional Engineers,' *EJ,* 26 (Oct. 1943) pp. 568–76; Edit.

'The Engineering Institute of Canada and the Provincial Associations of Professional Engineers,' *ibid.*, 14 (Oct. 1931) pp. 528–9.

46 'Report of Council Meetings,' *JEIC*, 2 (July 1919) p. 522; Edit. 'Ballot on Legislation,' *ibid.*, 2 (Sept. 1919) p. 606.

47 'G.H. Duggan, M.E.I.C.,' *ibid.*, 2 (June 1919) p. 460; 'H.H. Vaughan, M.E.I.C.,' *ibid.*, pp. 461-2; 'L.A. Thornton, M.E.I.C.,' *ibid.*, p. 462. Some senior EIC members disagreed with this prediction. See, e.g., C.C. Kirby to Editor, *ibid.*, 2 (Aug. 1919) p. 567; 'L.B. Elliot, M.E.I.C.,' *ibid.*, 2 (June 1919) p. 462.

48 *Cf.* 'An Act Respecting the Engineering Profession,' *ibid.*, p. 112. Although C.C. Kirby, a legislation committee member and a supporter of the model act, explained that section 7(i) was intended to exclude sub-professionals such as rodmen and draughtsmen from the act – positions the committee considered roughly analogous to law clerks, for example (C.C. Kirby to Editor, *ibid.* [July 1919] p. 521) – most junior engineers were unconvinced and vigorously protested the clause until it was revised. 'Toronto Branch,' *ibid.*, p. 527; 'Niagara Peninsula Branch,' *ibid.*, pp. 528–9; 'Toronto Branch,' *ibid.*, 3 (Feb. 1920) p. 71.

49 'G.H. Duggan, M.E.I.C.,' p. 461; 'H.H. Vaughan, M.E.I.C.,' p. 462.

50 See Peter Gillespie's remarks, 'Should Professional Engineers Organize Union?' *CE*, 38 (March 1920) p. 283.

51 Peters, 'Legislation Concerning the Status of Engineers,' p. 219. For the CMI's reaction to this remark, see Edit. 'The Status of Engineers,' *BCMI*, no. 78 (Oct. 1918) p. 838.

52 Edit. 'A Rose by Any Other Name Etc.,' *ibid.*, no. 70 (Feb. 1918) p. 83; Edit. 'EIC Seeking Closed Profession Says Mining Institute Secretary,' *CE*, 35 (Aug. 1918) p. 189.

53 Edit. 'Legislation and Engineering,' *BCMI*, no. 77 (Sept. 1918) p. 745.

54 Edit. 'A Rose by Any Other Name Etc.,' *ibid.*, p. 83.

55 F.S. Keith to Editor, *BCMI*, no. 77 (Sept. 1918) pp. 806–7.

56 Council Minutes, CMI, 17 Jan. 1919, p. 306; Toronto Branch Papers, Box no. 6; Minutes of Council Special Meeting (copy), 4 Dec. 1918, n.p.

57 'Legislation for Engineers,' *BCMI*, no. 84 (April 1919) p. 374.

58 See 'Status of the Engineer,' *CMJ*, 41 (March 1920) p. 212.

59 Council Minutes, CMI, 'Report of Committee on Engineering Legislation,' 17 Feb. 1920, p. 384.

60 Edit. 'Legislation and Engineering,' *BCMI*, p. 745.

61 See J.A. Reid to Editor, *JEIC*, 3 (Feb. 1920) p. 91.

62 Edit. 'Professional Mining Engineers,' *CMJ*, 43 (Nov. 1922) p. 761; Edit. 'Status of the Engineer,' *ibid.*, 41 (Feb. 1920) p. 168.

63 Edit. 'What Do Mining Engineers Think about Engineering Status Legislation?' *ibid.*, 42 (May 1921) pp. 375–6.

64 Council Minutes, CMI, 29 Jan. 1920, pp. 375–6; *ibid.*, 1 May 1920, p. 292; *ibid.*, 21 Jan. 1921, p. 37; 'Status of Engineers – Discussion,' *BCMI*, no. 95 (April 1920) p. 292; Edit. 'What Do Mining Engineers Think about Engineering Status Legislation?' p. 375.

65 Edit. 'Engineering Legislation,' *JEIC*, 2 (Oct. 1919) p. 680; 'Report of Council Meeting,' *ibid.*, p. 689; Fraser S. Keith to H. Mortimer-Lamb, *BCMI* (Nov. 1919) pp. 1154–5; Council Minutes, CMI, 20 Oct. 1919, p. 351.

66 Edit. 'Engineering Institute's Convention at Montreal,' *CE*, 42 (Jan. 1922) p. 187.

67 G.R.G. Conway, 'The British Columbia Engineer,' 25 (Oct. 1913) p. 639; C.H. McLeod, 'How Canadian Engineers Organize,' p. 342; Toronto Branch Papers, Box no. 5, Letter to D. Blanchard, 18 Jan. 1918; H.H. Vaughan to P. Gillespie, 22 Feb. 1918.

68 'Report of Council Meeting,' *JEIC*, 1 (Aug. 1918) p. 171; Toronto Branch Papers, Box no. 5, Vaughan to Gillespie, 22 Feb. 1918.

69 For background on the Advisory Conference Committee, see 'Ontario Provincial Division EIC,' *CE*, 37 (Nov. 1919) p. 500; 'Advisory Conference Committee on Engineering Legislation for Province of Ontario,' *ibid.*, 38 (April 1920) p. 365; 'Report of Ontario Committee on Legislation,' *ibid.*, 39 (Dec. 1920) p. 631; J.B. Challies to Editor, *JEIC*, 3 (March 1920) p. 148; 'Ontario Provincial Division,' *ibid.* (Jan. 1920) p. 23; 'Advisory Conference Committee on Engineering Legislation in Ontario,' *CMJ*, 41 (April 1920) p. 318.

70 'Report of the Ontario Committee on Legislation,' *CE*, 39 (Dec. 1920) p. 631.

71 Edit. 'Legislation and Engineering,' p. 746.

72 See chapter 7.

73 For background, see Edit. 'Joint Committee Doing Valuable War Work,' *CR*, 32 (April 1918) p. 269; 'Joint Committee of Technical Organizations,' *CMJ*, 41 (Feb. 1920) p. 148; 'The Engineer's Opportunity for Patriotic Service,' *CR*, 31 (Jan. 1917) p. 2; Edit. 'Technical Men and the War,' *EN*, 26 (Jan. 1917) p. 19; 'Joint Committee of Technical Organizations,' *ibid.*, 27 (April 1918) pp. 27–8; 'Joint Committee of Technical Organizations Hold Successful Annual Meeting,' *ibid.*, 28 (April 1919) pp. 32–4.

74 For a description of the origin, structure, and work of the CSA, see Canadian Engineering Standards Association, *Yearbook 1927* (Ottawa, 1927) pp. 6–10.

75 'Report J.C.T.O. Status Committee,' *CE*, 37 (Dec. 1919) pp. 517–18; Unsigned Letter to Editor, *JEIC*, 3 (Feb. 1920) pp. 91-3.

76 Edit. 'Professional Legislation in Ontario Delayed,' *CE*, 40 (May 1921) p. 447.

77 For a text of the Ontario bill, see 'Engineering Legislation for Ontario,' *EN*, 31 (Jan. 1920) pp. 35–40.

78 'Personals,' *JEIC*, 2 (Nov. 1919), p. 743.

79 'Professional Legislation in Ontario,' *CE*, 42 (March 1922) p. 314. For a detailed outline of the progress of the Ontario bill, see Willis Chipman's report to the Advisory Conference Committee: 'Legislation in Ontario,' *EJ*, 5 (Aug. 1922) pp. 427–8.
80 'Legislation in Ontario,' p. 427.
81 See 'The Professional Engineers' Act of Ontario,' *EJ*, 5 (July 1922) p. 369.
82 'Legislation in Ontario,' *ibid.*, p. 428.
83 *Ibid.*, p. 370; Research Directorate's Staff Study, 'The History and Organization of the Engineering Profession in Ontario' (1978), prepared for the Professional Organizations Committee, Ministry of the Attorney General, Ontario, Appendix D, p. 4.
84 Quoted in 'Engineering Legislation,' *CMJ*, 42 (30 Dec. 1921) p. 1012.
85 'Engineering Legislation,' *ibid.*, p. 1013.
86 R.E. Hore, 'An Equal Chance,' *ibid.*, 41 (April 1920) p. 265. These remarks were inspired by Herbert Hoover's inaugural address to the American Institute of Mining and Metallurgy. See *ibid.*, pp. 264–5.
87 'Engineering Legislation,' p. 1013.
88 'Saskatchewan, Engineering Progress on Act,' *CE*, 39 (Dec. 1920) p. 615; 'Saskatchewan's Bill Fails to Pass,' *ibid.*, p. 629; 'Engineering Legislation Making Progress,' *ibid.*, 38 (April 1920) pp. 354–5; 'Saskatchewan Engineers Will Incorporate,' *ibid.* (May 1920) p. 441; 'Saskatchewan Branch,' *JEIC*, 3 (May 1920) p. 269; 'Report of Council,' *ibid.*, 4 (Feb. 1921) p. 70; 'Annual General and Professional Meeting,' *ibid.* (March 1921) p. 194.
89 An Act to Incorporate the Association of Professional Engineers and for Other Purposes Connected Therewithin, *Statutes of Prince Edward Island*, 1955, c. 43.
90 Fraser S. Keith, 'Engineering Legislation in Canada,' p. 23; 'Engineering Legislation Making Progress – Quebec,' *CE*, 38 (April 1920) p. 355.
91 For an analysis of these acts, see Keith, 'Engineering Legislation in Canada,' pp. 23–4.
92 'Engineering Legislation Making Progress – Alberta,' *CE*, p. 354; Arthur L. Ford, 'The Legislation Situation in Alberta,' *JEIC*, 3 (June 1920) pp. 310–11; Edit. 'Engineering Legislation in Alberta,' *CE*, 39 (July 1920) p. 168.
93 See An Act to Amend and Consolidate the Engineering Profession Act, *Statutes of Alberta*, 1930, c.30, s.6, and An Act to Regulate the Professions of Engineering and Geology, *ibid.*, 1955, c.74, s.45(a).
94 'Toronto Branch,' *EJ*, 5 (Nov. 1922) p. 554.
95 Evans and Barker, *Century One*, p. 171; Research Directorate, 'History and Organization,' Appendix C, pp. 8–9.
96 'History and Organization,' Appendix D, pp. 4–6.

Note on sources

The most important primary source is the Engineering Institute of Canada Papers housed in the National Archives of Canada. CSCE/EIC Council Minutes provided insight into society politics. EIC membership application files, 1887–1922, are an invaluable source of biographical, educational, and career information. Quantified, they form a data base of nearly five thousand cases, which, together with published census data, produced a more precise picture of the structure and composition of the engineering profession.

While the EIC preserved little of its correspondence, there is a good collection of letters, as well as some committee reports and minutes, in the CSCE's Toronto Branch Papers, housed in the Fisher Rare Book Room of the University of Toronto Library. Less valuable, but still useful, are the Galbraith Papers and the Haultain Papers, in the University of Toronto Archives, and the C.H. McLeod Papers, in the McGill University Archives.

Engineering periodicals yielded the most important volume of research. CSCE/EIC publications, together with engineering news magazines, contain an astonishing array of significant, although largely unindexed information: proceedings and other society business; articles, speeches, committee reports, and news items; obituaries and biographies; correspondence; and statistical data.

Two secondary works were particularly useful for this study. Michael Bliss's article 'The Protective Impulse: An Approach to the Social History of Oliver Mowat's Ontario' in Donald Swainson (ed.), *Oliver Mowat's Ontario* (Toronto, 1972) pp. 174–88, contains some provocative ideas on the 'protectionist' behaviour of professional groups. Edwin Layton's book, *The Revolt of the Engineers* (Cleveland, 1971), although an examination of social responsibility and the American engineering profession, sets high standards of scholarship and raises important questions about engineering professionalism.

Index